The Selected Letters of
LEWIS CARROLL

Charles Lutwidge Dodgson

The Selected Letters of
LEWIS CARROLL

Edited by
Morton N. Cohen

with the assistance of
Roger Lancelyn Green

Pantheon Books, New York

Library of Congress Cataloging in Publication Data

Carroll, Lewis, 1832–1898.
The selected letters of Lewis Carroll.

Includes index.
1. Carroll, Lewis, 1832–1898—Correspondence.
2. Authors, English—19th century—Correspondence.
I. Cohen, Morton Norton, 1921–   . II. Green,
Roger Lancelyn. III. Title.
PR4612.A4   1982   828'.809   [B]   82-47870
ISBN 0-394-74965-0 (pbk.)   AACR2

Manufactured in the United States of America
First American Edition

To Gordon N. Ray

Preface to the Pantheon/Papermac Edition

"One of the deep secrets of Life," Charles Lutwidge Dodgson confided to his friend the actress Ellen Terry, is "that all, that is really *worth* the doing, is what we do for *others*." The letters assembled here, or a remarkably high percentage of them, spell out the way that Dodgson practised what he preached. Indeed, he spent much of his life in the service of others: writing for their instruction and amusement; paying for their schooling, for their lessons in French, music, and art; getting them jobs; guiding their careers; meeting their dentists' bills; buying them railway tickets; treating them to the theatre; giving them inscribed copies of his books and other presents; taking their photographs; inventing games and puzzles for them; tutoring them in mathematics and logic; giving them religious guidance; feeding and clothing them; and, of course, telling them stories.

Letter-writing itself was often for him another way of doing something for others, especially for the young girls whose friendship he so ardently cultivated. As he stood at his upright desk, he was often challenged to breathe life and laughter onto the dry leaves of letter paper ranged before him. The result is a stream of letters that Lewis Carroll's fancy alone could create – new self-contained microcosms of Wonderland, vehicles of fun and pleasure that underscore his devotion to others and prove him, in both senses of the phrase, a man of letters.

Of course, not everything he wrote was inspired by the comic muse. He was actually a serious man, formal and scholarly, shy and awkward, hard-working, fastidious, deeply religious. From his father's death in 1868, he was, as the eldest son, head of his family, and he took to heart his responsibilities to his three brothers and seven sisters. From the age of eighteen, he was a member of the oldest university in the land, Oxford; from twenty-three a mathematics don at Christ Church; and from twenty-nine an ordained clergyman. He wrote treatises on mathematics and logic as well as children's books and concerned himself with the mechanics of designing and publishing them. His far-reaching interests and avocations involved him deeply in photography, the theatre, art, literature, and the minutiae of college affairs; his voluminous reading took him into the worlds of science, medicine, psychic phenomena, and technology. All these interests elicited from his pen a flow of serious, reflective letters that provide posterity with a record of his life, his mind, his soul, and go beyond to document the behaviour, manners, and psychological tenor of his age. His less serious letters are, on the other hand, marvellously fanciful creations, many of them little jewels fashioned for child friends. These reveal the workings of the imagination we already know from the *Alice* books; they take the art of letter-writing into new provinces.

Dodgson was, surely, one of the world's most prolific letter-writers. By his own confession, he wrote "wheelbarrows full, almost." "One-third of my life seems to go in receiving letters," he claimed, "and the other two-thirds in answering them." Writing to the poet Christina Rossetti on August 16, 1882, he told her that her letter was the thirteenth he had written that day. He confessed to his young friend Mary Brown that some of the letters he had yet to answer were five and a half years old; he got about two thousand letters off every year, he told her, but even that was not enough. "I'm generally 70 or 80 names in arrears, and sometimes *one* letter will take me an afternoon," he wrote elsewhere. On New Year's Day 1892 he resolved to catch up. "I began by making a list of the people who are waiting (some of them 5 to 10 years) for letters. There are more than 60 of them." "Life seems to go in letter-writing," he wrote to Ellen Terry's sister Marion when he was fifty-five, "and I'm beginning to think that the proper definition of 'Man' is 'an animal that writes letters.' "

He was a systematic record-keeper, and in fact devised a Register of Letters Received and Sent, with a *précis* of each alongside its date and entry number. He began this record on January 1, 1861, less than a month before his twenty-ninth birthday, and maintained it diligently for the remaining thirty-seven years of his life. That Letter Register has not survived, but we know that the last number recorded there was 98,721. We also know that he kept a separate register for letters he sent and received between 1882 and 1892 as Curator of Senior Common Room at Christ Church. That register has not survived either, but by adding a modest estimate of five thousand entries one arrives at a hypothetical sub-total of 103,721. To that figure one must yet add an estimate of the number of letters sent and received before either register was begun, during the first twenty-nine years of his life, as a schoolboy at Richmond and Rugby and an undergraduate and young Oxford don. How many? If there were over 100,000 in his last thirty-seven years, what for the first twenty-nine? It is difficult to know. But, whatever the figure, the total is overpowering.

One hard reality emerges from these arithmetical speculations, and that is that letter-writing was no sham pastime for Dodgson. He took it seriously, and he spent long hours at it. "I find I [write] about 20 words a minute, and a page contains about 150 words, i.e., about $7\frac{1}{2}$ minutes to a page," he observed. "So the copying of 12 pages took about $1\frac{1}{2}$ hours: and the original writing $2\frac{1}{2}$ or more. In fact," he sums up his report on how long it took him to write a draft of a letter and to make a fair copy, "I began soon after $2\frac{1}{2}$, and ended about 7." But he comforted himself by recalling to the actress Mrs. Herbert Beerbohm Tree: "I have proved by actual trial that a letter, that takes an hour to *write*, takes only about 3 minutes to *read*!"

Sometimes he composed letters in bed at night (he invented a device called the Nyctograph to enable him to take notes under the covers, in the dark); and in the morning, fully dressed, standing before his writing-desk, he would choose the appropriate sheet of paper from the various sizes he kept in good supply, select his pen, and write, usually in purple ink, in a clear, easy hand that placed no strain upon the reader. One might conclude that letter-writing was a compulsion with him. But the saving grace is that he could laugh about it: "I hardly know which is me and which is the inkstand," he wrote. "The confusion in one's *mind* doesn't so much matter – but when it comes to putting bread-and-butter, and orange marmalade, into the *inkstand*; and then dipping pens into *oneself*, and filling *oneself* up with ink, you know, it's horrid!"

The light touch and the whimsy always come to his rescue; he rises above the ordinary, the basic, and whisks himself and his reader off to a world of nonsense. He creates puzzles, puns, pranks; he teases, he feigns, he fantasizes. He sends letters in verse, sometimes in verse set down as prose to see if his correspondent will detect the hidden metres and rhymes; letters written backwards so that one has to hold them up to a looking-glass to read them; letters with hoaxes and acrostics; rebus letters with other visual effects, with a beetle or a spider crawling across the page, with a sketch of what he himself looked like when he was lecturing. In the end he packs into tiny envelopes huge amounts of pleasure for his many friends. For them the postman's knock must surely have become one of the world's happiest sounds.

Yes, of course, he enjoyed composing these letters, and reaped a sense of fulfilment, psychic satisfaction – all of that – and he knew it. He admitted the possibility that doing good for others might be motivated by one's own pleasure. But, as he continued in his letter to Ellen Terry, "it is *not* selfishness, that my own pleasure should be *a* motive so long as it is not *the* motive that would outweigh the other, if the two came into collision."

Motive and manner of life meant everything to the man we have come to know as Lewis Carroll. He would have been abashed, even appalled, at the thought that his name (or even his pen name) would become a household word. For he was essentially a modest man, one who led a rather ordinary life for his time and station.

He was the son of an intelligent and sensitive clergyman in the north of England. He grew up in what appears to have been an agreeable family circle. The Dodgsons were a "good English family" on both sides, with a heavy sprinkling of clerics and an occasional bishop and military man here and there on the family tree. They could even make a claim to a distant relationship to Queen Victoria. It was an upper-crust family: conservative, steeped in tradition, self-conscious, reverential, pious, loyal, and devoted to social service. The father could be witty and whimsical at times, but, on the whole, he was occupied with his clerical duties and must have given the impression of a strong, solid, authoritarian, rather gloomy, high and dry churchman.

We know less about Lewis Carroll's mother. She died before Carroll's nineteenth birthday. She must have been a gentle creature, and, what with eleven children, a busy one. In his few allusions to her, Carroll shows genuine affection. But the evidence makes quite clear that Carroll's relationship with his father was more important. The two developed close sympathies, and in the course of being taught by his father while, as a boy, he was still at home, the young Carroll adopted the father as his ideal, a model to emulate. Dodgson *père* died in 1868, when Carroll was thirty-six, but even many years later, he characterized his father's death as "the greatest sorrow of my life."

Carroll the man had mostly pleasant memories of childhood. He grew up with a gaggle of sisters and brothers to play with, and he enjoyed walks and outings in the Yorkshire countryside. He was good at mechanical things and built a miniature railway in the garden and a puppet theatre for which he wrote original plays. He was also a great reader, had a good memory, liked to sketch and paint and to write poetry and short stories. But most of all, he had learned in the Dodgson family circle to live a purposeful life, and he dedicated his entire being to making his life meaningful to others and to society in general. Carroll was educated first by his father, then at the Richmond School in Yorkshire, next at Rugby in Warwickshire, and, as an undergraduate, at Christ Church, Oxford.

It was not until 1862, when he was thirty, that he first told the story of *Alice's Adventures in Wonderland* to the three daughters of his college dean as they rowed languidly on the River Isis. Even then, it took another three and a half years before the story could be read by all. It was this book and its sequel, *Through the Looking-Glass and What Alice Found There,* with their exceptional blend of humour and nonsense, that made Carroll world famous.

The *Alice* stories were by-products of a mind filled with many serious matters. By profession, Charles Dodgson was a mathematician and logician, and he wrote and published numerous works on these subjects. He was also deeply interested in art, and was one of the earliest art photographers. He liked to sketch as well, to stay abreast of the art movements of his day, and to visit art exhibitions. He was a tireless theatre-goer and fostered a love of the theatre in many of his child friends. He pursued friendship not only with literary lights but also with artists, actors, and playwrights of the time. It follows that many of his letters are to the famous people of the Victorian world of the arts.

For most of his life, Dodgson lived in college rooms. He allowed himself the pleasure of visits to London and outings with young friends, but no extravagant indulgences. He travelled abroad only once, always ate frugally when he ate at all, and he usually dressed simply, in black. For much of his life he helped support his six unmarried sisters and a good many other people—relatives, friends, even strangers. He was always willing to take on new students, and he was happy, albeit with genuine modesty, to give young and old alike religious and spiritual instruction. When he realized that his *Alice* books would bring in a modest income for the rest of his life, he actually asked the University of Oxford to reduce his salary.

Although he resigned his lectureship in 1881, before he turned fifty, he remained a Student of Christ Church until his death in 1898, a fortnight before his sixty-sixth birthday. In his Oxford setting, with occasional forays into the larger world, Charles Dodgson, the shy, stammering, sheltered academic don, managed to encompass two disparate worlds, writing serious tomes on the one hand and creating nonsensical flights into Wonderland on the other.

This selection of Dodgson's letters comes from the two-volume edition of *The Letters of Lewis Carroll* that was published in London by Macmillan and in New York by Oxford University Press in 1979. Those two volumes contain 1,305 of Dodgson's letters, of which 320 appear here, a selection which I hope captures the essence as well as the multiple interests and subtleties of the whole man. Where the two-volume edition strove to identify the recipients of Dodgson's letters and to give a biographical sketch of each one, I have included in this edition biographical information only where I believe it to be especially interesting or illuminating. Full biographical details are available in the original edition, as are identifications of most of Dodgson's quotations and allusions. There, too, readers will find an explanation of the principles used in transcribing the letters, and they can determine the location and source of each letter.

Although the Reverend Charles Lutwidge Dodgson lived a life away from the limelight, disliked publicity, and cherished privacy, he was aware that we must all make concessions to history, that we cannot, should not, try to place a restraining hand upon the truth from beyond the grave. Surely he would have taken some satisfaction in knowing that his letters could, more than three-quarters of a century after his death, still afford pleasure to others.

New York and London, 1982   Morton N. Cohen

Contents

List of Illustrations

Biographical Chronology

1832   Born (January 27), the eldest son (third of eleven children) of Charles Dodgson, Perpetual Curate of Daresbury, Cheshire, and Frances Jane (born Lutwidge).

1843   Father became Rector of Croft, Yorkshire, and family moved there.

1844–5   At Richmond School, Yorkshire (from August 1, 1844).

1846–9   At Rugby School (from January 27, 1846).

1850   Matriculated at Christ Church, Oxford (May 23).

1851   Took up residence at Christ Church (January 24).
Mother died (January 26).

1852   Student of Christ Church (December, 1852, until his death).

1854   B.A. (1st Class Honours in Mathematics; 2nd Class in Classics).

1855   Sub-Librarian, Christ Church (until 1857).
Mathematical Lecturer (until 1881).

1857   M.A.

1861   Ordained deacon (December 22).

1862   Told the story of Alice's adventures to the Liddell sisters on a boat trip (July 4).

1865   *Alice's Adventures in Wonderland* published (July).

1867   Journey on the Continent with H. P. Liddon (July 13–September 14).

1868   Father died (June 21).
Moved his family to Guildford (September 1).

1869   *Phantasmagoria* published.

1871   *Through the Looking-Glass and What Alice Found There* published (December).

1876   *The Hunting of the Snark* published (March).

1877   First took Eastbourne summer lodgings (July 31).

1879   *Euclid and His Modern Rivals* published.

1881   Resigned Mathematical Lectureship (but retained his Studentship) to devote more time to writing.

1882   Curator of Senior Common Room, Christ Church (December 1882 to February 1892).

1885   *A Tangled Tale* published.

1886   *Alice's Adventures Under Ground* published.

1887   *The Game of Logic* published (February).

1888   *Curiosa Mathematica*, Part I published.

1889   *Sylvie and Bruno* published.

1890   *The Nursery "Alice"* published.

1892   Resigned Curatorship of Senior Common Room, Christ Church (February).

1893   *Curiosa Mathematica*, Part II published.
        Sylvie and Bruno Concluded published.

1896   *Symbolic Logic, Part I* published (February 21).

1898   Died at Guildford (January 14) and buried there.
        Three Sunsets and Other Poems published.

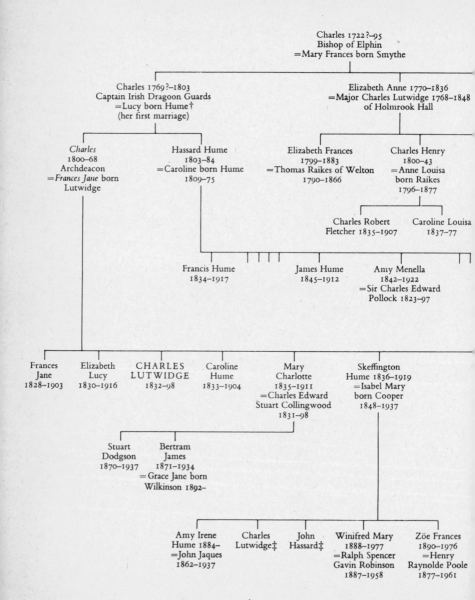

Charles 1722?–95
Bishop of Elphin
=Mary Frances born Smythe

Charles 1769?–1803
Captain Irish Dragoon Guards
=Lucy born Hume†
(her first marriage)

Elizabeth Anne 1770–1836
=Major Charles Lutwidge 1768–1848
of Holmrook Hall

Charles
1800–68
Archdeacon
=*Frances Jane* born
Lutwidge

Hassard Hume
1803–84
=Caroline born Hume
1809–75

Elizabeth Frances
1799–1883
=Thomas Raikes of Welton
1790–1866

Charles Henry
1800–43
=Anne Louisa
born Raikes
1796–1877

Charles Robert
Fletcher 1835–1907

Caroline Louisa
1837–77

Francis Hume
1834–1917

James Hume
1845–1912

Amy Menella
1842–1922
=Sir Charles Edward
Pollock 1823–97

Frances
Jane
1828–1903

Elizabeth
Lucy
1830–1916

CHARLES
LUTWIDGE
1832–98

Caroline
Hume
1833–1904

Mary
Charlotte
1835–1911
=Charles Edward
Stuart Collingwood
1831–98

Skeffington
Hume 1836–1919
=Isabel Mary
born Cooper
1848–1937

Stuart
Dodgson
1870–1937

Bertram
James
1871–1934
=Grace Jane born
Wilkinson 1892–

Amy Irene
Hume 1884–
=John Jaques
1862–1937

Charles
Lutwidge‡

John
Hassard‡

Winifred Mary
1888–1977
=Ralph Spencer
Gavin Robinson
1887–1958

Zöe Frances
1890–1976
=Henry
Raynolde Poole
1877–1961

‡Died in infancy

The Dodgson Family[*]

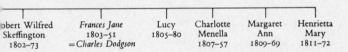

Other issue

obert Wilfred Skeffington 1802–73	*Frances Jane* 1803–51 = *Charles Dodgson*	Lucy 1805–80	Charlotte Menella 1807–57	Margaret Ann 1809–69	Henrietta Mary 1811–72

† Captain Charles Dodgson's widow married George Marwood born Metcalf 1746–1827. Their only child, Margaret Anne, married William Wilcox 1801–72, and from this marriage issued thirteen children, most of whom enter into C. L. Dodgson's letters.

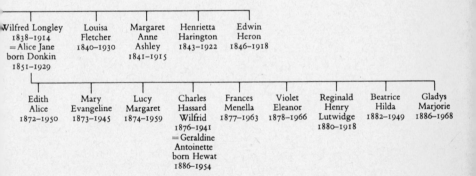

Wilfred Longley 1838–1914 = Alice Jane born Donkin 1851–1929

Louisa Fletcher 1840–1930

Margaret Anne Ashley 1841–1915

Henrietta Harington 1843–1922

Edwin Heron 1846–1918

Edith Alice 1872–1950

Mary Evangeline 1873–1945

Lucy Margaret 1874–1959

Charles Hassard Wilfrid 1876–1941 = Geraldine Antoinette born Hewat 1886–1954

Frances Menella 1877–1963

Violet Eleanor 1878–1966

Reginald Henry Lutwidge 1880–1918

Beatrice Hilda 1882–1949

Gladys Marjorie 1886–1968

* This pedigree is based on a more extensive one prepared by C. L. Dodgson's great-nephew Philip Dodgson Jaques. It includes C. L. Dodgson's immediate family and some distant relatives who enter into his letters.

The Selected Letters of
LEWIS CARROLL

I. The Dodgson Family and Lewis Carroll's Youth

Although Charles Lutwidge Dodgson remained a bachelor all his life, he was very much a family man. He was ever a devoted brother and son; and, from his father's death in 1868, he became, as eldest son, head of the family, a responsibility he took seriously.

For a time in the 1830s, Carroll's father was Perpetual Curate of Daresbury in Cheshire (where Lewis Carroll was born), then Rector of Croft in Yorkshire (where Carroll grew up), and eventually Chaplain to the Bishop of Ripon, Canon of Ripon, and Archdeacon of Richmond.

When Carroll was twelve, he left home to enter the Richmond School, not far from Croft, where his father was still rector. By then, Carroll was already proficient in Latin and mathematics. He remained at Richmond for only a year and a half, boarding with the headmaster and his large family. When he left, the headmaster wrote to Carroll's father, "I shall always feel a peculiar interest in the gentle, intelligent, and well-conducted boy who is now leaving us."

The next three years Carroll spent at Rugby. His memories of Rugby were not particularly pleasant; probably, being shy and contemplative by nature, he did not fit well into the rough-and-ready atmosphere of the boys' living quarters. But Rugby left its mark upon Carroll all the same. The strong, militantly Christian preaching of Dr. Thomas Arnold was still echoing in the school when Carroll was there, and he came away convinced that life on earth was a struggle between good and evil, between God and the Devil, and that it was his purpose on earth to fend off the Devil by means of self-denial, a strong will, and uncompromisingly righteous thought and behaviour. One must strive constantly to be virtuous, and one must do serious work in God's name. It is not surprising, given Carroll's family background and his training at school, that while he was still in his twenties, he was ordained a deacon in the Church of England.

But before then he went from Rugby to Oxford, to Christ Church, the same college where his father had made a double first. He himself achieved an excellent record and in 1852 was made Student of Christ Church (the equivalent of a Fellow elsewhere) and in 1855 was appointed Mathematical Lecturer.

To his nurse

[?1837]

My dear Bun,

I love you very much, and tend you a kitt from little Charlie with the horn of hair. I'd like to give you a kitt, but I tan't, betause I'm at Marke. What a long letter I've written. I'm twite tired.*

To his sisters Frances and Elizabeth and his brother Skeffington

Richmond School, Yorkshire
August 5 [1844]

My dear Fanny and Memy,

I hope you are all getting on well, as also the sweet twins, the boys I think that I like the best, are Harry Austin, and all the Tates† of which there are

---

* Charles Dodgson wrote this earliest of letters from an unknown address to his nurse at home when he was four or five years old. His hand was probably guided by one of his elders.

† James Tate was headmaster of Richmond Grammar School. Charles Dodgson started school four days before he wrote this letter. He lived with the Tates as a boarder.

7 besides a little girl who came down to dinner the first day, but not since, and I also like Edmund Tremlet, and William and Edward Swire, Tremlet is a very sharp little fellow about 7 years old, the youngest in the school, I also like Kemp and Mawley. The rest of the boys that I know are Bertram, Harry and Dick Wilson, and two Robinsons, I will tell you all about them when I return. The boys have played two tricks upon me which were these – they first proposed to play at "King of the cobblers" and asked me if I would be king, to which I agreed, then they made me sit down and sat (on the ground) in a circle round me, and told me to say "Go to work" which I said and they immediately began kicking me and knocking on all sides. The next game they proposed was "Peter, the red lion," and they made a mark on a tombstone (for we were playing in the church-yard) and one of the boys walked with his eyes shut, holding out his finger, trying to touch the mark, then a little boy came forward to lead the rest and led a good many very near the mark; at last it was my turn, they told me to shut my eyes well, and the next minute I had my finger in the mouth of one of the boys, who had stood (I believe) *before* the tombstone with his mouth open. For 2 nights I slept alone, and for the rest of the time with Ned Swire. The boys play me no tricks now. The only *fault* (tell mama) that there has been was coming in one day to dinner *just* after grace. On Sunday we went to church in the morning, and sat in a large pew with Mr. Fielding, the church we went to is close by Mr. Tate's house, we did not go in the afternoon but Mr. Tate read a discourse to the boys on the 5th Commandment. We went to church again in the evening. Papa wished me to tell him all the texts I had heard preached upon, please to tell him that I could not hear it in the morning nor hardly one sentence of the sermon, but the one in the evening was I Cor: i. 23. I believe it was a farewell sermon but I am not sure. Mrs. Tate has looked through my clothes and left in the trunk a great many that will not be wanted. I have had 3 misfortunes in my clothes etc., 1st I cannot find my tooth brush, so that I have not brushed my teeth for 3 or 4 days, 2nd I cannot find my blotting paper, and 3d I have no shoe horn. The chief games are, foot-ball, wrestling, leap frog, and fighting. Excuse bad writing.

Your affectionate brother,
Charles

To Skeff

My dear Skeff,
Roar not lest thou be abolished.

Yours, etc. –

To his sister Elizabeth

School House [Rugby]
October 9 [1848]

Dearest Elizabeth,

Thank you for your letter: in reply to your question, I *do* get a prize,* value one guinea. I have chosen for it Butler's *Analogy* in 2 vols. which exactly comes up to the value, one vol.: *Analogy*, the other *Sermons*. As to the other prize I am not yet decided: Papa has taken no notice of the book I had set my fancy on getting, Whiston's *Josephus*, in 2 vols., 24s.: will you ask him what he thinks of it? Clarendon's *Rebellion* is in double columns, and Hallam's looks very dry. Whiston would require a Bohn to make up the value. I was thinking of Wheatly on the Common Prayer.

I have *not* got any warm gloves yet but must do so soon. Now I think of it, I should like 10s. of my own money to be sent: I can settle about the gloves afterward. I must not forget to send my hearty thanks to Papa and Mamma for their kind present. I cannot in the least decide what to get, and should be glad of some advice on *this* head.

Thanks for your explanation of a *drawn* bonnet. I suppose *shot* silk or satin is to be explained on the same principles: I hope you never wear it. I am glad to hear of the 6 rabbits. For the new name after some consideration I recommend Parellelopipedon. It is a nice easy one to remember, and the rabbit will soon learn it.

The report is certainly a delightful one: *I* cannot account for it; I hope there is no mistake. As to the difference between Walker and myself (Papa seems satisfied about Harrison) it must be remembered that he is in the 6th and has hitherto been considered the best mathematician in the school. Indeed no one but me got anything *out* of the 6th (I hope you understand this last sentence). As to the tutor marks, we did not go the 1st week and the Prize examinations have prevented the 4th. The Lower Mathematical Prizeman, Fisher, unfortunately broke his arm yesterday by falling down: it had been broken before, or I do not think so slight a thing could have done it.

---

* Dodgson entered Rugby on January 27, 1846. He made an excellent record and won prizes in classics, composition, divinity, history, and mathematics.

Is W.L. and L.F.'s *Useful and Instructive Poetry* finished binding yet?*
I enclose for Papa *the* Geometrical problem worked out by Mr. Mayor. It is
one of the most beautifully neat ones I ever saw. Pray ask him to take *great*
care of it. There are some books I should like to have leave to get: these are
Butler's Ancient Atlas (on 2nd thoughts not yet). Liddell and Scott's
Larger *Greek–English Lexicon*. Mr. Price quite despises the little one and
says it is only fit for my younger brothers. It is hardly any use in Demosthenes.
Cicero's Epistles, this we do in school. If he consents will you ask him to send
the leave on a piece of paper by itself. With best love to all I remain –

Your most affectionate brother,

C.—L. or D

B

CD

To his sister Mary

Christ Church, Oxford†
March 6, 1851

Dearest Mary,

Many very happy returns of your birthday. I write this for you to get on
Saturday, as I suppose you will not get the letters on Sunday. I hope you
will "keep" it very happily on the Monday, and will imagine my presence
when the health is drunk. The other day I borrowed a book called Coxe's
Christian Ballads, thinking I might like to get a copy: however I found so
many things in it I did not like, and so few I did, that I decided on not buying
the book, but as some of the ballads are sold separate I got the 2 I like best,
which I enclose (one wants sewing). I think you will like them, but I can
hardly ask you to consider so small a purchase as a birthday present.

*Dodgson composed this family magazine for his seven-year-old brother Wilfred and
his five-year-old sister Louisa.

†Dodgson started life as an undergraduate at Christ Church, Oxford, on January 24,
1851.

Give Elizabeth my best thanks for her letter: I am tired of saying "nice long," so let it be always understood in future. I am very glad to see the improved account of Aunt Caroline. I have got all Dr. Hook's *Meditations*; the 2nd vol. contains Lent, the 3d Easter to Trinity, the 4th Trinity.

As Cousin Menella [Smedley] cannot tell you the meaning of "kakography," I must do my best: the word *now* means "bad or incorrect writing," but its original meaning was "vulgarity," and it is thus derived: "kay" or "kai," a Syriac verb, signifying "to wear": "kog" or "kogh" in Chaldee means "paper": and "graph" or "graf," is a Hebrew word meaning "flowers." Hence "kakography" meant "the wearing of paper flowers," and from this came to mean "vulgarity," as the wearing such flowers has always been considered among civilised nations as the height of vulgarity. In the same way "kakographist," meant originally, "she that wears paper flowers," and was a term of great reproach: its meaning is now altogether changed.

I am not so anxious as usual to begin my personal history, as the first thing I have to record is a very sad incident, namely my missing morning chapel; before however you condemn me, you must hear how accidental it was. For some days now I have been in the habit of – I will not say getting up, but of being called at ¼ past 6, and generally managing to be down soon after 7. In the present instance I had been up the night before till about ½ past 12, and consequently when I was called I fell asleep again, and was thunderstruck to find on waking that it was 10 minutes past 8. I have had no imposition, nor heard anything about it. It is rather vexatious to have happened so soon, as I had intended never to be late.

This afternoon I was sitting in my room when I heard a sudden shrieking of dogs, as if fighting: I rushed to the window, but the fight, if any, was over, having lasted for about the space of 3 seconds, and every thing and every body was flying from the scene of combat: six dogs went headlong down the steps, which lead into the quad, yelling at the very top of their voices; six sticks came flying after them, and after that came their six masters, all running their hardest, and all in different directions. For a little time none of the dogs knew which way to go, so they went darting about, tumbling over each other, screaming, and getting hit by the sticks, and their masters did the same only they screamed in a different manner: at last 3 dogs got away and ran straight home, screaming as they went, 2 others were hunted up and down the quad by their masters, I suppose with the intention of beating them, but were never sufficiently caught for that purpose, and the sixth went home with its master, but even *it* screamed all the way. Never

was such desperate vengeance taken for so small an offence: I should think
all the dogs will rue the day: the two combatants will never wish to fight
again, nor the others to be aiders or abettors.

I have got a new acquaintance of the name of Colley, who has been here
once or twice to tea, and we have been out walking together. Today we set
out for the justice court, to hear the trials conducted, as the assizes began on
Monday: it was a cold wretched day for our walk, and you may imagine
what a pleasant surprise it was to us to find that the assizes concluded yesterday, and the judges left Oxford last night.

Mr. Faussett has recovered, so our mathematical lectures have begun
again.

As to my being in London this Easter, the probability is that I shall come
straight home to Bletchley, and not trouble Uncle S[keffington] at all: the
holidays are too short to spare much time for meandering: if I had mentioned it in my last letter I should have said there was no *object* in my going
to London, but after the message in E.L.'s* letter civility forbids me to say a
thing, the very mention of which would be downright rudeness.

I have asked Papa 2 questions, which he seems to have forgotten to
answer, 1st what I am to do about a name plate, and 2nd what I am to do
about a Greek History, also 3dly whether I may get Horatius Zeunii. I am
using Mr. Ley's at present. The notes in Anthon are wretched.

In routing over my wardrobe the other day I discovered a curious and
far from satisfactory circumstance, namely that I have left all my silk neck
handkerchiefs at home. The only things of the kind I possess here are the
handkerchief I now have on, and a black satin tie for the evening. Will you
hunt them up at Croft and send them: if you cannot find them I will look
for them again but I do not think they are here.

I think this is one of the most magnificently long letters I have ever
written.

With best love to all, I remain

Your very affectionate Brother,
Charles Lutwidge Dodgson

* His sister Elizabeth's.

nexte we goe. yn forre Respon-
-siong, & ſ am me uppé toe
mine eyes yn worke.
Thine truly,
Charles.

Last page of letter to his sister Louisa, June 10, 1851

To his sister Louisa

Christ Church, Oxford
June 10, 1851

My beloved and thrice-respected Sister,

Verily I doe send greeting untoe thee, and wish thee all hail for thy byrthe-day, and theretoe manie happie returns off the same. And therewith I have made purchase off ane smalle boke, whilke I have hope ytte maie lyke thee toe possesse. For besydes manie pleasaunte and entertainynge thynges therein contained, ye moralle I trowe beeth both sound and healthful, whylke iss ane great matterre.

Forbie I have received ane epistle (for whilke I send thanks, and ytte lyketh me well) from mine systere Elyzabethe, and anon I shall enform her off my lectures, etc., gratefulle that she doth notte adde toe ye nombere thereoffe.

Ytte will pain thyne hearte, I wotte, toe heare thatte ye people offe Oxford hig-towne cannotte skylle to nurse babys; and trulie their mannere thereoffe is cruelle: herewithe I enclose a sketch of what I have wytnessed myne selfe, and to mie mynde the underneathe babie yn the nurse herre armes ys yn ane sorrie plight.

Onne Moone his daye nexte we goe yn forre Responsions, and I amme uppe toe mine eyes yn worke.

Thine truly,
Charles

To his sister Elizabeth

Spring Gardens, London
July 5, 1851

Dearest Elizabeth,

I must try to make up for my exceedingly short letter of yesterday. In the first place, for fear I forget it again, my Aunts send their best love, including Aunt Raikes.

I am afraid it will be impossible to give you any idea of all I have seen, but I will do my best. On Friday at 10 o'clock I went with Aunt Charlotte to the Exhibition,* to be joined afterwards by Aunts Henrietta, Margaret, and

* The Great Exhibition had opened on May 1.

Aunt Raikes. The building is within 10 minutes walk of Alfred Place, by means of some curious little short cuts through stable yards, etc.

I think the first impression produced on you when you get inside is of bewilderment. It looks like a sort of fairyland. As far as you can look in any direction, you see nothing but pillars hung about with shawls, carpets, etc., with long avenues of statues, fountains, canopies, etc., etc., etc. The first thing to be seen on entering is the Crystal Fountain, a most elegant one about 30 feet high at a rough guess, composed entirely of glass and pouring down jets of water from basin to basin: this is in the middle of the centre nave and from it you can look down to either end, and up both transepts. The centre of the nave mostly consists of a long line of colossal statues, some most magnificent. The one considered the finest, I believe, is the Amazon and Tiger. She is sitting on horseback, and a tiger has fastened on the neck of the horse in front. You have to go to one side to see her face, and the other to see the horse's. The horse's face is really wonderful, expressing terror and pain so exactly, that you almost expect to hear it scream. She is leaning back to strike at the tiger with a spear, and her expression is of steady determination without the least fear. A pair of statues of a dog and child struck me as being exceedingly good. In one the child is being attacked by a serpent, and the dog standing over to defend it. The child is crying with fear, and making I think an exceedingly ugly face. In the other the dog has conquered: the body of the serpent is lying at one side, and the head, *most thoroughly* bitten off, at the other. The dog seems to have quite chewed the neck of the serpent to make sure. The child is leaning over and playing with the dog, which is *really* smiling with pleasure and satisfaction. Then there is an enormous one of Godfrey of Bouillon, with the horse a great deal larger than an elephant; however I cannot describe to you $\frac{1}{100}$ of what I saw. The view down from the galleries is very striking. The different compartments on the ground floor are divided by carpets, shawls, etc., and you look down into one after another as you go along. There is a medieval compartment beautifully fitted up, and a suite of Austrian rooms, furnished, floored, etc., exactly as in Austria, the floors inlaid with different woods and very slippery, and the furniture wonderfully carved. There are some very ingenious pieces of mechanism. A tree (in the French Compartment) with birds chirping and hopping from branch to branch exactly like life. The bird jumps across, turns round on the other branch, so as to face back again, settles its head and neck, and then in a few moments jumps back again. A bird standing at the foot of the tree trying to eat a beetle is rather a failure (I am blotting dreadfully); the beetle is lying very conveniently before it, but it never succeeds in getting its head more than a quarter of an inch down, and that in uncomfortable little jerks, as if it was choking. I have to go to the Royal Academy so must stop: as the subject is quite inexhaustible, there is no hope of ever coming to a regular finish.

I want instructions what to do as to my various invitations: they are, to go on Tuesday to Tunbridge Wells, on Thursday to Gordon Square *till* Monday, on Monday to escort Cousin E. L. Raikes to Hastings, and after a day or two there, home. Those are the propositions: nothing is fixed. Last night I dined with the Stones, and afterwards to a music party at the Watsons. Some day, I forget which, I am to go to a music party at the Campbells. Also Mr. Brinley Richards' concert. Today I am going with my Aunt to The Diorama of Jerusalem. Let Fanny send her commission. I shall know next term what class I got in collections. In haste.

Your very affectionate Brother,
Charles

To his sister Elizabeth

[Christ Church, Oxford]
December 9, 1852

Dearest Elizabeth,

You shall have the announcement of the last piece of good fortune this wonderful term has had in store for me, that is, *a 1st class in Mathematics.* Whether I shall add to this any honours at collections I cannot at present say, but I should think it very unlikely, as I have only today to get up the work in The Acts of the Apostles, 2 Greek Plays, and the Satires of Horace and I feel myself almost totally unable to read at all: I am beginning to suffer from the reaction of reading for Moderations.

I heard this morning from Uncle Skeffington, telling me that he should expect me on Friday, to stay till Tuesday or Wednesday, when I am to migrate to Putney. It will be a most delightful trip for me, if only considered as an interval of rest. You will have very little of my company this Xmas, as we return on the 15th of January.

I am getting quite tired of being congratulated on various subjects: there seems to be no end of it. If I had shot the Dean, I could hardly have had more said about it.

Mr. Gordon has given me a copy of his Censor's speech (printed for private distribution): I will bring it home with me for Papa to read. I think it beautiful Latin; it is mostly about the Duke.*

I have decided against taking the rooms I thought of at first, but there is another set (in Tom) that I have got my eye on. I am going to write to Uncle S[keffington] and Mr. Greenall† (I promised to tell him the result of the Mathematics) so conclude.

Best love to all.

> Your very affectionate Brother,
> Charles L. Dodgson

To his sister Mary

> Christ Church, Oxford
> December 13, 1854

My dear Sister,

Enclosed you will find a list, which I expect you to rejoice over considerably: it will take me more than a day to believe it, I expect — I feel at present very like a child with a new toy, but I daresay I shall be tired of it soon, and wish to be Pope of Rome next. Those in the list who were of the Whitby party are, Fowler, Ranken, Almond, and Wingfield.‡ I have just given my Scout a bottle of wine to drink to my First. We shall be made Bachelors on Monday: I *think* I may be able to come home on the Tuesday, but I am not sure yet, and will write again about it. If you have not yet sent the London order will you get *The Life of R. Haydon* for me? That is, unless it happens to be in the Ripon Library. I hope that Papa did not conclude it was a 2nd by not hearing on Wednesday morning. I have just been to Mr. Price to see how I did in the papers, and the result will I hope be gratifying to you. The following were the sums total of the marks for each in the 1st class, as nearly as I can remember:

> Dodgson 279
> Bosanquet 261

* The Duke of Wellington, Chancellor of Oxford University, died on September 14 of that year.
† Gilbert Greenall, M.P. for Warrington, was an old family friend.
‡ Dodgson was one of a number of undergraduates who spent the summer vacation at Whitby reading mathematics with Professor Bartholomew Price.

Cookson 254
Fowler 225
Ranken 213

He also said he never remembered so good a set of men in. All this is very satisfactory. I must also add (this is a very boastful letter) that I ought to get the Senior Scholarship next term. Bosanquet will not try, as he is leaving Oxford, and the only man, besides the present First, to try, is one who got a 2nd last time. One thing more I will add, to crown all, and that is – I find I am the next 1st class Math. student to Faussett (with the exception of Kitchin, who has given up Mathematics) so that I stand next (as Bosanquet is going to leave) for the Lectureship. And now I think that is enough news for one post.

Your very affectionate Brother,
Charles L. Dodgson

To his sister Henrietta and brother Edwin

[Christ Church, Oxford]
January 31 [?1855]

My dear Henrietta,
My dear Edwin,

I am very much obliged by your nice little birthday gift – it was much better than a cane would have been – I have got it on my watch chain, but the Dean has not yet remarked it.

My one pupil has begun his work with me, and I will give you a description how the lecture is conducted. It is the most important point, you know, that the tutor should be *dignified*, and at a distance from the pupil, and that the pupil should be as much as possible *degraded* – otherwise you know, they are not humble enough. So I sit at the further end of the room; outside the door (*which is shut*) sits the scout; outside the outer door (*also shut*) sits the sub-scout; half-way down stairs sits the sub-sub-scout; and down in the yard sits the *pupil*.

The questions are shouted from one to the other, and the answers come back in the same way – it is rather confusing till you are well used to it. The lecture goes on, something like this.

Tutor. "What is twice three?"
Scout. "What's a rice tree?"

Sub-Scout. "When is ice free?"
Sub-sub-Scout. "What's a nice fee?"
Pupil (timidly). "Half a guinea!"
Sub-sub-Scout. "Can't forge any!"
Sub-Scout. "Ho for Jinny!"
Scout. "Don't be a ninny!"
Tutor (looks offended, but tries another question). "Divide a hundred by twelve!"
Scout. "Provide wonderful bells!"
Sub-Scout. "Go ride under it yourself."
Sub-sub-Scout. "Deride the dunder-headed elf!"
Pupil (surprised). "Who do you mean?"
Sub-sub-Scout. "Doings between!"
Sub-Scout. "Blue is the screen!"
Scout. "Soup-tureen!"

And so the lecture proceeds.
　　Such is Life – from

Your most affectionate brother,
Charles L. Dodgson

To his cousin W. E. Wilcox

Christ Church, Oxford
May 11, 1859

My dear William,
　　I have had it in my head for some time back to write you an account of my visit to the Isle of Wight, only I doubted if there was enough to tell to make it worth while – now however that you yourself ask for it, you must be thankful for what you get, interesting or not – truly *bis dat qui cito dat.** (I trust there is some latent appropriateness in the quotation.) Wilfred must have basely misrepresented me if he said that I followed the Laureate down to his retreat, as I went, not knowing that he was there, to stay with an old College friend at Freshwater. Being there, I had the inalienable right of a freeborn Briton to make a morning call, which I did, in spite of my friend

---

* "He gives twice who gives in a trice."

Collyns having assured me that the Tennysons had not yet arrived. There was a man painting the garden railing when I walked up to the house, of whom I asked if Mr. Tennyson were at home, fully expecting the answer "no," so that it was an agreeable surprise when he said "he's there, sir" and pointed him out, and behold ! he was not many yards off, mowing his lawn in a wide-awake and spectacles. I had to introduce myself, as he is too short-sighted to recognise people, and when he had finished the bit of mowing he was at, he took me into the house to see Mrs. Tennyson, who, I was very sorry to find, had been very ill, and was then suffering from almost total sleeplessness. She was lying on the sofa, looking rather worn and haggard, so that I stayed a very few minutes. She asked me to come to dinner that evening to meet a Mr. Warburton (brother of the *Crescent and the Cross*), but her husband revoked the invitation before I left, as he said he wished her to be as little excited as possible that evening, and begged I would drop in for tea that evening and dine with them the next day. He took me over the house to see the pictures, etc. (among which my photographs of the family were hung "on the line," framed in those enamel – what do you call them – cartons?). The view from the garret windows he considers one of the finest in the island, and showed me a picture which his friend Richard Doyle had painted of it for him, also his little smoking-room at the top of the house, where of course he offered me a pipe, also the nursery, where we found the beautiful little Hallam (his son) who remembered me more readily than his father had done.

I went in the evening, and found Mr. Warburton an agreeable man, with rather a shy, nervous manner: he is a clergyman, and inspector of schools in that neighbourhood. We got on the subject of clerical duty in the evening, and Tennyson said he thought clergymen as a body didn't do half the good they might if they were less stuck-up, and showed a little more sympathy with their people. "What they want," he said, "is force and geniality – geniality without force will of course do no good, but force without geniality will do very little" – all very sound theology to my thinking. This was up in the little smoking-room, to which we had adjourned after tea, and where we had about 2 hours' very interesting talk. The proof-sheets of "The King's Idyls" were lying about, but he would not let me look at them. I looked with some curiosity to see what sort of books occupied the lowest of the swinging bookshelves, most handy to his writing-table: they were all without exception Greek or Latin – Homer, Aeschylus, Horace, Lucretius, Virgil, etc. It was a fine moonlight night, and he walked through the garden with me when I left, and pointed out an effect of the moon shining through thin white cloud which I had never noticed before – a sort of golden ring, not close round its edge like a halo, but at some distance off. I believe sailors consider it a sign of bad weather. He said he had often noticed it, and had alluded to it in one of his early poems: you will find it in "Margaret."

The next day I went to dinner, and met Sir John Simeon, who has an estate some miles off there, an old Christ Church man, who has turned Roman Catholic since. He is one of the pleasantest men I ever met, and you may imagine that the evening was a delightful one: I enjoyed it thoroughly, especially the concluding 2 hours in the smoking-room.

I took over my books of photographs, but Mrs. Tennyson was too tired to look at them that evening, and I settled to leave them and come for them next morning, when I could see more of the children, who had only appeared for a few minutes during dinner.

Tennyson told us that often on going to bed after being engaged on com-position, he had dreamed long passages of poetry ("you, I suppose," turning to me, "dream photographs") which he liked very much at the time, but forgot entirely when he woke. One was an enormously long one on fairies, where the lines from being very long at first, gradually got shorter and shorter, till it ended with 50 or 60 lines of 2 syllables each! The only bit he ever remembered enough to write down was one he dreamed at 10 years old, which you may like to possess as a genuine unpublished fragment of the Laureate, though I think you will agree with me that it gives very little indication of his future poetic powers –

> May a cock-sparrow
> Write to a barrow?
> I hope you'll excuse
> My infantine muse.

Up in the smoking-room the conversation turned upon murders, and Tennyson told us several horrible stories from his own experience: he seems rather to revel in such descriptions – one would not guess it from his poetry. Sir John kindly offered me a lift in his carriage back to the hotel, and as we were standing at the door before getting in, he said, "you don't object to a cigar in the carriage, do you?" On which Tennyson growled out, "he didn't object to *two pipes* in that little den upstairs, and *a feebliori** he's no business to

---

* A pun on *a fortiori*.

object to one cigar in a carriage." And so ended one of the most delightful evenings I have spent for many a long day. I lunched with them the next day, but saw very little of Tennyson himself, and afterwards showed the photographs to Mrs. T. and the children, not omitting to get Hallam's auto-graph, in a large bold text-hand, under his portrait. The children insisted on reading out the poetry opposite to the pictures, and when they came to their father's portrait (which has for a motto "The Poet in a golden clime was born," etc.), Lionel puzzled over it for a moment, and then began boldly "The Pope —"! on which Mrs. Tennyson began laughing, and Tennyson growled out from the other side of the table "Hollo! what's that about the Pope?" but no one ventured to explain the allusion.

I asked Mrs. Tennyson for an explanation of "The Lady of Shalott," which has been so variously interpreted. She said that the original legend is in Italian, and that Tennyson only gave it as he found it, so that it is hardly fair to expect him to furnish an interpretation as well.

By-the-bye do you think that those lines in *The Times*, called "The War," and signed "T," are Tennyson's? I have made a bet with a friend here that they are not, and am going to try and find out: many people seem to think they are.

Well! you ought to be very much obliged to me for writing so long a letter (and I hate letter-writing as a general rule), and I am going to conclude it with rather an odd request. I have been thinking of writing an account of my Tennyson visit to Menella Smedley. Now it will probably be long before I get time for it, and the letter would be in substance much the same as this. Would you mind forwarding this for her perusal, as she is my only other appreciative correspondent. It is of course less compliment to her than writing direct, and possibly she may not feel at all grateful for it, but it is better than none.

So no more at present from

> Your faithful Cousin,
> Charles L. Dodgson

P.S. 5 minutes to 3 A.M.! This comes of beginning letter-writing at night.

To his family

[Christ Church, Oxford]
[December 18, 1860]

...proposition we had been doing ! – he was less influenced by the presence of Majesty, and remembered it. She*was only a minute or two in the Hall, during which the Dean pointed out some of the chief pictures, and presented the Sub-dean. With her were Prince Albert, Princess Alice, Prince of Wales, Prince Alfred, and suite. I had never seen her so near before, nor on her feet, and was shocked to find how short, not to say dumpy, and (with all loyalty be it spoken), how *plain* she is. She is *exactly* like the little full-length photograph published of her. I have got the whole set of the Royal Family, and will bring them home with me.

You will be sorry to hear that I have failed, finally and completely, in getting H.R.H. to sit for his photograph. I will give you the history of my proceedings in the matter, which will show you that I did not fail for want of asking, and that, if ever impudence and importunity deserved to succeed, *I* did.

When the Royal party returned to Frewen Hall,† I called to enter my name (as usual) in the visiting book, and to see General Bruce, whom I reminded of the promised photograph, and also asked him to take some opportunity of introducing me to H.R.H. as I had never had an opportunity of thanking him for consenting to sit. This he promised to do, and also said he would arrange for a sitting.

Weeks passed, and I heard no more of it. When it was so near the end of term as to be "now or never," I wrote to tell him that I had got out my chemicals, and found they worked very fairly, and hoped he would come without delay. He answered that the Prince feared it could not be done in such rainy weather. I wrote once more to say that if *that* was the only objection, it *could* be done, but if there was any *other* reason against it, I withdrew my request. I happened to meet General Bruce, who at once entered

---

* Queen Victoria visited Christ Church, where the Prince of Wales was an undergraduate, on December 12, 1860, accompanied by the Prince Consort, their second daughter, Princess Alice, and their second son, Prince Alfred.

† Beside the Oxford Union, where the Prince of Wales lived while at Oxford. Major-General Robert Bruce was Governor to the Prince of Wales.

on the subject, and admitted that the Prince's *real* reason was that he was utterly weary of being photographed, having been so often victimised. Though I thought this hardly sufficient excuse for not keeping his promise, of course I could only beg that he might be no more troubled on the subject.

Last Wednesday we were asked to an evening party at the Deanery to meet the Prince. I need not say that I got hold of General Bruce, and claimed the fulfilment of his promise to introduce me, which he most readily did. The Prince shook hands very graciously, and I began by apologising for having been so troublesome about the photograph. He looked perhaps a *little* ashamed of himself, and said something about the weather being unfavourable. I asked him if the Americans had victimised him much as a sitter, and he said "yes, but they had not succeeded well," and we talked for 2 or 3 minutes about photographs, my pictures of the Liddells, and the *tableaux vivants* which were to form the entertainment of the evening. When I say "we," it should rather be, that *I* talked to *him*, for he was anything but suggestive of conversation himself, seeming rather shy and silent.

I told him that as I could not get the photograph of himself, I meant to take one from his published picture (by Richmond) for my album, and hoped he would at least give me his *autograph*, which he promised to do. I also said if he would like copies of any of my photographs, I should think it an honour for him to accept them, and he thanked me, saying he should like some of them, or something to that effect.

When the talk came to a pause, and he did not seem inclined to go on, I drew back, and the interview came to an end. You will not wonder at these minute details, knowing how unique a thing an interview with Royalty is to me.

The *tableaux vivants* were *very* successful, but I must leave the description of them for viva voce. Lady Williamson was there, and supplied the costumes, and herself appeared in one scene. One of the prettiest was Tennyson's *The Sleeping Princess*, acted entirely by the children. The grouping was capital, I believe by Lady W. I was sure it could not be by Mrs. Liddell, of whose taste in that line I have already had melancholy experience in my photographs. I shall try and get them to go through it by daylight in the summer. It would make a beautiful photograph.

To return to the Prince, I wrote a note to General Bruce, asking if I might bring my album to Frewen Hall, and *see* the autograph done, pleading that that would much increase its value in my eyes. He wrote appointing 10 on Saturday, and added that the Prince would at the same time select some of the photographs. I sent over the box of albums, and went at 10. General

Bruce joined me in the hall (a sort of morning room), and the Prince came in directly afterwards, and seemed very friendly and more at his ease than he was at the Deanery. He saw that I was noticing his dog (an enormous Newfoundland, given him in America), and began to talk to me about it, telling me, in answer to my question, that it was not yet a year old. When the box was opened, he looked through the second album, especially admiring the "cherry" group, the Chinese group, and the large one of the 2 Haringtons.

He said he had no time to finish looking through them then, and proposed they should be left, but on my saying (an awful breach of court etiquette, no doubt), that I was expecting some friends that morning to see them (the John Slatters), he fixed on Tuesday (today) to have them sent over again. He consented to give the autograph then, but would not use my gold pen, as I wanted, saying that he wrote best with quill, and went to fetch a good one, with which he signed, adding the place and date at my suggestion. There ends my interview with Royalty. I have sent over the box this morning, and General Bruce is to send me a list of those of which he would like to have copies. We must do them if possible in the Easter Vacation: I expect there will be no lack of volunteers to print for the Prince – of course none but *first-raters* must be sent.

By this time you will have had *about* enough on this subject.

I spent the *whole* of yesterday in sorting letters and bills, and have made up a great bundle of letters interesting as autographs, which I shall bring home for exhibition, and may be able to spare Mary one or two of the most worthless (Mary: "kind and thoughtful brother !").

I don't *think* I shall go by London at all this time. I should have done so if Edwin had joined me, but it is rather dull work going about there alone, and my business will do just as well at the end of the Vacation as now. We have to be here again by the 19th. – The little Haringtons have just been in (you see I have other visitors than the Liddells) to invite me to lunch tomorrow. I am going out now bill-paying, which cheerful occupation will probably last till post-time, so I here conclude one of the longest letters I have written for some time. Make the most of it.

Your very affectionate brother,
Charles L. Dodgson

To the Diocesan Registrar, Oxford

Croft Rectory, Darlington
August 5, 1861

Dear Sir,

I am intending to offer myself at the Bishop of Oxford's examination in September, to be ordained Deacon.* I gave his Lordship notice of this about 4 months ago. Would you kindly inform me what else is necessary (of papers to be sent in, etc.) before presenting myself for examination, and when and where I ought to appear? Believe me

Yours truly,
Charles L. Dodgson
(M.A. and Student of Christ Church)

* Dodgson was ordained a deacon on December 22, 1861, but he never took priest's orders.

II. Alice and Photography

When the Dean of Christ Church, Thomas Gaisford, died in June 1855, he was succeeded by Henry George Liddell, chaplain to Queen Victoria's husband, headmaster of Westminster School, and co-author with Robert Scott of the formidable *Greek Lexicon*.

With the Dean and his *Lexicon* came his wife, a son, and three daughters. The second daughter, Alice, became, in time, Lewis Carroll's "ideal child friend" and the model for the heroine of the fantasy that he created, spontaneously, on July 4, 1862, when he and a fellow don, Robinson Duckworth, took the three Liddell girls on a rowing party.

Actually the story almost never got recorded. It was put onto paper only because, as Alice herself recalled in later years, "on the next day I started to pester him to write down the story for me." She "kept going on, going on at him" until he promised to set it down for her. The rest is history.

Although we think of Carroll primarily in connection with the *Alice* books, his interest in technological advances, and in gadgets generally, made the camera an object that he wanted to possess and experiment with. He bought one as early as 1856, when photography itself was still in its infancy. For Carroll, taking good and careful pictures, pictures that would please and delight for their sheer artistic qualities, became much more than just a hobby; and to this day he keeps his place among the important early photographic artists in all histories on the subject.

Carroll began by taking sittings of his family and friends and of his university associates. But before long he moved on to London and other venues with his cumbersome camera to photograph some of the luminaries of his time. He managed to photograph the Terry family, the Rossetti family, John Everett Millais and his family, his friends the George MacDonalds, the Tennysons, John Ruskin, Prince Leopold, Frederick the Crown Prince of Denmark, and various judges and churchmen.

In time he turned to children and devoted himself to photographing them. So successful was he that the historian of photography Helmut Gernsheim has written that he was "the most outstanding photographer of children in the nineteenth century."

To Lorina, Alice and Edith Liddell

Christmas 1861

Little maidens, when you look

On this little story-book,

Reading with attentive eye

Its enticing history,

Never think that hours of play

Are your only HOLIDAY,

And that in a HOUSE of joy

Lessons serve but to annoy:

If in any HOUSE you find

Children of a gentle mind,

Each the others pleasing ever—

Each the others vexing never—

Daily work and pastime daily

In their order taking gaily—

Then be very sure that they

Have a *Life* of HOLIDAY.*

* This acrostic, in Dodgson's own hand, appears on the front inner cover of a copy of Catherine Sinclair's *Holiday House* (1839, 2nd ed. 1856). On the fly-leaf Dodgson wrote: "L. A. and E. Liddell/a Christmas gift/from C. L. Dodgson."

To Annie Rogers

My dear Annie,   [? 1862]

                    I send you
            A picture, which I hope will
            B one that you will like to
            C. If your Mamma should
            D sire one like it, I could
            E sily get her one.

                                        Your affectionate friend,
                                             C. L. Dodgson

To Hallam Tennyson*

                                        Christ Church, Oxford
                                        January 23, 1862

My dear Hallam,

Thank you for your nice little note. I am glad you liked the knife, and I think it a pity you should not be allowed to use it "till you are older." However, as you *are* older now, perhaps you have begun to use it by this time: if you were allowed to cut your finger with it, once a week, just a little, you know, till it began to bleed, and a good deep cut every birthday, I should think that would be enough, and it would last a long time so. Only I hope that if Lionel ever wants to have *his* fingers cut with it, you will be kind to your brother, and hurt him as much as he likes.

If you will send me word, some day, when your two birthdays are, perhaps I may send *him* a birthday present, if I can only find something that will hurt him as much as your knife: perhaps a blister, or a leech, or something of that sort.

Give him half my love, and take the rest yourself.

                                        Your affectionate friend,
                                             Charles L. Dodgson

* The Poet Laureate's younger son.

To Tom Taylor*

Christ Church, Oxford
December 20, 1863

Dear Sir,

Do you know Mr. Tenniel enough to be able to say whether he could undertake such a thing as drawing a dozen wood-cuts to illustrate a child's book, and if so, could you put me into communication with him? The reasons for which I ask (which however can be of but little interest if your answer be in the negative) are that I have written such a tale for a young friend, and illustrated it in pen and ink. It has been read and liked by so many children, and I have been so often asked to publish it, that I have decided on doing so. I have tried my hand at drawing on the wood, and come to the conclusion that it would take much more time than I can afford, and that the result would not be satisfactory after all. I want some figure-pictures done in pure outline, or nearly so, and of all artists on wood, I should prefer Mr. Tenniel. If he should be willing to undertake them, I would send him the book to look over, not that he should at all follow my pictures, but simply to give him an idea of the sort of thing I want. I should be much obliged if you would find out for me what he thinks about it, and remain

Very truly yours,
C. L. Dodgson

My address will be "Croft Rectory, Darlington" till the end of the year, and then "The Residence, Ripon" till the 15th.

To Robinson Duckworth†

Christ Church, Oxford
April 12, 1864

Dear Duckworth,

Will you dine with me in Hall on Thursday? or on Saturday? And should you be disposed any day soon for a row on the river, for which I could procure some Liddells as companions.

Ever truly yours,
C. L. Dodgson

* The popular and prolific dramatist, who later became editor of *Punch*, gave Dodgson an introduction to John Tenniel, the *Punch* cartoonist.
† Then Fellow of Trinity College, Oxford, Duckworth was the other adult present on the memorable river picnic in July 1862 when Dodgson first told the story of Alice in Wonderland.

To Mary MacDonald*

Christ Church, Oxford
May 23, 1864

My dear Child,

It's been so frightfully hot here that I've been almost too weak to hold a pen, and even if I had been able, there was no ink – it had all evaporated into a cloud of black steam, and in that state it has been floating about the room, inking the walls and ceiling till they're hardly fit to be seen: today it is cooler, and a little has come back into the ink-bottle in the form of black snow – there will soon be enough for me to write and order those photographs your Mamma wants.

This hot weather makes me very sad and sulky: I can hardly keep my temper sometimes. For instance, just now the Bishop of Oxford came in to see me – it was a civil thing to do, and he meant no harm, poor man: but I was so provoked at his coming in that I threw a book at his head, which I am afraid hurt him a good deal (Mem: this isn't quite true, so you needn't believe it. Don't be in such a hurry to believe next time – I'll tell you why. If you set to work to believe everything, you will tire out the believing-muscles of your mind, and then you'll be so weak you won't be able to believe the simplest true things. Only last week a friend of mine set to work to believe Jack-the-giant-killer. He managed to do it, but he was so exhausted by it that when I told him it was raining (which was true) he *couldn't* believe it, but rushed out into the street without his hat or umbrella, the consequence of which was his hair got seriously damp, and one curl didn't recover its right shape for nearly 2 days. (Mem: some of *that* is not quite true, I'm afraid.)) Will you tell Greville I am getting on with his picture (to go into the oval frame, you know) and I hope to send it in a day or two. Also tell your Mamma that I'm sorry to say none of my sisters are coming to London this summer.

With my kind regards to your Papa and Mamma, and love to you and the other infants, I remain

Your affectionate Friend,
Charles L. Dodgson

The only unlucky thing that happened to me last Friday was *your* writing to me. There!

* Daughter of poet-novelist George MacDonald and his wife, who wrote plays and produced amateur theatricals. Dodgson was a good friend of the family.

To Tom Taylor

Christ Church, Oxford
June 10, 1864

My dear Sir,

You were kind enough to wish me to let you know some while before I came to town on my photographic visit, that you might see whether you could entrap any victims for me. My plans are not definitely settled yet, but, so far as I can see, I shall be in town on or before the 20th (though I could come sooner if there were reason to do so). After that I shall be photographing at various friends' houses for 2 or 3 weeks. I am obliged to speak vaguely, as my plans will be liable to change from day to day.

I have many children sitters engaged, among others, Mr. Millais',* who will make most picturesque subjects. Believe me

Ever yours truly,
C. L. Dodgson

P.S. I should be very glad if you could help me in fixing on a name for my fairy-tale, which Mr. Tenniel (in consequence of your kind introduction) is now illustrating for me, and which I hope to get published before Xmas. The heroine spends an hour underground, and meets various birds, beasts, etc. (*no* fairies), endowed with speech. The whole thing is a dream, but *that* I don't want revealed till the end. I first thought of "Alice's Adventures Under Ground," but that was pronounced too like a lesson-book, in which instruction about mines would be administered in the form of a grill; then I took "Alice's Golden Hour," but that I gave up, having a dark suspicion that there is already a book called "Lily's Golden Hours." Here are the other names I have thought of:

$$\text{Alice among the} \begin{cases} \text{elves} \\ \text{goblins} \end{cases} \quad \text{Alice's} \begin{cases} \text{hour} \\ \text{doings} \\ \text{adventures} \end{cases} \quad \text{in} \begin{cases} \text{elf-land} \\ \text{wonderland.} \end{cases}$$

Of all these I at present prefer "Alice's Adventures in Wonderland." In spite of your "morality," I want something sensational. Perhaps you can suggest a better name than any of these.

---

* The Pre-Raphaelite painter John Everett Millais.

Calendar of events connected with the composing and publishing of *Alice's Adventures in Wonderland*

To Alexander Macmillan*

Christ Church, Oxford
November 11, 1864

Dear Sir,

I have been considering the question of the *colour* of *Alice's Adventures*, and have come to the conclusion that *bright red* will be the best – not the best, perhaps, artistically, but the most attractive to childish eyes. Can this colour be managed with the same smooth, bright cloth that you have in green?

Truly yours,
C. L. Dodgson

To Mary MacDonald

Christ Church, Oxford
November 14, 1864

My dear Mary,

Once upon a time there was a little girl, and she had a cross old Uncle – his neighbours called him a Curmudgeon (whatever that may mean) – and this little girl had promised to copy out for him a sonnet Mr. Rossetti had written about Shakespeare. Well, and she didn't do it, you know: and the poor old Uncle's nose kept getting longer and longer, and his temper getting shorter and shorter, and post after post went by, and no sonnet came — I leave off here to explain how they sent letters in those days: there were no gates, so the gate-posts weren't obliged to stay in one place – consequence of which, they went wandering all over the country – consequence of which, if you wanted to send a letter anywhere, all you had to do was to fasten it on to a gate-post that was going in the proper direction (only they sometimes changed their minds, which was awkward). This was called "sending a letter by the post." They did things very simply in those days: if you had a lot of money, you just dug a hole under the hedge, and popped it in: then you said you had "put it in the bank," and you felt quite comfortable about it. And the way they travelled was – there were railings all along the side of the road, and they used to get up, and walk along the top, as steadily as they could, till they tumbled off – which they mostly did very

* Co-founder of the publishing firm Macmillan & Co.

soon. This was called "travelling by rail." Now to return to the wicked little girl. The end of her was, that a great black WOLF came, and — I don't like to go on, but nothing was found of her afterwards, except 3 small bones.

I make no remark. It is rather a horrid story.

Your loving friend,
C. L. Dodgson

To Alexander Macmillan

Croft Rectory, Darlington
August 24, 1866

My dear Sir,

Thanks for your letter and information, with which I am very well satisfied. Your magnificent idea of printing *3000* more alarms me a little: *I* should have thought *1000* a large enough venture, considering the sale hitherto – but if your mention of "a less expensive paper" implies (as I presume it must do) that you propose to lower the price of the book, I am inclined to defer to your judgement in the matter. My idea at first was that 7s. 6d. was too dear.

If however you think we had better keep to 7s. 6d., *then* the paper must be the same as we used before. I can *not* consent to the one being reduced without the other, so that people might say "here is an inferior article sold at the old price."

Let me know when you are ready to print again, that I may send you a list of corrections which I am preparing.

If we decide on the 3000, it would be well, I think, to print on the title-pages "fifth thousand," "sixth thousand," etc.

I should be glad to know what you think of my idea of putting it into French, or German, or both, and trying for a Continental sale. I believe I could get either version well done in Oxford. It would have to be got up, and sold, at a much cheaper rate, if one may judge of their light literature by the specimens that reach England.

It will probably be some time before I again indulge in paper and print. I have, however, a floating idea of writing a sort of sequel to *Alice*, and if it ever comes to anything, I intend to consult you at the very outset, so as to have the thing properly managed from the beginning.

Sincerely yours,
C. L. Dodgson

To Annie Rogers

[1867]

My dear Annie,

This is indeed dreadful. You have no idea of the grief I am in while I write. I am obliged to use an umbrella to keep the tears from running down on to the paper. Did you come yesterday to be photographed? and were you *very* angry? why wasn't I there? Well the fact was this – I went out for a walk with Bibkins, my dear friend Bibkins – we went many miles from Oxford – fifty – a hundred say. As we were crossing a field full of sheep, a thought crossed my mind, and I said solemnly, "Dobkins, what o'clock is it?" "Three," said Fipkins, surprised at my manner. Tears ran down my cheeks. "It is the HOUR," I said. "Tell me, tell me, Hopkins, what day is it?" "Why, Monday, of course," said Lupkins. "Then it is the DAY!" I groaned. I wept. I screamed. The sheep crowded round me, and rubbed their affectionate noses against mine. "Mopkins!" I said, "you are my oldest friend. Do not deceive me, Nupkins! What year is this?" "Well, I *think* it's 1867," said Pipkins. "Then it's the YEAR!" I screamed, so loud that Tapkins fainted. It was all over: I was brought home, in a cart, attended by the faithful Wopkins, in several pieces.

When I have recovered a little from the shock, and have been to the seaside for a few months, I will call and arrange another day for photographing. I am too weak to write this myself, so Zupkins is writing it for me.

Your miserable friend,
Lewis Carroll

To Lilia MacDonald*

The Residence, Ripon
January 5, 1867

My dear Lily,

I have ordered a little book *The Fountain of Youth* to be sent you as a New Year's gift, and hope this note may reach you in time to warn you of its coming, that it may not be too great a shock for your nerves. The book is intended for you to look at the outside, and then put it away in the bookcase: the *inside* is not meant to be read. The book has got a moral – so I need hardly say it is *not* by Lewis Carroll.

* Eldest of the MacDonald children.

The moral is, that if ladies *will* insist on being considered as children, long after their hair has begun to get gray and their faces to be covered with wrinkles (I know a family in Kensington where the eldest daughter does this – and she is *nearly* 57 !) they will end at last in being hermitesses, and building 50 small crosses up the side of a hill. However, never mind the moral. I hope you will be a child still when I see you next.

There are 2 reasons for not sending love to your brothers and sisters – one is, they *will* keep sending it back to me; as if they didn't value it a bit; the other is, it will lose all its warmth on the way this bitter weather. The trees look *so* lovely about here – as if you had taken the summer woods and frozen all the green out of them: it quite looks like Fairy Land.

With love to all you young ones, I remain

Your affectionate "Uncle,"
C. L. Dodgson

I hope you will succeed in getting to the Pantomime today. Thank your Mama for her letter which came this morning. My sisters send their kind regards to your Mama, and best New Year's wishes for you all.

To his brother Edwin

Christ Church, Oxford
March 11, 1867

My dear Edwin,

I expect this will be a pretty long letter, as it has to detail a "sperience" which was very interesting to me, and may perhaps be so to you. When I had seen the *Living Miniatures* at the Haymarket on my way here at the beginning of term (I think I gave you some account of *that*) I wrote to Mr. Coe, the manager of the little company, to ask where I could get photographs of the children, and telling him how much I had liked the performance. In answering my letter, he thanked me for the interest I took in his entertainment, and giving me some account of the trouble he had had in getting it up, and training the children. Then I wrote to thank him in turn, and saying that I should have liked if possible to photograph them myself, but there would be no chance till July. I think it was in his answer to this, that he said, if I came to town before the thing came to an end, he hoped I would come behind the scenes and see how the whole thing was managed. I decided at first against doing so, thinking that probably the whole charm of the thing depended on the footlights – but finally I thought it *would* be an interesting thing to see it once, and that it would probably be my last chance (as the performance has not paid, and so will probably not be tried again) of seeing the mechanism of a theatre without its company. So I took a day in town, and wrote to Mr. Coe to say I would call on him, and to Wilfred to say I was coming, and would call at his office in hopes of his being able to join me for the day. *That* part of the business failed, as all I found at his office was my own letter lying on the table. However, after some shopping, and a visit to the Gallery of Female Artists, I called at Mr. Coe's, a little before 2. I found him a very pleasant and gentlemanly person, and we had some talk about the lessons he gives in elocution. He says he has given lessons to various clergymen, barristers, and lecturers, and I am by no means sure that I shall not go to him to get a few hints. I also saw Mrs. Coe for a minute, who seemed a very nice sort of person, quite lady-like. We soon went off to the theatre, and in at the stage-door. I had told him I wanted to see the theatrical machinery, so he set one of the officials to take me round, under the stage, etc. The only curious part was below: the stage rests on a perfect forest of pillars, every part of it being supported separately by cross-beams, so that almost every bit of it can be lowered separately as a trap: and there is one gigantic trap on which he said 8 people could go up at once – fancy 8 ghosts rising all together. While I was seeing these things Mr. and Mrs. Coe were getting the children ready, and when I went to the green-room to wait, one of them was already there, a little boy dressed as an officer, one of the best of the company, with whom I had a little talk.

Gradually all the children made their appearance, along with Mr. and Mrs. Coe, and several matronly people, who seemed to be mothers of some of them. Though the green-room was in broad daylight, and the little actresses were liberally rouged, the effect was still exceedingly pretty. There was not much real beauty, but 2 or 3 of them would have been much admired, I think, if they had been born in higher stations in life. By this time the overture had begun, but before the curtain drew up there was a new bit to be rehearsed as "Mr. Grumble-gudgeon Mite," a wonderful little boy of $5\frac{1}{2}$, was to sing a comic song for the first time, and some lines of conversation had been written to introduce it. I had no idea before that they ever did such a thing as rehearse, close to the curtain, with the audience on the other side of it, however I suppose the music prevented any of it being heard. I went on the stage to see this done, and the conversation was repeated, and the "business" (the moving about) gone through till Mr. Coe was satisfied. Then he put me into the prompter's box, where I had an excellent view of the stage, and signalled the curtain up. There was no prompter (he said they had not needed one, even the first day) and there was no one to send the children on at the right moment, but the whole thing went on like a piece of clock-work: the children were always ready at the right moment to go on, and Mr. Coe said he could safely leave the theatre, and they would get through the whole thing without a hitch. Mrs. Coe soon joined me in the prompter's box, with the youngest of the company in her arms, Annette Solomon by name, a very pretty little Jewish child, who had no talking to do, but only to go on and dance an Irish Jig. When I saw the performance before, it had seemed rather a shame to send on so small a child, who looked so shy and scared – but all that, I found, was entirely unreal: she was a very conversational little creature, not a bit shy, and so far from disliking her part, she was only anxious to do a great deal more. The part of Mrs. Mite (taken by a very clever child) involves a good deal of talking, including a violent "scene" with her sour-tempered little husband, and this was the part Annette had set her heart on. Later on in the piece, when I was sitting talking to Mr. Coe, with the tiny creature on my knee, she suddenly interrupted the conversation to say to him, very earnestly, and apropos to nothing "I *wish* I might act Mrs. Mite! I know all her part, and I'd get an encore for every word!" Mrs. Coe told me that was quite true: she has learnt it quite perfect, of her own accord. After her dance was over, she was always turning up at every corner, trotting about the place, evidently enjoying it thoroughly. In fact all the children seemed to regard the whole thing as a treat – the going "on" most of all – but when off they watched the other children with quite as much interest, and applauded them quite as vehemently, as any audience could have done. Such a feeling as jealousy never seemed to enter into their heads.

The first piece is a comedy representing an evening-party, and furnished room for some songs and figure-dances such as "Sir Roger de Coverly," etc. The burlesque was a much prettier thing to see: in the green-room Mrs. Coe was putting the last touches to the little fairies, who looked extremely pretty in their muslin and spangles. Fairies look very well over the footlights, in "the golden groves of bliss" or what not: but in my opinion they are much better worth looking at when wandering about among the carpenters and scene shifters: the contrast adds wonderfully to their picturesqueness.

Once I was standing in one of the side-entrances watching a dance that

"Pearl" was executing on the stage, with much applause from the audience: and close by me one of the little fairies, *out* of sight of the audience, was going through identically the same dance, step for step, and with quite as much grace and spirit as the real performer. I told Mrs. Coe of this, and she said "Oh, if we let the children dance as much as they liked, we should soon have all their shoes worn out." The prettiest bit perhaps was the snow-storm. It looks very well from the front, when the cottage-door is opened, and through it you see the snow falling, and hear a chorus of voices singing "Home, sweet home," and then "enter a group of fairies" disguised as travellers in grey cloaks and hoods: but it is more interesting to see from behind, the cut paper being showered down by a man on the top of a pair of steps, and the group of fairies, who had been joined by Mrs. Coe and "Sylvius" the hero (acted by a very clever little French girl), singing their chorus before going on. Mrs. Coe was titivating Sylvius' dress, turning her round and round to pull her sleeves into shape, but the child never left off singing for a moment. I lost a good deal of the performance itself, as I kept wandering about, sometimes chatting with Mrs. Coe in the green-room, and sometimes watching the children, who were all over the place, but never in any one's way, and making themselves useful whenever they were wanted. I saw the little Annette (who is only 4) carrying a heap of things, almost as big as herself, to the green-room.

There was no other visitor behind: all else seemed there on business. I did not try to make acquaintance with the children (except the smallest 2 fairies), thinking that, as they are only poor children, and *not* in the profession, they would not be the better for being noticed and made to think much of themselves – though certainly I *never* saw such clever little things – the sharpest of the sharp race of London children. They had very nice manners, and talked extremely well. In fact you might introduce most of them into a drawing-room without any one guessing their lowly birth. I stayed till the thing was all over, and then bid good-bye to Mr. and Mrs. Coe and went off to Paddington, getting here again by 8 p.m.

If I take my camera to town in the summer, I shall certainly get some of the children to photograph – though there is little chance of the costumes being then in existence.

After I got back here, an idea occurred to me, and I sent off to Mr. Coe that medley-song of "Miss Jones."* I daresay you remember what I mean.

* A "medley-song" which Dodgson composed in 1862 with the help of some of his sisters.

He writes to say he thinks it very funny, and if one of his boys can manage it he will introduce it into the performance. I have also presented him, as an appropriate return for his entertainment, with a copy of *my* "juvenile entertainment," *Alice*. I have vague hopes (though I haven't suggested the idea to him) that it may occur to him to turn it into a pantomime. I fancy it would work well in that form.

Well, I've very seldom written so long a letter as this, and I don't *quite* know what you've done to deserve it: however, take it, and be thankful you have so generous and communicative a brother.

By the way, I think William Wilcox would be interested to hear my adventures in Greenland. Would you send the letter on for him to read, with my love. If I had an abundance of leisure, I would write him a special account: but I haven't – I hope he won't mind having it second-hand.

It would injure the exquisite symmetry of this composition if I were to introduce any other subject, so I'll wind up here.

Your ever affectionate brother,
C. L. Dodgson

To Agnes Argles

Christ Church, Oxford
November 28, 1867

Dear Miss Dolly,

I have a message for you from a friend of mine, Mr. Lewis Carroll, who is a queer sort of creature, rather too fond of talking nonsense. He told me you had once asked him to write another book like one you had read – I forget the name – I think it was about "malice." "Tell her," he said, "that I have just written a little story which is printed in *Aunt Judy's Magazine* and that I have ordered a copy of it to be sent to her."

"Very well," I said, "is that all the message?"

"One thing more," he said, as a few tears trickled down his cheeks, "tell her I *hope* she wasn't angry with me for talking nonsense about her name. You know I sometimes talk nonsense –" ("always" said I) "– and if she was, I *hope* she's forgiven me by this time!" Here the tears came showering over me like rain (I forgot to say that he was leaning out of an upper window, talking to me), and, as I was nearly wet through, I said, "Leave off that, or I won't send her any message at all!" So he drew in his head and shut the window.

If you have any message for him, you had better send it to

Yours very truly,
Charles L. Dodgson

To Margaret Cunnynghame

Christ Church, Oxford
January 30, 1868

Dear Maggie,

I found that the "friend," that the little girl asked me to write to, lived at Ripon, and *not* at Land's End – a nice sort of place to invite to! It looked rather suspicious to me – and soon after, by dint of incessant enquiries, I found out that she was called "Maggie," and lived in a "Crescent"! Of course I declared "after *that*" (the language I used doesn't matter), "I will *not* address her, that's flat! So do not expect me to flatter."

Well, I hope you soon will see your beloved Pa come back – for consider, should you be *quite* content with only Jack? Just suppose they made a blunder! (Such things happen now and then.) Really, now, I shouldn't wonder if your "John" came home again, and your father staid at school! A most awkward thing, no doubt. How would you receive him? You'll say perhaps "you'd turn him out." That would answer well, so far as concerns the *boy*, you know – but consider your Papa, learning lessons in a row of great inky school-boys! This (though unlikely) *might* occur: "Haly" would be grieved to miss him (don't mention it to *her*).

No carte has yet been done of me that does real justice to my *smile*; and so I hardly like, you see, to send you one – however, I'll consider if I will or not – meanwhile, I send a little thing to give you an idea of what I look like when I'm lecturing. The merest sketch, you will allow – yet still I think there's something grand in the expression of the brow and in the action of the hand.

Have you read my fairy-tale in *Aunt Judy's Magazine*?* If you have, you will not fail to discover what I mean when I say "Bruno yesterday came to remind me that *he* was my godson!" On the ground that I "gave him a name"!

Your affectionate friend,
C. L. Dodgson

P.S. I would send, if I were not too shy, the same message to "Haly"† that she (though I do not deserve it, not I!) has sent through her sister to me. My best love to yourself – to your Mother my kindest regards – to your small, fat, impertinent, ignorant brother my hatred. I think that is all.

To Mary MacDonald

Christ Church, Oxford
March 13, 1869

Well! You *are* a cool young lady indeed! After keeping me all these weeks waiting for an answer, you quietly write on another subject, just as if nothing had happened! I wrote, or have written (observe, Madam, that I put it in the preterite or past tense: it isn't likely I ever *shall* write again about it) on the 26th of January last, offering you a copy of the German edition of *Alice*. Well, the days rolled on – and the nights too (as nearly as I can remember, one between every two days, or thereabouts), and *no answer* came. And the weeks rolled on, and the months too, and I got older, and thinner, and sadder, and still NO ANSWER came. And then my friends said – how white my hair was getting, and that I was all skin and bone, and other pleasant remarks – and – but I won't go on, it is too dreadful to relate, except that, through all these years and years of waiting and anxiety (all of which have elapsed since the 26th of January last – you see, we live so fast at Oxford) still NO ANSWER ever came from this granite-hearted young person! And then she calmly writes and says, "Oh, do come and see the

---

* "Bruno's Revenge" had appeared in the December 1867 issue of *Aunt Judy's Magazine*.

† Margaret's elder sister was Clara Halyburton; their two brothers, John and Hugh, also enter the letter, Hugh in the postscript.

race!"* And I answer with a groan, "I *do* see the race – the human race – it is a race *full of ingratitude* – and of all that race none is more ungratefuller, more worser – more – my pen chokes, and I can say no more!

P.S. – I'm afraid I shan't be in town – else I should be glad to come, if only to have the opportunity of saying, "Monster of ingratitude! Avaunt!"

To Marion Terry[†]

The Chestnuts, Guildford
August 2, 1869

My dear Polly,

Did you really take my messages for earnest, and are you really offended, you extraordinary ~~creature~~ ~~young person~~ ~~child~~ ~~individual~~ ? (Don't you see what difficulties I'm in? Why can't you help me out with a word, like a good – (difficulty again) – member of the Human Species?) I'm quite nervous as to every word I say, for fear of offending you again!

However, I am glad you and Flo like your books after all – thanks for all the notes, and particularly to Mrs. Lewis for her kind wishes about my coming to Inverness. I only wish there were a cheap balloon running between Guildford and Inverness – that would do it, say, in 6 hours: return tickets, 15 shillings; and I shouldn't doubt long about coming! As it is, I must defer the pleasure of meeting you and the other interesting ~~young person~~ ~~infant~~ (same difficulty) till you are back in Cambridge Gardens, when I hope to find that you will have forgiven my unkind messages.

---

* The Oxford and Cambridge Boat Race, held in 1869 on March 17 and viewable from the MacDonalds' home on the river at Hammersmith.

† Ellen Terry's younger sister, also an actress. Two other sisters mentioned here, Florence and Kate ("Mrs. Lewis"), were also actresses until they married. At the time, the Terrys were living at 3 Cambridge Gardens, near Ladbroke Grove.

~~Compliments~~
~~Kind regards~~
~~Respects~~
~~Love~~ to Flossie.

~~Yours truly,~~
~~Your sincere,~~
~~affectionate friend,~~
C. L. Dodgson

To a girl named Christie

[? October 1869]

My dear Christie,
    I greatly fear
    I'm wanted here,
    Which makes it clear
    I can't appear
    At your "pour rire" –
    Would I were freer!
    So, with a tear
    (At which don't sneer),
    I am, my dear,
    Your most sincere
        C. L. Dodgson

P.S. If you see Ina Watson, please tell her I'm very angry with her. *She*'ll know why.

To Georgina Watson*

The Chestnuts, Guildford
[After October 5, 1869]

My dear Ina,
    Though I don't give birthday *presents*, still I may write a birthday letter. I came to your door to wish you many happy returns of the day, but the cat

---

* "Ina" Watson was one of three sisters whose family lived near Dodgson's own family in Surrey. He composed a number of original puzzles for the girls, and he photographed them.

The

My [deer] Ina,

Though [eye] don't give birthday presents, still [eye]

April

... write a birthday [letter].

June

[eye] came 2 your [door] 2 wish U many happy returns of the day, [barrel] the [cat] met me, [hand] took me for a [rat], [hand] hunted me [hand] and [hand] till [hand] could hardly [well] However somehow [eye] got into the [house], [hand] there a [mouse] met me, [hand] took me for [stone] a [cat], and pelted me

Rebus letter to Georgina Watson

with [image] , [image] ,
[image] . Of course [eye] ran
into the street again, [hand] a
[fox] met me [hand] took me
for a [cart] , [hand] dragged me
all the way 2 the [image] ,
[basket] the worst of all was when
a [wheelbarrow] met me [hand] took
me for a [horse] . I was
harnessed 2 it, [hand] had
. 2 draw it miles and miles,
all the way 2 Merrow. So
U C I couldn't get 2 the
room where U were.
    However I was glad to

hear U were hard at work learning the [table] for a birthday treat.

I had just time 2 look into the kitchen, and your birthday feast getting ready, a nice [dish] of crusts, bones, pills, cotton-bobbins, and rhubarb and magnesia — "Now," I thought, "she will be happy!" and with a [face] I went on my way —

Your aff.te friend

CLD

met me, and took me for a mouse, and hunted me up and down till I could hardly stand. However *some*how I got into the house, and there a mouse met me, and took me for a cat, and pelted me with fire-irons, crockery, and bottles. Of course I ran into the street again, and a horse met me and took me for a cart, and dragged me all the way to the Guildhall, but the worst of all was when a cart met me and took me for a horse. I was harnessed to it, and had to draw it miles and miles, all the way to Merrow. So you see I couldn't get to the room where you were.

However I was glad to hear you were hard at work learning the multiplication tables for a birthday treat.

I had just time to look into the kitchen, and saw your birthday feast getting ready, a nice dish of crusts, bones, pills, cotton-bobbins, and rhubarb and magnesia. "Now," I thought, "she will be happy!" and with a smile I went on my way.

Your affectionate friend,
C.L.D.

To Edith Jebb*

[Leicester]
January 18, 1870

My dear Edith,

Did you happen to notice that curious-looking gentleman who was in the railway-carriage with me, when I left Doncaster? I mean the one with a nose this shape – (I don't know any name for that sort of nose) and eyes like this He was peeping with one eye out of the window, just when I was leaning out to whisper "good-bye" into your ear (only I forgot where your ear was exactly, and somehow fancied it was just above your chin), and when the train moved off he said, "She seems to be VS. Y?" Of course I knew he meant "very sorry. Why?" So I said, "She was sorry because I had said I meant to come again." He rubbed his hands together for half an hour or so, and grinned from ear to ear (I don't mean from one ear to the other, but from one ear round again to the same) and at last he said, "SSSS." I thought at first he was only hissing like a snake, so I took

* Edith Jebb was the youngest daughter in a large family of "beautiful children" whom Dodgson met at Whitby while on a seaside holiday in the summer of 1865.

no notice – but at last it crossed my mind that he meant "She shows some sense," so I smiled and replied, "SSS" (meaning of course "Sensibly said, Sir!") but he didn't understand me, and said in rather a cross tone, "Don't hiss at me like that! Are you a cat or a steam-engine? SS." I saw that this meant "Silence, stupid!" and replied, "S," by which you will guess at once that I meant to say "Sertainly." All he said after that was, "Your head is MT," and as I couldn't make out what he meant, I didn't say anything. But I thought I had better tell you all about it at once, that you might tell the police, or do anything else you thought ought to be done. I believe his name was "HTIDE BBEJ" (isn't it a curious name?).

Yours affectionately,
Lewis Carroll

To Edith Jebb

Christ Church, Oxford
February 1, 1870

My poor dear puzzled Child,

I won't write you such a hard letter another time. And can't you really guess what the gentleman meant when he said, "Your head is MT"? Suppose I were to say to you, "Edith my dear! My cup is MT. Will you B so kind as 2 fill it with T?" Shouldn't you understand what I meant? Read it loud and try again.

Another thing I want to say is, please don't think that I expect long letters from you in return for my letters. I like writing letters to you, but I *don't* like you to take so much trouble in answering them. Next time they leave you alone and you would like a letter, tell me – and I shall be *quite* content if your answer is nothing but this:

"My dear Mr. Dodgson,
            I remain
                    Yours aff^{tely}
                            Edith."

You see even that short note would tell me *something*. I should know that you "remain affectionate," which would be worth hearing, as of course you *might* have written

"I remain
        Yours dislikingly."

Next time you see that little girl who sat next you at tea, just ask her, from me, if she is as disagreeable as ever. I rather want to know.

Ever yours aff^{tely}
C. L. Dodgson

What other names have you beside "Edith"? Tell me, and I will make you a "monogram" (like ‍) for writing all the initials at once.

To Mary Marshal

Christ Church, Oxford
April 19, 1870

My dear Child,

I took your letter and the book-marker to Mr. Lewis Carroll this morning. He sends you his thanks for the book-marker but he was very unwilling to take it. "I meant the book for a *present*," he said: "I don't want anything in exchange!" However I persuaded him to take it at last. When he saw your letter he said you were too old for the book, and that I must have made a mistake about your age; he thought you might be "*thirty*" not "*thirteen*." "No child of thirteen ever wrote such a hand as that!" he cried. However I told him you certainly were a child, and that you had been to a very good school at the bottom of the sea.

He is writing another book about Alice, telling how she went through the looking-glass into that wonderful house that you see in the looking-glass over the chimney-piece – but I don't know when it will be finished.

He sends you his kind regards, and I send mine to your Grandpapa and Grandmamma. I am glad you got home safe on Wednesday. Mr. Carroll says I ought to have seen you safe to your journey's end, and that *he* would have behaved better if he had been in my place!

Very truly yours,
C. L. Dodgson

To Agnes Hughes*

[?1871]

My dear Agnes,

You lazy thing! What? I'm to divide the kisses myself, am I? Indeed I won't take the trouble to do anything of the sort! But I'll tell *you* how to do it. First, you must take *four* of the kisses, and – and that reminds me of a very curious thing that happened to me at half-past four yesterday. Three visitors came knocking at my door, begging me to let them in. And when I opened the door, who do you think they were? You'll never guess. Why, they were three cats! Wasn't it curious? However, they all looked so cross and disagreeable that I took up the first thing I could lay my hand on (which happened to be the rolling-pin) and knocked them all down as flat as pancakes! "If *you* come knocking at *my* door," I said, "*I* shall come knocking at *your* heads." That was fair, wasn't it?"

Yours affectionately,
Lewis Carroll

To Agnes Hughes

[?1871]

My dear Agnes,

About the cats, you know. Of course I didn't leave them lying flat on the ground like dried flowers: no, I picked them up, and I was as kind as I could be to them. I lent them the portfolio for a bed – they wouldn't have been comfortable in a real bed, you know: they were too thin – but they were *quite* happy between the sheets of blotting-paper – and each of them had a pen-wiper for a pillow. Well, then I went to bed: but first I lent them the three dinner-bells, to ring if they wanted anything in the night.

You know I have *three* dinner-bells – the first (which is the largest) is rung when dinner is *nearly* ready; the second (which is rather larger) is rung when it is quite ready; and the third (which is as large as the other two put together) is rung all the time I am at dinner. Well, I told them they might ring if they

---

* Amy and Agnes Hughes were the daughters of the Pre-Raphaelite painter Arthur Hughes. Dodgson became acquainted with the family in the 1860s.

happened to want anything – and, as they rang *all* the bells *all* night, I suppose they did want something or other, only I was too sleepy to attend to them.

In the morning I gave them some rat-tail jelly and buttered mice for breakfast, and they were as discontented as they could be. They wanted some boiled pelican, but of course I knew it wouldn't be good for them. So all I said was "Go to Number Two, Finborough Road, and ask for Agnes Hughes, and if it's *really* good for you, she'll give you some." Then I shook hands with them all, and wished them all goodbye, and drove them up the chimney. They seemed very sorry to go, and they took the bells and the portfolio with them. I didn't find this out till after they had gone, and then I was sorry too, and wished for them back again. What do I mean by "them"? Never mind.

How are Arthur, and Amy, and Emily? Do they still go up and down Finborough Road, and teach the cats to be kind to mice? I'm *very* fond of all the cats in Finborough Road.

Give them my love.

Who do I mean by "them"?

Never mind.

Your affectionate friend,
Lewis Carroll

To Amy Hughes

[? 1871]

My dear Amy,

How are you getting on, I wonder, with guessing those puzzles from "Wonderland"? If you think you've found out any of the answers, you may send them to me; and if they're wrong, I won't tell you they're right!

You asked me after those three cats. Ah! The dear creatures! Do you know, ever since that night they first came, they have *never left me*? Isn't it kind of them? Tell Agnes this. She will be interested to hear it. And they *are* so kind and thoughtful! Do you know, when I had gone out for a walk the other day, they got *all* my books out of the bookcase, and opened them on the floor, to be ready for me to read. They opened them all at page 50, because they thought that would be a nice useful page to begin at. It was rather unfortunate, though: because they took my bottle of gum, and tried to gum pictures upon the ceiling (which they thought would please me), and by accident they spilt a quantity of it all over the books. So when they were shut up and put by, the leaves all stuck together, and I can never read page 50 again in any of them!

However, they meant it very kindly, so I wasn't angry. I gave them each a spoonful of ink as a treat; but they were ungrateful for that, and made dreadful faces. But, of course, as it was given them as a treat, they had to drink it. One of them has turned black since: it was a white cat to begin with.

Give my love to any children you happen to meet. Also I send two kisses and a half, for you to divide with Agnes, Emily, and Godfrey. Mind you divide them fairly.

Yours affectionately,
C. L. Dodgson

To Margaret Cunnynghame

[Christ Church, Oxford]
April 10, 1871

No, no! I cannot write a line,
   I cannot write a word:
The thoughts I think appear in ink
   So shockingly absurd.

To wander in an empty cave
   Is fruitless work, 'tis said:
What must it be for one like me
   To *wander in his head*?

You say that I'm "to write a verse" –
   O Maggie, put it quite
The other way, and kindly say
   That I'm "averse to write"!

C.L.D.

To Mabel and Emily Kerr*

Christ Church, Oxford
May 20, 1871

A Double Acrostic

Thanks, thanks, fair Cousins, for your gift
   So swiftly borne to Albion's isle –
Though angry waves their crests uplift
   Between our shores, for many a league !

("So far, so good," you say: "but how
   Your Cousins?" Let me tell you, Madam.
We're both descended, you'll allow,
   From one great-great-great-grandsire, Noah.)

Your picture shall adorn the book
   That's bound, so neatly and moroccoly,
With that bright green which every cook
   Delights to see in beds of cauliflower.

The carte is very good, but pray
   Send me the larger one as well !
"A cool request !" I hear you say.
   "Give him an inch, he takes an acre !

"But we'll be generous, because
   We well remember, in the story,
How good and gentle Alice was,
   The day she argued with the Parrot !"

Lewis Carroll

* Emily and Mabel Kerr were two young girls living in Canada, who had sent Dodgson their photograph through their aunt, Mrs. Edwin Hatch. Dodgson replied with this double acrostic, based on the girls' first names. The last word in each stanza is a red herring; for each one, substitute the correct rhyme, arrange the five words vertically, and then read downwards: their first and last letters spell out *Mabel* and *Emily*.

```
M    il     E
A    da     M
B    roccol I
E    l      L
L    or     Y
```

To Mary Crofts

2 Wellington Square, Hastings
April 12, 1873

My dear Mary,

Please thank whoever it was that sent me my boots – and the pen, which I forgot to ask for in my telegram. I will now explain to you how it was I came to leave the boots behind. You see, Ethel came to help me to pack. She is a very useful little body (though, by the bye, she is *most* useful when she does nothing – because, when she does anything, it is generally mischief) and I was very glad to have her help, though it lost me my time, my temper, and my boots. In the first place, there was the confusion of having another person in the room: for instance, I said, "Oh dear! I *must* shave before I go: my beard is nearly down to my feet!" and I made a gallon or so of lather ready, and got out two or three razors – but then, as it happened, we were both running about the room in such a hurry to get things packed, that I couldn't remember which was which – so, by mistake, I shaved *her* instead. I daresay you remarked how beautifully smooth her chin was when she came down to dinner? However, that's not nearly the worst. The worst is now to come, and explains how the boots got left behind. I said, "Now, Ethel, there really isn't a moment to lose! We *must* get things packed! Remember, all the *large* things are to go into the portmanteau, and all the *small* things into the carpet-bag. Now go to work!" Then we began running round and round the room like mad things. The first thing Ethel did was to put the bed into the portmanteau. That was a natural mistake, but I told her it *must* be taken out again, because there are beds enough in the house here – and besides, it didn't belong to me. Then somehow, as we were running round, I took her up, among some other small things, and popped her into the bag, and just at the same moment she took *me* up (as she saw I was a large thing, and didn't notice in her hurry that I was alive) and crammed me into the portmanteau. It was very unfortunate, because we were a long time in getting out again, and that made me quite forget the boots. Now you understand how it was.

Love to the rest.

Your affectionate friend,
C. L. Dodgson

To Alexandra Kitchin[*]

Christ Church, Oxford
August 21, 1873

My dear Xie,

Poor, poor Hugh and Brook! Have you quite forgotten that you've got *three* brothers? Why mayn't *they* choose photographs too? I said "the children," you know. But perhaps you will say they are *not* children, but that you and Herbert are the only two *children*, and they are two little old men. Well, well, perhaps they are: and then of course they won't care about photographs: but they do *look* very young, I *must* say.

The day after you went, I passed by your garden, and saw the little pug-dog wandering in and out, and it turned up its nose at me. So I went up to it and said, "It is not good manners to turn up your nose at people!" Its eyes filled with tears, and it said, "I wasn't doing it at *you*, Sir! It was only to keep myself from crying." "But what are you crying about, little pug-dog?" said I. The poor little dog rubbed its paws over its eyes, and said, "Because my Ex—" "Because your Extravagance has ruined you?" I said. "Then let it be a lesson to you *not* to be extravagant. You should only spend a halfpenny a year." "No, it's *not* that," said the little dog. "It's because my Ex—" "Because your Excellent master, Mr. Kitchin, is gone?" I said. "*No!*" said the little dog. "*Do* let me finish the word! It's because my Exie is gone!" "Well! What of that?" I said. "She's only a child! She's not a bone!"

"No," said the pug: "she's not a bone."

"Now, tell me the truth," I said. "Which do you like the best? Xie, or a bone?"

The little dog thought for a minute, and then he said, "She's very 'bonne,' you know: that means 'good' in French. But she's not so good as a bone!"

Wasn't it an interesting conversation? Tell me what photographs Hugh and Brook choose: and give my love to them, and to Herbert: and take a *leetle* tiny slice of it for yourself.

Yours very affectionately,
C. L. Dodgson

---

[*] Dodgson enjoyed a special friendship with the Kitchins. The father, George W. Kitchin, was a colleague at Christ Church and later Dean of Winchester and of Durham. Mrs. Kitchin was a sympathetic soul with a sense of humour. Dodgson photographed the children; "Xie," the eldest, was one of his favourite sitters.

To Beatrice Hatch

[Christ Church, Oxford]
November 13, 1873

My dear Birdie,

I met her just outside Tom Gate, walking very stiffly, and I think she was trying to find her way to my rooms. So I said, "Why have you come here without Birdie?" So she said, "Birdie's gone! and Emily's gone! and Mabel isn't kind to me!" And two little waxy tears came running down her cheeks.

Why, how stupid of me! I've never told you who it was, all the time! It was your new doll. I was very glad to see her, and I took her to my room, and gave her some Vesta matches to eat, and a cup of nice melted wax to drink, for the poor little thing was *very* hungry and thirsty after her long walk. So I said, "Come and sit down by the fire, and let's have a comfortable chat." "Oh, no! *no*!" she said. "I'd *much* rather not! You know I do melt so *very* easily!" And she made me take her quite to the other side of the room, where it was very cold: and then she sat on my knee, and fanned herself with a penwiper, because she said she was afraid the end of her nose was beginning to melt.

"You've no *idea* how careful we have to be, we dolls," she said. "Why, there was a sister of mine – would you believe it? – she went up to the fire to warm her hands, and one of her hands dropped right off! There now!"

"Of course it dropped *right* off," I said, "because it was the *right* hand." "And how do you know it was the *right* hand, Mister Carroll?" the doll said.

So I said, "I think it must have been the *right* hand, because the other hand was *left*."

The doll said, "I shan't laugh. It's a very bad joke. Why, even a common wooden doll could make a better joke than that. And besides, they've made my mouth so stiff and hard, that I *can't* laugh, if I try ever so much!"

"Don't be cross about it," I said, "but tell me this. I'm going to give Birdie and the other children one photograph each, whichever they choose. Which do you think Birdie will choose?" "I don't know," said the doll: "you'd better ask her."

So I took her home in a Hansom Cab. Which would you like, do you think? Arthur as Cupid? or Arthur and Wilfrid together? or you and Ethel as beggar children? or Ethel standing on a box? or one of yourself?

Your affectionate friend,

Lewis Carroll

To Gaynor Simpson

[The Chestnuts, Guildford]
December 27, 1873

My dear Gaynor,

My name is spelt with a "G," that is to say "*Dodgson*." Any one who spells it the same as that wretch (I mean of course the Chairman of Committees in the House of Commons) offends me *deeply*, and *for ever*! It is a thing I *can* forget, but *never can forgive*! If you do it again, I shall call you "'aynor." Could you live happy with such a name?

As to dancing, my dear, I *never* dance, unless I am allowed to do it *in my own peculiar way*. There is no use trying to describe it: it has to be seen to be believed. The last house I tried it in, the floor broke through. But then it was a poor sort of floor – the beams were only six inches thick, hardly worth calling beams at all: stone arches are much more sensible, when any dancing, *of my peculiar kind*, is to be done. Did you ever see the Rhinoceros, and the Hippopotamus, at the Zoological Gardens, trying to dance a minuet together? It is a touching sight.

Give any message from me to Amy that you think will be most likely to surprise her, and believe me

Your affectionate friend,
Lewis Carroll

To Florence Terry

Christ Church, Oxford
January 1874

My dear Florence,

Ever since that heartless piece of conduct of yours (I allude to the affair of the Moon and the blue silk gown) I have regarded you with a gloomy interest, rather than with any of the affection of former years – so that the above epithet "dear" must be taken as conventional only, or perhaps may be more fitly taken in the sense in which we talk of a "dear" bargain, meaning to imply how much it has cost us; and who shall say how many sleepless nights it has cost *me* to endeavour to unravel (a most appropriate verb) that "blue silk gown"?

Will you please explain to Tom about that photograph of the family group, which I promised him? Its history is an instructive one, as illustrating my habits of care and deliberation. In 1867 the picture was promised him, and an entry made in my book. In 1869, or thereabouts, I mounted the picture on a large card, and packed it in brown paper. In 1870, or 1871, or thereabouts, I took it with me to Guildford, that it might be handy to take with me when I went up to town. Since then I have taken it two or three times to London, and on each occasion (having forgotten to deliver it to him) I brought it back again. This was because I had no convenient place in London to leave it in. But *now* I have found such a place. Mr. Dubourg has kindly taken charge of it – so that it is now much nearer to its future owner than it has been for 7 years. I quite hope, in the course of another year or two, to be able to remember to bring it to your house: or perhaps Mr. Dubourg may be calling, even sooner than that, and take it with him. You will wonder why I ask *you* to tell him instead of writing myself. The obvious reason is that you will be able, from sympathy, to put my delay in the most favourable light – to make him see that, as hasty puddings are not the best of puddings, so hasty judgements are not the best of judgements, and that he ought to be content to wait, even another 7 years, for his picture, and to sit "like patience on a monument, smiling at grief." This quotation, by the way, is altogether a misprint. Let me explain it to you. The passage originally stood "*They* sit, Like patients on *the* Monument, smiling at *Greenwich*." In the next edition "Greenwich" was printed short "Green$^{\underline{h}}$" and so got gradually altered into "Grief." The allusion of course is to the celebrated Dr. Jenner, who used to send all his patients to sit on the top of the Monument (near London Bridge) to inhale fresh air, promising them that, when they were well enough, they should go to "Greenwich Fair." So of course they always looked out towards Greenwich, and sat smiling to think of the treat in store for them. A play was written on the subject of their inhaling the fresh air, and was for some time attributed to him (Shakespeare), but it is certainly not in his style. It was called *The Wandering Air*, and was lately revived at the Queen's Theatre.* The custom of sitting on the Monument was given up when Dr. Jenner went mad, and insisted that the air was worst up there, and that the *lower* you went the *more airy* it became. Hence he always called those little yards, below the pavement, outside kitchen windows, "*the kitchen airier*," a name that is still in use.

* Charles Reade's play based on the Tichborne Case, *The Wandering Heir*, was then playing at the Queen's Theatre; Ellen Terry would take over the female lead the following month.

All this information you are most welcome to use, the next time you are in want of something to talk about. You may say you learned it from "a distinguished etymologist," which is perfectly true, since any one who knows me by sight can easily distinguish me from all other etymologists.

What parts are you and Polly now playing? Believe me to be (conventionally)

Yours affectionately,
C. L. Dodgson

III. Home at Guildford and Holidays at the Seaside

When Lewis Carroll's father died in 1868, he went house-hunting in Guildford. In August he bought "The Chestnuts," a house that then enjoyed a rural prospect but is now in the centre of town. The Dodgsons made the move from Croft Rectory on September 1. From then on, Carroll regularly visited the family at Guildford and exercised a fraternal concern over the house and its occupants.

In the summers, he preferred holidays at the seaside. These began in his early days at Whitby; then he went for a number of summers in the 1860s and 1870s to the Isle of Wight. In 1877 he took lodgings in Eastbourne, at the home of a Mrs. Dyer, the wife of a postman. Here he had "a nice little first-floor sitting-room with a balcony, and bedroom adjoining," and for the rest of his life he spent his summers as the Dyers' star, if somewhat exacting, lodger.

To Lord Salisbury

Christ Church, Oxford
May 9, 1875

My dear Lord Salisbury,

I do not know if you have taken any interest in the not very inviting subject of "Vivisection," which I believe will soon come before Parliament for debate and (I hope) for restrictive legislation. If you *have*, you probably know much more of its literature than I do: if not, I hope it is not an impertinence to call your attention to a most able and interesting essay, in the last number of the *New Quarterly Review*, by Miss Frances Power Cobbe (who wrote that very powerful volume of Essays, *The Hopes of the Human Race*). It seems to me that there is terrible need of legislation – not so much in the interests of the poor tortured animals as of the demoralised and brutalised medical students. I venture also to enclose a fly-leaf, printed by the Society for Prevention of Cruelty to Animals, containing a letter of Dr. Hoggan, and one that I wrote to the *Pall Mall* based on *his* letter.

I have another motive for writing today. I have just heard from Miss Ellen Terry (the much-talked-of Portia in the *Merchant of Venice*, now acting at the Prince of Wales' Theatre): she says "when you can come to town, please let me know if you would care to take two nice children to see the affair, and then I will send you the best box in the house." Now I wrote to Gwenny some days ago to ask if she and Maud would come there with me on the 17th or 18th (I have accepted a box for one of those nights, whichever she can most conveniently give). If they *may* come, or if (supposing Maud to be considered too old, or myself too young, for *her* to come) then if Gwenny and Jem may come, I shall be delighted to take them. If *not*, I should like to know at once, that I may find two other children. May I beg the favour of a line by return of post – not of course from one so busy as your Lordship, but from one who perhaps can spare a minute from her "Conic Sections!" Believe me, my dear Lord,

Sincerely yours,
C. L. Dodgson

To R. H. Collins

Christ Church, Oxford
May 28, 1875

Dear Mr. Collins,

You will think me strangely ignorant of etiquette, or at least of court etiquette, but I feel some difficulty on the subject of the Prince's photographic visit on Wednesday.* Two of my sisters are now staying with me: in the ordinary case of a friend coming to be photographed, one would as a matter of course introduce him to the ladies, and ask them to show him some of my photographs in the intervals of sitting in the studio – but this is of course an exceptional case, and very possibly the Prince may prefer that he and you should be allowed to come and go without being troubled in

---

* Prince Leopold, Duke of Albany, Queen Victoria's youngest son, was a Christ Church undergraduate. Dodgson writes to the Prince's tutor, (Sir) Robert Hawthorn Collins. The Prince came to be photographed on the appointed Wednesday, June 2, and Dodgson got two sittings.

any other way than is entailed by the photography. I am anxious not to add in any way to the trouble which H.R.H. has so kindly undertaken to go through, and specially anxious not to do anything which can look like taking an advantage of his kindness. "Give him an inch, he takes an ell" is a saying which Royal personages probably have to quote more often than any one else.

My rooms are not so scanty but that I can easily arrange that your visit shall be without anything but photography to trouble the Prince.

Very truly yours,
C. L. Dodgson

I need hardly add that the ladies do not know that I am writing this.

To Gertrude Chataway

Christ Church, Oxford
October 13, 1875

My dear Gertrude,

I never give birthday *presents*, but you see I *do* sometimes write a birthday *letter*: so, as I've just arrived here, I am writing this to wish you many and many a happy return of your birthday tomorrow. I will drink your health, if only I can remember, and if you don't mind – but perhaps you object? You see, if I were to sit by you at breakfast, and to drink your tea, you wouldn't like *that*, would you? You would say "Boo! hoo! Here's Mr. Dodgson's drunk all my tea, and I haven't got any left!" So I am very much afraid, next time Sybil looks for you, she'll find you sitting by the sad sea wave, and crying "Boo! hoo! Here's Mr. Dodgson has drunk my health, and I haven't got any left!" And how it will puzzle Dr. Maund, when he is sent for to see you! "My dear Madam, I'm very sorry to say your little girl has got *no health at all*! I never saw such a thing in my life!" "Oh, I can easily explain it!" your Mother will say. "You see she *would* go and make friends with a strange gentleman, and yesterday he drank her health!" "Well, Mrs. Chataway," he will say, "the only way to cure her is to wait till his next birthday, and then for *her* to drink *his* health."

And then we shall have changed healths. I wonder how you'll like mine! Oh, Gertrude, I wish you wouldn't talk such nonsense!

Please give these papers, with my love, to Violet and Dulcie, to gum in at the end of their *Looking-Glasses*, and send one to Alice next time you write.

And now with best love and half-a-dozen kisses for yourself, I remain

Your loving friend,
Lewis Carroll

Gertrude Chataway in fisherman's jersey and cap, drawn by Dodgson.

To Mrs. J. Chataway

Christ Church, Oxford
October 25, 1875

Dear Mrs. Chataway,

I send you some verses, written last night and finished this morning (please don't show them to any one but Mr. Chataway, just at present), as to which I shall be much obliged if you will kindly give me leave to print them, if I should find occasion to do so. They embody, as you will see, some of my recollections of pleasant days at Sandown – but they do *not* embody, as they might well have done, my grateful feelings to yourself, for the society, so liberally granted to me at all times and seasons, of one of the sweetest children it has ever been my happiness to meet. May she grow up to be (as I cannot doubt she will, unless she meets with quite other influences than those she is under now) as delightful a woman as she is a child, and be the household-treasure of some happy man, "far on in summers that I shall not see!"

Sincerely yours,
C. L. Dodgson

Girt with a boyish garb for boyish task,
　　Eager she wields her spade – yet loves as well
Rest on a friendly knee, the tale to ask
　　That he delights to tell.

Rude spirits of the seething outer strife,
　　Unmeet to read her pure and simple spright,
Deem, if you list, such hours a waste of life,
　　Empty of all delight!

Chat on, sweet Maid, and rescue from annoy
　　Hearts that by wiser talk are unbeguiled!
Ah, happy he who owns that tenderest joy,
　　The heart-love of a child!

Away, fond thoughts, and vex my soul no more!
Work claims my wakeful nights, my busy days:
Albeit bright memories of that sunlit shore
Yet haunt my dreaming gaze!

Lewis Carroll
Christ Church
October 25, 1875

To Mrs. J. Chataway

Christ Church, Oxford
October 28, 1875

Dear Mrs. Chataway,

Many thanks for the delicious ½ carte of Gertrude. I can't feel sure from your letter whether you have or have not noticed that the verses embody her name. They do it in two ways – by letters, and by syllables – the only acrostic of that kind I have ever seen. Will that make any difference in the leave you give to print the verses? If I print them, I shan't tell anyone it is an acrostic – but someone will be sure to find it out before long. In haste,

Sincerely yours,
C. L. Dodgson

To Mrs. J. Chataway

Christ Church, Oxford
November 7, 1875

Dear Mrs. Chataway,

With the exception of my Publisher, Printer, and Artist, and my own family, I have told nobody yet of my intention of bringing out a little Christmas book. And I think *you* are the next person to whom the announcement ought to be made, because I have taken, as a dedication, the verses I sent you the other day in MS. It will be a very small book – not 40 pages – a poem (supposed to be comic) with a frontispiece by Mr. Holiday. The advertisements will appear about the middle of this month, I suppose, and till then I should be glad if you would not let the *name* of the book go beyond your own family-circle. I don't mind the fact, that the book is in the press, being known – but the name ought to be *new* when it appears. It is called *The Hunting of the Snark*, and the scene is laid in an island frequented by the Jubjub and Bandersnatch – no doubt the very island in which the Jabberwock was slain (see *Through the Looking-Glass*).

When I receive the 2 cartes of Gertrude in beach-attire – may I order a few unmounted prints of the best from Debenham? I want to insert them in a few copies of the book, opposite to the Dedicatory verses – if you remember which it was I admired most, perhaps you would order half-a-dozen unmounted prints, which would save time. Believe me

Yours very sincerely,
C. L. Dodgson

I send love, and a kiss, to Gertrude. But I shan't do it again, unless she sends some message to me!

To Gertrude Chataway

Christ Church, Oxford
December 9, 1875

My dear Gertrude,

This really will *not* do, you know, sending one more kiss every time by post: the parcel gets so heavy that it is quite expensive. When the postman brought in the last letter, he looked quite grave. "Two pounds to pay, sir!" he said. "*Extra weight*, sir!" (I think he cheats a little, by the way. He often makes me pay two *pounds* when I think it should be *pence*). "Oh, if you please, Mr. Postman!" I said, going down gracefully on one knee (I wish you could see me go down on one knee to a Postman – it's a very pretty sight). "Do excuse me just this once! It's only from a little girl!"

"Only from a little girl!" he growled. "What are little girls made of?" "Sugar and spice," I began to say, "and all that's ni—" but he interrupted me. "No! I don't mean *that*. I mean, what's the good of little girls, when they send such heavy letters?" "Well, they're not *much* good, certainly," I said, rather sadly.

"Mind you don't get any more such letters," he said, "at least, not from that particular little girl. *I know her well, and she's a regular bad one!*" That's not true now, is it? I don't believe he ever saw you, and you're not a bad one, are you? However, I promised him we would send each other *very* few more letters. "Only two thousand four hundred and seventy, or so," I said. "Oh!" he said. "A little number like *that* doesn't signify. What I meant is, you mustn't send *many*." So you see we must keep count now, and when we get to two thousand four hundred and seventy, we mustn't write any more, unless the postman gives us leave.

I sometimes wish I was back on the shore at Sandown; don't you?

Your loving friend,
Lewis Carroll

Why is a pig that has lost its tail like a little girl on the sea-shore?
Because it says, "I should like another Tale, please!"

To Magdalen Millard

Christ Church, Oxford
December 15, 1875

My dear Magdalen,

I want to explain to you why I did not call yesterday. I was sorry to miss you, but you see I had so many conversations on the way. I tried to explain to the people in the street that I was going to see you, but they wouldn't listen; they said they were in a hurry, which was rude. At last I met a wheelbarrow that I thought would attend to me, but I couldn't make out what was in it. I saw some features at first, then I looked through a telescope, and found it was a countenance; then I looked through a microscope, and found it was a face! I thought it was rather like me, so I fetched a large looking-glass to make sure, and then to my great joy I found it was me. We shook hands, and were just beginning to talk, when myself came up and joined us, and we had quite a pleasant conversation. I said, "Do you remember when we all met at Sandown?" and myself said, "It was very jolly there; there was a child called Magdalen," and me said, "I used to like her a little; not much, you know – only a little." Then it was time for us to go to the train, and who do you think came to the station to see us off? You would never guess, so I must tell you. They were two very dear friends of mine, who happen to be here just now, and beg to be allowed to sign this letter, as

Your affectionate friends,
Lewis Carroll, and C. L. Dodgson

To Alice Crompton

[Christ Church, Oxford]
April 7, 1876

Alice dear, will you join me in hunting the Snark?
   Let us go to the chase hand-in-hand:
If we only can find one before it gets dark,
   Could anything happen more grand?

Ever ready to share in the Beaver's despair,
   Count your poor little fingers and thumbs;
Recollecting with tears all the smudges and smears
   On the page where you work at your sums!

May I help you to seek it with thimbles and care?
   Pursuing with forks and hope?
To threaten its life with a railway-share?
Or to charm it with smiles – but a maiden so fair
   Need not trouble herself about soap!

                             Lewis Carroll

To Mrs. J. Chataway

Christ Church, Oxford
June 28, 1876

My dear Mrs. Chataway,
   Tuesday will suit me quite well. You had better drive to "Tom Gate, Christ Church." To save you from possible extortion, I may as well mention that the *legal* charge for one (or for two) would be 1*s*. With your party, 2*s*. would be an ample fare. If it is really a bad day, I will not expect you. (*N.B.* I don't mean "cloudy." Cloudy days are often *best* for photography.)
                          Sincerely yours,
                          C. L. Dodgson

P.S. If you should decide on sending over Gertrude and not coming yourself, would you kindly let me know what is the minimum amount of dress in which you are willing to have her taken? With that information, I will then be guided by *her* likings in the matter: children differ very much – with some that I know (Londoners chiefly) I would not venture to propose even taking off their shoes: but with a child like your Gertrude, as simple-minded as Eve in the garden of Eden, *I* should see no objection (provided she liked it herself) to photographing her in Eve's original dress. And I think, if you were here and could see the photographs I have done of children in that primitive costume, that you would agree that it is quite possible to make such a picture that you might frame it and hang it up in your drawing-room.

But, much as I should myself like to have such a picture of her, if *you* at all object, or if *she* has changed her mind since I saw her (she was quite willing to be taken so, last September), of course I give it up, though I do not, once in a hundred cases, get so well-formed a subject for art.

To Gertrude Chataway

Christ Church, Oxford
July 21, 1876

My dear Gertrude,
   Explain to me how I am to enjoy Sandown without *you*. How can I walk on the beach alone? How can I sit all alone on those wooden steps? So you see, as I shan't be able to do without you, you will have to come. If Violet [Martineau] comes, I shall tell her to invite you to stay with her, and then I shall come over in the *Heather-Bell* and fetch you. If ever I do come over, I see I couldn't go back the same day: so you will have to engage me a bed somewhere in Swanage: and if you can't find one, I shall expect *you* to spend the night on the beach, and give up your room to *me*. Guests, of course, must be thought of before children; and I'm sure in these warm nights the beach will be quite good enough for *you*. If you *did* feel a little chilly, of course you could go into a bathing-machine, which every-body knows is *very* comfortable to sleep in. You know they make the floor of soft wood for that very purpose. I send you 7 kisses (to last a week) and remain

Your loving friend,
Lewis Carroll

To Mrs. J. Chataway

Christ Church, Oxford
October 21, 1876

Dear Mrs. Chataway,

I am charmed to hear you can come. Thursday will do well. If you *could* come on Wednesday afternoon, it would be ten times better, and the only additional expense would be beds – not many shillings. I would engage you beds at the lodgings opposite, where my sisters lodge when they visit me, and you would live over here, only sleeping there. Would you want one room or two? By coming on Wednesday we could begin the photos at 9 on Thursday: morning light is so much the best – and I would ask Mr. Sampson to come and dine with us on Wednesday. (Excuse a rambling style: I write amid interruptions of pupils.)

A question now arises, which I would be glad if you and Mr. Chataway would settle at once. I have a little friend here, Lily Gray, child of Dr. Gray, and one of my chief beach friends at Sandown this year. She is 5, a graceful and pretty child, and one of the sweetest children I know (nearly as sweet as Gertrude) – and she is so perfectly simple and unconscious that it is a matter of entire indifference to her whether she is taken in full dress or nothing. My question is, are you going to allow Gertrude (who I think is also perfectly simple and unconscious) to be done in the same way? If so, I could make such *lovely* groups of the two (e.g. Lily sitting on Gertrude's knee), and I would ask Mrs. Gray to bring Lily over on Thursday morning. Of course if you or she would not like it, I withdraw my request: but I would like to know beforehand, that I may arrange with Mrs. Gray. I did a very successful one of Lily, so dressed, yesterday.

Gertrude need not bring spade or bucket: I have both here.

Very sincerely yours,
C. L. Dodgson

To Gertrude Chataway

Christ Church, Oxford
October 28, 1876

My dearest Gertrude,

You will be sorry, and surprised, and puzzled, to hear what a queer illness I have had ever since you went. I sent for the Doctor, and said "Give me some medicine, for I'm tired." He said "Nonsense and stuff! You don't want medicine: go to bed!" I said "No: it isn't the sort of tiredness that wants bed. I'm tired in the *face*." He looked a little grave, and said "Oh, it's your *nose* that's tired: a person often talks too much when he thinks he nose a great deal." I said "No: it *isn't* the nose. Perhaps it's the hair." Then he looked rather graver and said "*Now* I understand: you've been playing too many hairs on the piano-forte." "No, indeed I haven't!" I said, "and it isn't exactly the *hair*: it's more about the nose and chin." Then he looked a good deal graver and said "Have you been walking much on your chin lately?" I said "No." "Well!" he said, "it puzzles me very much. Do you think that it's in the lips?" "Of course!" I said, "that's exactly what it is!" Then he looked very grave indeed, and said "I think you must have been giving too many kisses." "Well," I said, "I did give *one* kiss to a baby-child, a little friend of mine." "Think again," he said, "are you sure it was only *one*?" I thought again, and said "Perhaps it was eleven times." Then the Doctor said "You must not give her *any* more till your lips are quite rested again." "But what am I to do?" I said, "because, you see, I owe her a hundred and eighty-two more." Then he looked so grave that the tears ran down his cheeks, and he said "You may send them to her in a box." Then I remembered a little box that I once bought at Dover and thought I would some day give it to *some* little girl or other. So I have packed them all in it very carefully: tell me if they come safe, or if any are lost on the way.

If I had thought of it while you were here, I would have measured you against my door, where I have Xie's height marked, and other little friends. Please tell me your exact height (without your shoes), and I will mark it now.

I hope you're rested after the eight pictures I did of you.

Your most loving friend,
Lewis Carroll

To Mrs. J. Chataway

Christ Church, Oxford
October 28 [1876]

My dear Mrs. Chataway,

I feel I should be rather taking an unfair advantage of circumstances if I retained that negative (much as I prize it) of Gertrude in her "Swanage

costume," without knowing whether *Mr.* Chataway approves of it – as he
had no opportunity of pronouncing an opinion on the new suggestion. If he
should wish it, I will erase those three negatives, after doing a print of each
for you (as I suppose you would like to have one yourself). Of course I hope
he will *not* wish it.

If I *may* keep prints of them, the next question is, may I show them to
anybody? My own idea would be to put them among the others I have done
of the same kind (some in less dress), and then they would only be shown on
exceptional occasions and to exceptional friends. I would have shown you
the collection, if you had come with Gertrude only (but I did not venture
to offer it under the circumstances), and I am by no means sure you would
not have admired them enough to modify your views about Gertrude!
However, I feel highly privileged as it is, and am most grateful to you for
all the trouble you have had in bringing her over.

Very sincerely yours,
C. L. Dodgson

To Mrs. J. Chataway

Christ Church, Oxford
November 1, 1876

My dear Mrs. Chataway,

Thanks for your letter. You speak of "erasing a negative" with a calmness
which a photographer would not share with regard to any of his artistic
offspring. A good negative is to a photographer (at least in *my* case it is) as
valuable, artistically, as a print: and it has the advantage of not fading, which
prints nearly always do. So I hope at least you will be in no hurry to have
the negative (I mean the *good* one of the 3 in bathing-drawers: the other 2
I will erase forthwith) destroyed. It is locked up safe, where no printer can
get at it: and it is entered on a list "to be erased," as a direction to my
Executors, when the negatives come into their possession.

I have got a print of it ready for you. Would you like it mounted on a
"cabinet" card (which will hold it well) or on a larger card, so as to have
a broad margin?

This wintry weather makes my studio too cold for sitters: but I hope to
have it artificially warmed, so as to be able to take pictures through the
winter.

Best love to Gertrude. I have got her height marked on my door: it is exactly the same as my little actress-friend, Lizzie Coote, aged 13 !

Yours very sincerely,
C. L. Dodgson

To Mrs. J. Chataway

Christ Church, Oxford
November 26, 1876

My dear Mrs. Chataway,

After all the trouble I have put you to for my own gratification – first in bringing over my little friend to be photographed, and secondly in making concessions (much against inclination, I fear) to my rather *outré* and unconventional notions of Art, it is a real satisfaction to me to find that some of the results give you pleasure. The one with the hands round the knees I should enjoy as much as you do, if only the face were *quite* clear – but that I'm afraid it isn't. I hope I may have another opportunity of trying it: it is a very happily conceived attitude, I think.

For the "night-gown" one, you know, you have *her* to thank: *I* had wished to leave off, it was getting so dark – but she made me go on for the all-prevailing reason that she thought it would please *you*.

The warming apparatus is complete, and I hope to test it by photographing Dulcie some day this week.

I send my best love to Gertrude, and thanks for her *ad libitum* supply of kisses. As she leaves the number to *me* to settle, I will call it "two," which I think is a reasonable allowance, and I send her *one* in return.

Very sincerely yours,
C. L. Dodgson

I have quite forgotten, I see, to answer your question. I charge 1s. 6d. each for cabinets, 1s. each for cartes. *Any* of them can be done as cartes: you can easily see, by cutting a hole in a piece of paper, how much will go into a carte. I wait to know whether Miss Chataway will accept a copy of any one of them; and also which Gertrude would like.

I have been so busy that I haven't yet had time to mount you a print of the standing one in "full dress."

To his cousin Mrs. W. E. Wilcox*

Christ Church, Oxford
February 7, 1877

My dear Fanny,

I have a favour to ask of you. I have taken a liberty (which I hope you will forgive) of getting Margaret to tell me about your circumstances, that I might offer help towards educating the children. I rejoice to be able to do such a thing, for dear William's sake. And now will you kindly let me send you £30 a year, paid half-yearly in advance. Just now it is of course more needed for my godson – but I don't want it to be considered as restricted to *him*. Please spend it in any way that best suits your plans.

With love to the children, I am

Ever yours affectionately,
C. L. Dodgson

P.S. Of course I can only promise this during my life, and, if I had heavy losses, I *might* not be able to continue it. But I see no reason to fear having to withdraw or reduce it.

To Mrs. E. Hatch

Christ Church, Oxford
March 14, 1877

Dear Mrs. Hatch,

You know that photo I did of Birdie, seated in a crouching attitude, side view, with one hand to her chin, in the days before she had learned to consider dress as *de rigueur*? It was a gem the equal of which I have not much hope of doing again: and I should very much like, if possible, to get Miss Bond, of Southsea (the best photographic colourist living, *I* think) to colour a copy. But I am shy of asking her the question, people have such different views, and it *might* be a shock to her feelings if I did so. *Would* you kindly

---

* Dodgson's favourite cousin, William Edward Wilcox, died in December 1876. Margaret (mentioned in the second line) was the sister of the deceased, and Dodgson's godson (line 6) the elder son of the deceased. Two younger children were Theodore and Menella.

do it for me? However particular she may be, I don't think she could reasonably take offence at being asked the question by a lady, and that lady the mother of the child in question. What I want you to do is to send her a description of the photograph (you may as well tell her that I took it), and simply ask her if she would be willing to colour a print of it. Then if she says "no," there is no harm done: but if I hear from you that she says "yes," I can then easily negotiate myself.

I have long intended to come and hunt up your new house, but at present am so ignorant of the address that I must send you this through Mr. Hatch. Believe me

Sincerely yours,
C. L. Dodgson

Miss Bond,
Park Lodge,
Southsea

To Bert Coote*

The Chestnuts, Guildford
June 9 [?1877]

My dear Bertie,

I would have been very glad to write to you as you wish, only there are several objections. I think, when you have heard them, you will see that I am right in saying "No."

The first objection is, I've got no ink. You don't believe it? Ah, you should have seen the ink there was in *my* days! (About the time of the battle of Waterloo: I was a soldier in that battle.) Why, you had only to pour a little of it on the paper, and it went on by itself! *This* ink is so stupid, if you begin a word for it, it can't even finish it by itself.

The next objection is, I've no time. You don't believe *that*, you say? Well, who cares? You should have seen the time there was in *my* days! (At the time of the battle of Waterloo, where I led a regiment.) There were always 25 hours in the day – sometimes 30 or 40.

The third and greatest objection is, my *great* dislike for children. I don't know why, I'm sure: but I *hate* them – just as one hates arm-chairs and

---

* The Cootes were another stage family that Dodgson had become acquainted with. They consisted of a brother and two sisters, Bert, Carrie, and Lizzie.

plum-pudding! You don't believe *that*, don't you? Did I ever say you would? Ah, you should have seen the children there were in my days! (Battle of Waterloo, where I commanded the English army. I was called "the Duke of Wellington" then, but I found it a great bother having such a long name, so I changed it to "Mr. Dodgson." I chose that name because it begins with the same letter as "Duke.") So you see it would never do to write to you.

Have you any sisters? I forget. If you have, give them my love. I am much obliged to your Uncle and Aunt for letting me keep the photograph.

I hope you won't be much disappointed at not getting a letter from

Your affectionate friend,
C. L. Dodgson

To P. A. W. Henderson

Christ Church, Oxford
June 18, 1877

Dear Mr. Henderson,

I have been told so often, and so forcibly, that I *ought* (as an amateur-photographer whose special line is "children"), to apply for leave to take your 2 little girls (whom I don't even know by sight yet), that I write to say I expect to be here till the end of the month, and shall be much pleased if you, or Mrs. Henderson, could at any time look in with them – *not* [to] be photographed then and there (I never succeed with strangers), but to make acquaintance with the place and the artist, and to see how they relished the idea of coming, another day, to be photographed.

Truly yours,
C. L. Dodgson

To his cousin Menella Wilcox

Grosvenor House, 44 Grand Parade, Eastbourne
July 14, 1877

My dear Nella,

If Eastbourne was only a mile off from Scarborough, I would come and see you tomorrow: but it *is* such a long way to come! There was a little girl running up and down on the parade yesterday and she always ended her run exactly where I was sitting: she just looked up in my face and then off she went again. So, when she had been about six times, I smiled at her, and she smiled at me and ran away again: and the next time I held out my hand, and she shook hands directly; and I said, "Will you give me that piece of seaweed?" and she said, "No!" and ran away again. And the next time I said, "Will you cut off a little bit of the seaweed for me?" And she said, "But I haven't got a pair of scissors!" So I lent her that folding pair of scissors, and she cut off a little bit very carefully, and gave it to me, and ran away again. But in a moment she came running back and said, "I'm frightened that my mother won't like you to keep it!" So I gave it back again, and I told her to ask her mother to get a needle and thread and sew the two bits of seaweed together again: and she laughed and said she would keep the two bits in her pocket. Wasn't she a queer little vegetable? I'm glad *you* don't keep running away all the time while we're talking.

Is Matilda Jane* quite well? And has she been running out in the rain again without her shoes on?

Give my love to your Mamma, and to *your* Aunt Lucy: not to *my* Aunt Lucy, because *she's* at Guildford.

Your affectionate Cousin,
Charles L. Dodgson

To Mrs. V. Blakemore

[7 Lushington Road, Eastbourne]
Tuesday night [August 14, 1877]

Dear Mrs. Blakemore,

After the experience of tonight,† I feel that far the best thing for Dolly is not to hear my name mentioned again: and for you just to ignore my presence, when you have her with you, and on no account to urge her to make any further effort at speaking to me. I will gladly do without ever seeing her again, if only she will be happy again, poor little thing. I have been nothing but a cause of grief and suffering to her. I will not even try to tell you how painful a thought that is to *me*, whose deepest and purest pleasures in this world have been in giving pleasure to children.

---

* Her doll.

† The Blakemore family, it appears, teased "Dolly" about her friendship with Dodgson, and when he encountered Mrs. Blakemore and Dolly, by chance, on the evening he wrote this letter, Dolly went into a "fit of almost hysterical crying."

Please let me give you one bit of warning about her – it occurred to me very forcibly tonight, when watching from a distance the crowd of sympathising relations gathered round her: and that is that the more of a "scene" you make over her when her nerves give way (and she has evidently got a highly sensitive nervous system) the more likely you make it that she will grow up a victim to that terrible malady, hysteria. Believe me

Sincerely yours,
C. L. Dodgson

To Mrs. V. Blakemore

[7 Lushington Road, Eastbourne]
[August 20?, 1877]

Dear Mrs. Blakemore,

Pray don't let this be a worry to you any longer: and pray don't let any circumstances interfere with our friendship. (I mean by "our" that between yourself and me. The other friendship, that between Dolly and me, is a little one-sided, I fear, but there's no helping it. I am sure you have taken trouble enough about it.) When Mr. Blakemore returns, I shall hope for the pleasure of seeing him and you here, and of at last having an opportunity of showing my photographs.

Sincerely yours,
C. L. Dodgson

Your letter was quite natural under the circumstances. I wonder you took my bachelor-theories as patiently as you did! It is I rather that should apologise.

I think I saw Dolly on the Pier last night: but I suppose it's best to ignore her.

To Mrs. V. Blakemore

[7 Lushington Road, Eastbourne]
Wednesday [August 15, 1877]

Dear Mrs. Blakemore,

I think the Government ought to be much obliged to us for using so many postage-stamps! I agree so heartily in your objection to leaving children to the care of servants that I can't imagine what I can have said to suggest the contrary: I should like the whole race of nurses to be abolished: children should be with their mother as much as possible, in my opinion. Only this morning I was saying to myself, as I walked on the beach and heard the screams of a child whose nurse was thwarting its wishes – apparently out of mere malice – "I think children must have an enormous amount of *original righteousness* not to be utterly ruined by their nurses!" There is one nursemaid I should like to point out to you: more than once I have thought of tracing her home and writing to the mother of the children: she worries them so incessantly that one wonders they have any tempers left at all.

Now I have an experiment to propose that I think *might* put an end to Dolly's misery – and *indeed* it is for *her* sake, rather than mine, that I wish it: although of course it would be a great pleasure to *me* also to have things on a natural footing again – it is that you should come here, and bring Dolly, and *nobody else*. The only chance of our meeting naturally is that we should *not* meet in the presence of the whole party, who are associated in her mind with all the teasing she has had about me, but with her mother only. Of course the *business* of the visit must be to show *you* photographs, etc., and I will only notice *her* so far as may seem pleasant to her. But I feel pretty sure that, when once she has got used to my presence, we shall be very good friends indeed. If the thing, after fair trial (say 5 or 10 minutes) is an obvious failure, I will trust to you to terminate the visit, as suddenly as you like. But I have great hope it will be a success, and shall be truly glad if it turns out so.

I shall be in at 12 tomorrow, if I do not hear from you, or at any other hour you like to fix.

Please don't notice me on the Pier tonight.

Yours sincerely,
C. L. Dodgson

If I rightly understand your postscript to mean that you *did* send the fruit, I can only repeat what I said before – *many* thanks for the kind thought.

P.S. I think the visit *might* have ended differently, if Dolly had known where she was coming, and had come of her own free-will. Also, if you could have hardened your heart enough to say "Well, you may cry if you like, but I can't have you on my knee till you're good," and had put her down in the corner, and insisted on her staying *there*: I think that, in that case, 15 minutes of entire neglect *might* have made a change. (I wonder if you noticed, as I did, that when she thought you were not petting her quite enough, she roared a little louder to recall your attention?) Both these ideas seem worth considering, *if* you ever bring her again.

Now, I have one more experiment to suggest. Would you come again without Dolly, and bring one or two little nieces, as near Dolly's age as possible? (*They* won't go into fits, will they?) I should like to show you my photographs under more comfortable circumstances, and I will show *them* the little bear, and other treasures. I wouldn't on any account suggest to them to say a word to Dolly: they are pretty sure, without any prompting, to tell her what they have seen. *If* she should express any wish to come, I would not be too ready to bring her. *I* think she ought to be made to under-stand distinctly that she did *not* behave properly when she came: that point settled, you might say you would take her *some* day, along with her little cousin, if she *really* means to behave better. If she never *volunteers* any remark about coming again, I think you had better never mention my name to her.

If you will come, please name your own day and hour.

Sincerely yours,
C. L. Dodgson

To Mrs. V. Blakemore

The Chestnuts, Guildford
October 2, 1877

Dear Mrs. Blakemore,

Please to give my love and my best thanks to *Edith* (I call her so rather than "*Dolly*," believing that to be her own wish) for the pocket-book. It will be very useful to me (it just happens to fill one of the few gaps in my wants in life) and I shall remember her (probably – I had better not be *too* confident) every time I see it!

I am making up for my long idleness at Eastbourne by writing 6 or 8 hours a day, and hope to get my book published by Xmas: but I fear it won't be suitable to present to Dolly Edith, unless she likes Geometry as much as fairies.

No summer that I have ever spent has given me so many child-friends as this, and I am very glad to think that I can now (a thing I despaired of for many weeks) include Edith in the list.

Thank you very much for all the trouble you took to win me the smiles of your little one – they are well worth the winning!*

With kindest remembrances to Mr. Blakemore, I am

Sincerely yours,
C. L. Dodgson

To Agnes Hull

Christ Church, Oxford
December 10, 1877

My dear Agnes,

At last I've succeeded in forgetting you! It's been a very hard job, but I took 6 "lessons-in-forgetting," at half-a-crown a lesson. After three lessons, I forgot my own name, and I forgot to go for the next lesson. So the Professor said I was getting on very well: "but I hope," he added, "you won't forget to pay for the lessons!" I said *that* would depend on whether the other lessons were good or not: and do you know? the last of the 6 lessons was so good that I forgot *everything*! I forgot who I was: I forgot to eat my dinner: and, so far, I've quite forgotten to pay the man. I will give you his address, as perhaps you would like to take lessons from him, so as to forget *me*. He lives in the middle of Hyde Park, and his name is "Mr. Gnome Emery." It *is* such a comfort to have forgotten all about Agnes, and Evey, and —— and —— and I feel as happy as the day is short! (I would have said "as the day is *long*," only, you see, this is winter, not summer.)

Oh, child, child! Why have you never been over to Oxford to be photographed? I took a first-rate photograph, only a week ago, but then the sitter (a little girl of 10) had to sit a minute and a half, the light is so weak now. But if you could get any one to bring you over, I could do one, even now. I expect to be here till nearly Christmas. What's the use of having a grown-up sister, if she can't escort you about England? After Christmas I hope to go to town, and take some children to Pantomimes. My first duty will be to take my friend Evelyn Dubourg (they give me a bed when I come to town) to some theatre or other. She says she is "keeping young" in

---

* After Dodgson abandoned all hope of making a friend of Dolly Blakemore, he again met mother and daughter by chance: "Dolly . . . not only spoke to me without crying," Dodgson wrote in his diary, "but actually asked me to come in with them! I did so, just to break the ice: but only stayed a minute. . . . In the afternoon I went in again, and stayed about an hour . . . , and it really looks as if we were good friends at last—after 5 weeks estrangement." In the end, a long and happy friendship developed.

order to go with me. *She* isn't grown-up yet (she isn't quite 16 yet, but will be in about a week) so she may be excused for childish tastes. After I've taken *her*, I should like to take two of you – or say two and a half, not more. "But what *is* half a child?" you will say. Well, you see, most children are partly arms and partly legs: but if a child is *all* arms, or *all* legs (it doesn't matter which) *that's* what I call "half a child." I enclose a riddle I've made for you. The answer is a word of two syllables. Also some anagrams for your grown-up sister. Love to Evey, and – believe me

Your loving friend,
Lewis Carroll

To Jessie Sinclair*

Christ Church, Oxford
January 22, 1878

My dear Jessie,

I liked your letter better than anything I have had for some time. I may as well just tell you a few of the things I like, and then, whenever you want to give me a birthday present (my birthday comes once every seven years, on the fifth Tuesday in April) you will know what to give me. Well, I like, *very* much indeed, a little mustard with a bit of beef spread thinly under it; and I like brown sugar – only it should have some apple pudding mixed with it to keep it from being too sweet; but perhaps what I like best of all is salt, with some soup poured over it. The use of the soup is to hinder the salt from being too dry; and it helps to melt it. Then there are other things I like; for instance, pins – only they should always have a cushion put round them to keep them warm. And I like two or three handfuls of hair; only they should always have a little girl's head beneath them to grow on, or else whenever you open the door they get blown all over the room, and then they get lost, you know.

Tell Sally it's all very well to say she can do the two thieves and the five apples, but can she do the fox and the goose and the bag of corn? That the man was bringing from market, and he had to get them over a river, and the boat was so tiny he could only take one across at a time; and he couldn't ever leave the fox and the goose together, for then the fox would eat the goose; and if he left the goose and the corn together, the goose would eat the corn. So the only things he *could* leave safely together were the fox and

---

* Dodgson got to know the Sinclairs, still another acting family, through his friendship with the Cootes. The Sinclair children were Sarah (Sally), Jessie, Kate, and Harry.

the corn, for you never see a fox eating corn, and you hardly ever see corn eating a fox. Ask her if she can do *that* puzzle.

I think I'll come and see you again – suppose we say once every two years; and in about ten years I really think we shall be good friends. Don't you think we shall? I shall be very glad to hear from you whenever you feel inclined to write, and from Sally too, if *she* likes to try her hand at writing. If she can't write with her hand, let her try with her foot. Neat footwriting is a very good thing. Give my love to her and Kate and Harry; only mind you keep a little for yourself.

Your affectionate friend,
Lewis Carroll

Thank your Mama for her letter which has just come.

To Edith Blakemore

Christ Church, Oxford
January 27, 1878

My dear Edith,

I send you my best thanks for your birthday-wishes, and the handkerchiefs, and the album (how pretty it is) that has just room for *one* picture. So I have put one into it – some child or other, that I made friends with at some seaside-place or other – Eastbourne I think it was.

But really you mustn't go on sending me such a shower of presents. I shall be wet through with them soon: and then I shall catch cold, and the doctor will say "You ought to have held up your umbrella when you knew your birthday was coming."

I send you my love and a kiss, and am

Your affectionate friend,
C. L. Dodgson

To Sarah Sinclair

Christ Church, Oxford
February 9, 1878

My dear Sallie,

Please tell Jessie I meant it *all* for nonsense, so I hope she won't give me a pincushion, for I've got three already. I've forgotten what I said in my letter to her, and *she* knows it all by heart; so you see this is what has happened – the letter has gone out of *my* mind into *her* mind: it is just like a person going into a new house. I wonder if it found Jessie's mind warm and comfortable, and if it liked it as well as its old house? I *think*, when it first got in, it looked round and said, "Oh, dear, oh dear! I shall *never* be comfortable in this new mind! I wish I was back in the old one! Why, here's a great awkward sofa, big enough to hold a dozen people! And it's got the word 'KINDNESS' marked on it. Why, I shan't be able to have it all to myself. Now, in my *old* house there was just *one* chair – a nice soft armchair that would just hold me; and it had the word 'SELFISHNESS' marked on the back; so other people couldn't come bothering in, because there were no chairs for them. And what a stupid little stool that is by the fire, marked 'HUMILITY'! Ah, you should have seen what a nice high stool there was in my old house! Why, if you sat on it you nearly knocked your head against the ceiling! And it was marked 'CONCEIT,' of course; that's a much nicer name than 'HUMILITY.' Well, let's see what's in the cupboard. In my old house there was just *one* large bottle of vinegar, with a label on it, 'SOUR TEMPER,' but *this* cupboard is stuffed full of jars! Let's see what the names are. Oh dear, oh dear! Why, they're all full of sugar, and the labels are 'LOVE OF SALLIE,' 'LOVE OF KATE,' 'LOVE OF HARRY'! Oh, I can't have all this rubbish here! I shall throw them all out of the window!"

I wonder what *this* letter will say when it gets into *your* mind! And what will it find there, do you think? I send my love for Jessie and Kate and Harry and you, and four kisses: that's just one a-piece. I hope they won't get broken on the way.

Yours affectionately,
Lewis Carroll

Thank Jessie for letter.

To Agnes Hull

Christ Church, Oxford
October 17, 1878

WELL! Of all the *mean* things ever done by a young lady of ten to save *one penny*, I think the sending that *precious* little book, on which I have spent so many *sleepless* hours, by book-post, so as to make sure that all its corners should get well bruised on the way, and the book itself should be read all through by the post-office clerks (who always read such books just after putting coals on the fire, so as to leave black thumb-marks all through it), and that the beautiful leather cover should be scratched by the post-office cats – was about the *meanest*! You hardly deserve to have it back again, you dreadful child! Of course I know your *real* motive – that you thought, if you sent it by post, I should expect you to write a note with it, and you were too proud to do *that*! Oh, this pride, this pride! How it spoils a child who would otherwise be quite endurable! And pride of birth is the worst of all. Besides, *I* don't believe the Hull family is as old as you say: it's all nonsense that idea of yours, that Japhet took the surname Hull because he was the one that built the hull of the Ark. I'm not at all sure that it *had* a hull. And when you say his wife was called Agnes, and that you are named after her, you know you're simply inventing. And anyhow, *I'm* descended from Japhet too: so you needn't turn up your nose (and chin, and eyes, and hair) so *very* high!

The negatives are dried and varnished, and all but the two large ones of you shall go to the printer here. Those two I want to send to London, to be left somewhere where the Tunbridge-Wells printer can call for them. That will be a nice little job for Evie....

Give them my love and three – oh no, it's no use sending any, because you never hand them on, and you *don't* deserve any more yourself.

Your loving friend,
Lewis Carroll

To Agnes Hull

[Christ Church, Oxford]
October 22, 1878

Why, how *can* she know that no harm has come to it? Surely *I* must know best, having the book before me from morning to night, and gazing at it *for hours together* with tear-dimmed eyes? Why, there were several things I didn't even mention, for instance, the number of beetles that had got crushed between the leaves. So when *I* sign myself "your loving" *you* go down a step, and say "your affectionate"? Very well, then *I* go down *another* step, and sign myself "yours truly, 'Lewis Carroll.'"

To Henry Sinclair

Christ Church, Oxford
March 22, 1879

Dear Mr. Sinclair,

Mrs. Neate has written to tell me of the sorrow that has fallen on you and on your dear children, and it has made me very sad to think of you and of them in the first utter blankness and desolation that follows the death of one that has been very dear. I wish I could say anything to relieve your pain: but that I fear is more than man can do. God alone can bind up the wound that He, for reasons beyond *our* understanding, has made: and He alone can enable us to say, even in our deepest sorrow, "Thy will be done." All *I* can do is to offer you my true sympathy – which I do most sincerely – and *that* I know, from my own experience, is comforting and strengthening. And another thing I can do for you, and will do: that is to pray for you; and for your dear little ones, that they may be guided through the life they must now face without a mother's care, so that they may one day meet her again, where "God shall wipe away all tears from their eyes."

When my own dear father died (the deepest sorrow *I* have known in life) there was one text that I often dwelt on and found sweet and soothing: and I will set it down, in the hope that you too may find comfort in it. "Then are they glad, because they are at rest: and so He bringeth them unto the haven where they would be." Surely *she*, whom you mourn, has reached that blessed haven. And is it not sweet to think that, after all her suffering here, she is at rest, and shall suffer no more, for ever and ever? Give the children my best love, if they are now with you, and believe me

Yours most truly,
C. L. Dodgson

I hope, if ever I can be of service to you or the children, in the years to come, that you will always count on me as a friend, and let me know your trouble.

To Mrs. A. L. Mayhew

Christ Church, Oxford
May 26, 1879

Dear Mrs. Mayhew,

Two, out of the three negatives which I did on Saturday, are decidedly good: the one of Ruth alone as "Comte de Brissac," standing: and the one of Ethel in the same dress, seated: the group is not so good, as Ethel moved a little. I would have liked to have done Ethel in Jersey and bathing-drawers (the dress worn by the children at Sandown) but did not like to do it without first getting leave.

If Saturday afternoon is fine, I shall be glad to have Janet as soon after 2 as she can be got here. If you cannot come yourself, Ruth and Ethel might bring her – or, if you have other places you wish to go to, and like to leave her for an hour or two, I shall be most happy to take charge of her: but in either of these cases I should like to know *exactly* what is the minimum of dress I may take her in, and I will strictly observe the limits. I hope that, at any rate, we may go as far as a pair of bathing-drawers, though for *my* part I should much prefer doing without them, and shall be very glad if you say she may be done "in any way she likes herself."

But I have a much more alarming request to make than *that*, and I hope you and Mr. Mayhew will kindly consider it, and not hastily refuse it. It is that the same permission may be extended to Ethel. Please consider my reasons for asking the favour. Here am I, an amateur-photographer, with a deep sense of admiration for *form*, especially the human form, and one who believes it to be the most beautiful thing God has made on this earth – and who hardly ever gets a chance of photographing it! Did I ever show you those drawings Mr. Holiday did for me, in order to supply me with some graceful and unobjectionable groupings for children without drapery? He drew them from life, from 2 children of 12 and 6 – but I thought sadly, "*I* shall never get 2 children of those ages who will consent to be subjects!" and now at last I seem to have a *chance* of it. I could no doubt hire *professional* models in town: but, first, they would be ugly, and, secondly, they would *not* be pleasant to deal with: so my only hope is with *friends*. Now your Ethel is beautiful, both in face and form; and is also a perfectly simple-minded child of Nature, who would have no sort of objection to serving as model for a friend she knows as well as she does me. So my humble petition is, that you will bring the *3* girls, and that you will allow me to try some groupings of Ethel and Janet (I fear there is no use naming Ruth as well, at her age, though *I* should have no objection!) without any drapery or suggestion of it.

I need hardly say that the pictures should be such as you might if you liked frame and hang up in your drawing-room. On no account would I do a picture which I should be unwilling to show to all the world – or at least all the artistic world.

If I did not believe I could take such pictures without any lower motive than a pure love of Art, I would not ask it: and if I thought there was any fear of its lessening *their* beautiful simplicity of character, I would not ask it.

I print all such pictures *myself*, and of course would not let any one see them without your permission.

I fear you will reply that the one *insuperable* objection is "Mrs. Grundy" – that people will be sure to hear that such pictures have been done, and that they will *talk*. As to their *hearing* of it, I say "of course. All the world are welcome to hear of it, and I would not on any account suggest to the children not to mention it – which would at once introduce an objectionable element" – but as to people *talking* about it, I will only quote the grand old monkish (?) legend:

> They say:
> Quhat do they say?
> *Lat them say!*

It only remains for me to add that, though my *theories* are so out-of-the-way (as you may perhaps think them), my *practice* shall be strictly in accordance with whatever rules you like to lay down – so you may at any time send the children by themselves, in perfect confidence that I will try *no* experiments you have not previously sanctioned.

I write all this, as a better course than coming to say it. *I* can be more sure of saying exactly what I mean – and you will have more leisure to think it over.

Sincerely yours,
C. L. Dodgson

To A. L. Mayhew

Christ Church, Oxford
May 27, 1879

Dear Mr. Mayhew,

I answer Mrs. Mayhew's kind note, to *you* – because I have chanced upon an unanswered note of yours, asking me to turn "horse" into "field."

Now I can turn "horse" into many other forms, but "field" seems to me
to give only "yield" or "fiend": can *you* get it any further?*

As to the photography, I am heartily obliged to Mrs. Mayhew for her
kind note. It gives more than I had ventured to hope for, and does not
extinguish the hope that I may yet get *all* I asked. You will think me very
sanguine in saying this: but I will make it plain.

First, the permission to go as far as bathing-drawers is very charming, as
I presume it includes *Ethel* as well as Janet (otherwise there would be no
meaning in bringing more than Janet) though I hardly dare hope that it
includes *Ruth*. I can make some charming groups of Ethel and Janet in
bathing-drawers, though I cannot exaggerate how much better they would
look without. Also the bathing-drawers would enable me to do a full front
view of Ethel, which of course could not be done without them: but why
should you object to my doing a *back* view of her without them? It would be
a *perfectly* presentable picture, and far more artistic than with them. As to
Janet, at *her* age they are surely unnecessary, whatever view were taken.

Now comes my reason for hoping that you and Mrs. Mayhew will after
all give *carte blanche* as to dress – at any rate for Ethel and Janet. It is that I pay
Mrs. Mayhew the compliment of believing that she states her *real* reason for
objecting to the entire absence of drapery. Oh the trouble I have sometimes
had with ladies, who *will* give fictitious reasons for things, and, when those
break down, invent others, till at last they are driven to speak the truth! But
I don't believe this of Mrs. Mayhew. I feel pretty sure that neither she nor
you would have admired, as you have done, all those studies of naked
children (which of course were done from live children), if you had objected
on general principles to children ever being pictured in that condition. And
therefore I was really pleased to read in Mrs. Mayhew's note that her reason
for objecting to absolute undress was because she felt "sure that the children

---

* They are playing at Doublets, a word game that Dodgson invented and published.
We cannot find Dodgson turning *horse* into *field*, but he certainly was able to turn *horse*
out to *grass*:

HORSE
h o use
r o use
r o ute
r outs
b outs
b oats
br ats
br ass
GRASS

themselves would decidedly object." Those words were very welcome reading, because *I* happen to feel sure, and for good reasons, that they would not only not "decidedly" object, but that they wouldn't object *at all*. For I had told them (I hope there was no harm in doing so) of the pictures I *wished* to take, but had said that of course Mrs. Mayhew must give leave before I could do them. Both Ruth and Ethel seemed quite sure that *Janet* wouldn't object in the least to being done naked, and Ethel, when I asked her if *she* would object, said in the most simple and natural way, that she wouldn't object at all. I didn't ask Ruth, as I felt no hope of leave being given by the higher powers in her case.

Now don't crush all my hopes, by telling me that all that Mrs. Mayhew said was merely a *façon de parler*, and that all the time you and Mrs. Mayhew object absolutely to the thing, however much the children themselves would like it!

At *any* rate, I trust you will let me do some pictures of *Janet* naked: at her age, it seems almost absurd to even suggest any scruple about dress.

My great hope, I confess, is about *Ethel*, who is (artistically) worth ten Janets. Do consider *her* case in reference to the fact that she herself is quite indifferent about dress.

If the worst comes to the worst, and you won't concede any nudities at all, I think you ought to allow *all three* to be done in bathing-drawers, to make up for my disappointment!

Sincerely yours,
C. L. Dodgson

P.S. I hope Mrs. Mayhew won't mind my suggesting that I never photograph well when a large party come. If Ruth and Ethel bring Janet, there is really no need for her to come as well – that is, *if* you can trust me to keep my promise of abiding strictly by the limits laid down. If you *can't* trust my word, then please never bring or send any of the children again! I should certainly prefer, in that case, to drop the acquaintance. I get on pretty well with three people on the premises: better, usually, with two: what I like best of all is to have *two* hours of leisure-time before me, *one* child to photograph, and *no* restrictions as to costume! (It is a descending Arithmetical Series – 2, 1, 0.)

To Mrs. A. L. Mayhew

Christ Church, Oxford
May 28, 1879

Dear Mrs. Mayhew,

Thanks for your letter. After my last had gone, I wished to recall it, and take out the sentence in which I had quite gratuitously suggested the possibility that you *might* be unwilling to trust me to photograph the children by themselves in undress. And now I am more than ever sorry I wrote it, as it has accidentally led to your telling me what I would gladly have remained ignorant of. For I hope you won't think me *very* fanciful in saying I should have no pleasure in doing any such pictures, now that I know I am ~~not thought fit for~~ only permitted such a privilege ~~except~~ on condition of being under chaperonage. I had rather do no more pictures of your children except in full dress: please forgive all the trouble I have given you about it.

Just now, for quite another reason, I would like to defer further photography. I have just received a distressing letter of domestic news, and feel so worried and anxious that I have no spirit for doing more photographs – even of a kind which I *could* do without a sense of not being trusted.

After a little while I hope to call again and arrange for another visit.

Sincerely yours,
C. L. Dodgson

I await answer about "field."

To Mrs. A. L. Mayhew

Christ Church, Oxford
June 9 [1879], 5:15 p.m.

Dear Mrs. Mayhew,

One of my strongest reasons for disliking viva voce discussions of any matter where there is a difference of opinion is that I am so liable to say what I do not mean. Now I have no doubt I gave you the impression, just now, that, if a child comes to me to be photographed and one more person comes, I would rather that other person were another child and *not* the mother. I have *no* such feeling, and therefore write to explain my real meaning, which I entirely failed to express viva voce.

I don't at all object to having as many as *three* here at a time (though I like two better and one best of all). But suppose three people came, two to be photographed and one more, it would be a matter of entire indifference to me whether that other one were a child or the mother, *provided it were also so to her.*

I hope I have now made my meaning clear. If I were sure that, whatever forms of photography you would allow me to try when you are here, you would *also* allow when you are *not* here, I should be delighted to do them *either* way: and if Ethel and Janet, for instance, had come to be done in bathing-dress, I should on the whole have preferred that the third person should be *you*, and not Ruth.

But the fact I have so unfortunately learnt, that you consider your presence *essential*, which is the same as saying "I cannot trust you," has taken away all the pleasure I could have in doing any such pictures, and most of my desire to photograph them again in any way.

It is not pleasant to know that one is not trusted. You said that you could, in conversation, explain away that disagreeable impression, and I was hoping, while you were talking this afternoon, that you would say something to show that I had made a mistake: but I fear there was nothing to say.

I cannot tell you how sorry I am for the annoyance I have caused you by starting so unlucky a topic.

Yours very truly,
C. L. Dodgson

Forgive my not having had those negatives printed. They are put away with my other old negatives, and the memories they recall are too disagreeable for me to care to get them out again just now.

To Mrs. P. A. W. Henderson

Christ Church, Oxford
Saturday [July 12?, 1879]

Dear Mrs. Henderson,

I hope my mention of my admiration of children's feet did not make you think I meant to propose taking *Annie* with bare feet. I shall propose no such thing, as I don't think she knows me well enough, and is also too nervous a child, to like it. So I hope she has heard nothing of it, as it might make her afraid to come.

With children who know me well, and who regard dress as a matter of indifference, I am very glad (when mothers permit) to take them in any amount of undress which is presentable, or even in none (which is more presentable than many forms of undress) but I don't think your Annie is at all a child of that sort. If you ever meet with any such "children of Nature," I shall be glad to hear of them.

Very truly yours,
C. L. Dodgson

To Mrs. P. A. W. Henderson

Christ Church, Oxford
July 20, 1879

Dear Mrs. Henderson,

Miss E. G. Thomson, the artist-friend I told you of, comes to me to-morrow, to spend the day: and I'm sure she would thoroughly enjoy helping to arrange the children for a few photographs, if they would like to come. If they themselves are *quite* willing to come, and if her presence will not make them shy of being undressed, I should be very glad if they could be left here at about 11½, and if they may have their dinner here, we will bring them home when we set forth to lionise Oxford. But if the fact of Miss T. being here makes them *at all* unwilling to come, please don't press it on them.

There would be another advantage in their coming while Miss Thomson is here, and that is, that she will perhaps be able to make a sketch or two of them, out of which (with the help of photographs as a guide to the features) she might make *a* really pretty drawing. I have commissioned her to make *some* drawing for me, but we haven't yet settled the subject: I don't think she *could* have a better subject than Annie.

I have only mentioned the *children*, as you talked of sending them alone: but if you are not too busy to come yourself, it would make the thing all the pleasanter. Even if too busy in the morning, couldn't you come to luncheon at 1½? That will make a nice party, 2 ladies and 2 gentlemen, and A. and F., of course, as I am asking Mr. Bayne to luncheon.

Love to the children.

Sincerely yours,
C. L. Dodgson

It is very pleasant to me to think that the children are so absolutely at their ease with me, and I assure you I take it as a great compliment and privilege that you are willing to trust me with them so entirely. I have never seen anything more beautiful in childhood than their *perfect* simplicity. *

To Agnes Hull

Christ Church, Oxford
November 26, 1879

My darling,

You are very cruel. I was very much pleased with the beginning of your letter, and then you took away nearly all the pleasure by telling me it is only because I am going to take you to the Lyceum that you are so affectionate! I don't care a bit for such affection. Do *you* care for the affection of a cat, that only purrs and rubs itself against you as long as it thinks there is cream in the cupboard?

So please write next time just as you would if there was *no* Lyceum. And please come with me to the Lyceum on the afternoon of December 20, as it happens oddly enough that I've got two tickets for then, and I was puzzling who to offer the other ticket to. I shall be on my way back from Hatfield to Guildford that day, so you mustn't mind if my manner is a little grand at first: you see I shall come fresh from being among lords and ladies, so how can I help despising an untitled child? But it'll soon pass off, and my chin will settle down again to its usual level. I hope you won't be *very* much frightened at coming without Alice: I'll bring a little hay for you to munch if you feel faint. No end of love and kisses to Evie and Jessie. I'm afraid there's no use in saying "and the same to you," for, if I never leave off kissing *them*, how in the world can I begin on *you*?

Your ever loving friend,
Lewis Carroll

To Agnes Hull

Christ Church, Oxford
December 18, 1879

My darling Aggie,

(I notice the cooling down of affection in *your* letter, but I shan't take the hint!) Really you mustn't begin to believe my letters to be all meant seriously,

---

* For a continuation of the themes struck in these two letters to Mrs. Henderson, see p. 97, below.

or I shall be so frightened I shan't dare to write to you: of course when I said I thought Evie was angry because I wasn't going to take her to *Madame Favart*, I was only talking nonsense. It's a way I have.

And so you think we're going to meet *soon*? And that there isn't time for many more letters? Now to *me* it seems, oh such a long way off! Hours and hours: 30 or 40 at least. And I should say there is plenty of time for *fifteen* more letters – 4 today, 8 tomorrow, and 3 on Saturday morning. You'll get so used to hearing the postman's knock, that at last you'll only say, "Oh, another letter from Mr. Dodgson, of course!" and when the maid brings it in, you'll only say, "Haven't time to read it: put it in the fire!"

My love to Alice, and tell her not to be nervous about the examination. In the Oxford examinations the best candidates are always fancying they will get plucked, but they come out, after all, crowned with beautiful wreaths of cauliflowers – and so will she, no doubt.

But I must leave off *this* letter, or I shan't have comfortable time for my other 4 letters to you today.

Your loving friend,
C.L.D.

Best love to

To Ellen Terry

[The Chestnuts, Guildford]
[January 12?, 1880]

. . . You gave me a treat on Saturday such as I have very seldom had in my life. You must be weary by this time of hearing your own praises, so I will only say that Portia was all I could have imagined, and more. And Shylock is superb – especially in the trial-scene.

Now I am going to be very bold, and make a suggestion, which I do hope you will think well enough of to lay it before Mr. Irving. I want to see that clause omitted (in the sentence on Shylock) –

That, for this favour,
He presently become a Christian.

It is a sentiment that is entirely horrible and revolting to the feelings of all who believe in the Gospel of Love. Why should our ears be shocked by such words merely because they are Shakespeare's? In his day, when it was held to be a Christian's duty to force his belief on others by fire and sword – to burn man's body in order to save his soul – the words probably conveyed no shock. To all Christians now (except perhaps extreme Calvinists) the idea of forcing a man to abjure his religion, whatever that religion may be, is (as I have said) simply horrible.

I have spoken of it as a needless outrage on religious feeling: but surely, being so, it is a great artistic mistake. Its tendency is directly contrary to the spirit of the scene. We have despised Shylock for his avarice, and we rejoice to see him lose his wealth: we have abhorred him for his bloodthirsty cruelty, and we rejoice to see him baffled. And now, in the very fulness of our joy at the triumph of right over wrong, we are suddenly called on to see in him the victim of a cruelty a thousand times worse than his own, and to honour him as a martyr. This, I am sure, Shakespeare never meant. Two touches only of sympathy does he allow us, that we may realise him as a man, and not as a demon incarnate. "I will not pray with you"; " I had it of Leah, when I was a bachelor." But I am sure he never meant our sympathies to be roused in the supreme moment of his downfall, and, if he were alive now, I believe he would cut out those lines about becoming a Christian.

No interpolation is needed – (I should not like to suggest the putting in a single word that is not Shakespeare's) – I would read the speech thus:

> That lately stole his daughter:
> Provided that he do record a gift,
> Here in the court, etc.

And I would omit Gratiano's three lines at Shylock's exit, and let the text stand:

> *Duke.* "Get thee gone, but do it."   (*Exit Shylock.*)

The exit, in solemn silence, would be, if possible, even grander than it now is, and would lose nothing by the omission of Gratiano's flippant jest....

To Alexandra Kitchin

Christ Church, Oxford
February 15, 1880

My dear Unknown Quantity,

Second thoughts are best. (I have got to be so sure of that, that nearly all my thoughts now *are* second thoughts. I have *no* first thoughts, as a general rule.) And on second thoughts, I said, "I will give her *both* the cards." (I hope you'll like "Ariel" as well as the Owls: true, I condemned it yesterday, but that was all gross exaggeration (nearly all my statements *are* gross exaggerations, as a general rule).)

"But why *two*?" you will say. "This is *too* much! He is *too* kind! I am *too* delighted!"

To all which I reply, "*Voilà tout!*"

Perhaps – who can say? (*I* never can, as a general rule) the second one is to express my gratitude to you for getting me that photo of your 3 friends. "What! Gratitude before he gets it?" you will say.

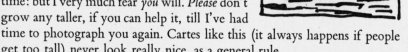

"Well, yes." You see, *events* lately have confused me so much (*you* won't understand this allusion, but your Mamma will understand it and will pity me) that my feelings work backwards – mostly – as a general rule. So whenever I remember receiving that photo from you, I always feel grateful: and when I've *got* it, why *then* I shall indulge in *hope*!

I'm afraid it'll be another 6 weeks or so before I can invite you to bring Dorothy to my studio. *She* won't have grown too tall by that time: but I very much fear *you* will. *Please* don't grow any taller, if you can help it, till I've had time to photograph you again. Cartes like this (it always happens if people get too tall) never look really nice, as a general rule.

So, my dear Multiplication-Sign, I sign myself (with a nervousness which your Mamma will understand and pity)

Affectionately yours,
Lewis Carroll

To Adelaide Paine

Christ Church, Oxford
March 8, 1880

My dear Ada,

(Isn't that your short name? "Adelaide" is all very well, but you see when one is *dreadfully* busy one hasn't time to write such long words – particularly when it takes one half an hour to remember how to spell it – and even then one has to go and get a dictionary to see if one has spelt it right, and of course the dictionary is in another room, at the top of a high bookcase – where it has been for months and months, and has got all covered with dust – so one has to get a duster first of all, and nearly choke oneself in dusting it – and when one *has* made out at last which is dictionary and which is dust, even *then* there's the job of remembering which end of the alphabet "A" comes – for one feels pretty certain it isn't in the *middle* – then one has to go and wash one's hands before turning over the leaves – for they've got so thick with dust one hardly knows them by sight – and, as likely as not, the soap is lost, and the jug is empty, and there's no towel, and one has to spend hours and hours in finding things – and perhaps after all one has to go off to the shop to buy a new cake of soap – so, with all this bother, I hope you won't mind my writing it short and saying, "My dear Ada.") You said in your last letter you would like a likeness of me: so here it is, and I hope you will like it. I won't forget to call the next time but one I'm in Wallington.

Your very affectionate friend,
Lewis Carroll

To Mrs. P. A. W. Henderson

Christ Church, Oxford
May 31, 1880

Dear Mrs. Henderson,

I do hope you did not think I had taken a step not warranted by the circumstances, in allowing the children to live for 3 hours in their favorite costume, up in the studio. But I felt so confident that, when you told Annie they must not be taken naked because it was too cold, it was your *only* reason, that I thought that objection cleared away by the fact that the studio was, I should think, at nearer 80° than 70°.

Their innocent unconsciousness is very beautiful, and gives one a feeling of reverence, as at the presence of something sacred: and, if you had only those two girls, I should see no objection (in spite of "Mrs. Grundy") in their repeating the performance, if they wished, next year, or even for 2 or 3 years to come. But, for the sake of their little brother, I quite think you may find it desirable to bring such habits to an end after this summer. A boy's head soon imbibes precocious ideas, which might be a cause of unhappiness in future years, and it is hard to say how soon the danger may not arise. So I shall be quite prepared to find, next year, that they have learned to prefer *dressed* pictures. I am not so selfish as to wish for pictures, however valuable as works of art, the taking of which involved any risk for others.

And I shall always feel proud of having been treated with such exceptional confidence.

I am going away for about 10 days, in a day or two, and shall not be able to print these pictures till I return. Then I shall be here till about the end of June.

Very sincerely yours,
C. L. Dodgson

To Evelyn Dubourg*

[Christ Church, Oxford]
July 3, 1880

So E.D. is *de rigueur*? Very good. It is not the *only* E.D. I have met with possessing this character. But why "of course"? Are there *no* exceptions? Surely, if you go to morning parties in evening dress (which you *do*, you know), why not to evening parties in morning dress?

Anyhow, I have been invited to *three* evening parties in London this year, in each of which "Morning Dress" was specified.

Again, doctors (not that *I* am a real one – only an amateur) must always be in trim for an instant summons to a patient. And when you invite a doctor to dinner (say), do you not always add "Morning Dress"? (I grant you it is done by initials in *this* case. And perhaps you will say you don't understand M.D. to stand for "Morning Dress"? Then take a few lessons in elementary spelling.)

Aye, and many and many a time have I received invitations to evening parties wherein the actual colours of the Morning Dress expected were stated!

For instance, "Red Scarf: Vest Pink." That is a *very* common form, though it is usually (I grant you) expressed by initials.

---

* Evelyn was the daughter of the author and dramatist Augustus William Dubourg, who was one of Dodgson's earliest friends in the theatre. Dubourg tried to help Dodgson get *Alice* put onto the London stage, but that was to happen only later, and by other means.

But I spare you. No doubt you are by this time duly ashamed of your too-sweeping assertion, and anxious to apologise. Will you plead that you know not how to apologise, and that ladies never *do* apologise to gentlemen? Then take a few lessons in elementary manners.

Yours affectionately,
Lewis Carroll

To his cousin and godson *W. M. Wilcox*

Christ Church, Oxford
November 23, 1880

Dear Willie,

Often and often I have been thinking of writing to you, but good resolutions are very like pie-crust – in one way, that they're very easily broken – but not, I hope, in another way, that if you keep them waiting a long time, they go bad.

You must have time in the long evenings, now, I should think, when games different from cricket and football are possible: so you might like to try my new game *Mischmasch** with some young friend. I hope the rules are clear enough: but, if you can't understand them, I will try to explain.

I hope you are thriving, in body and mind, at school: and that you are not quite so idle as *I* used to be at school: and that, as you grow older and older, you will be more of a help and comfort to your mother. She generally tells me a good deal about you when she writes.

Your ever affectionate cousin and godfather,
C. L. Dodgson

P.S. I enclose another bit of paper, thinking you might like to amuse yourself by taking it to the post-office, to see if anything happens when you hand it in. It is a curious and interesting experiment.†

---

* Mischmasch is a word game for two players or two sets of players that Dodgson invented during the summer of 1880. "The essence of the game," he wrote in the introduction, "consists of one Player proposing a 'nucleus' (i.e. a set of two or more letters, such as 'gp,' 'emo,' 'imse'), and in the other trying to find a 'lawful word' . . . containing it. Thus, 'magpie,' 'lemon,' 'himself,' are lawful words containing nuclei 'gp,' 'emo,' 'imse.' "

† Dodgson enclosed a money order for his godson.

To Catherine Laing

Christ Church, Oxford
November 30, 1880

Dear Madam,

I beg you will excuse the liberty I take in addressing you, though personally a stranger to you: but I have just learned – within the last hour – that a dictionary is in course of publication, under your directions as I understand, in which my name has been included, coupled with the anonymous name ("Lewis Carroll") under which I have published some books. And I lose not a moment in writing to request – most earnestly and urgently – that you will erase the paragraph in which I am mentioned. If you could for a moment realise how deep, and how lasting, an annoyance such publicity would be to me, you would, I feel sure, grant my request at once. But it is hard to convey it in words. I use a name, not my own, for writing under, for the one sole object, of avoiding *personal* publicity: that I may be able to come and go, unnoticed, in all public places. And it would be a real unhappiness to me to feel myself liable to be noticed, or pointed out, by strangers.

I know not if you have ever seen any writings of mine. If not, I have nothing to appeal to. But if you have, and if they have ever given you any pleasure, do not, I entreat you, repay it by the cruelty of breaking through a disguise which it is my most earnest wish to maintain. Believe me

Faithfully yours,
C. L. Dodgson

To Catherine Laing

Christ Church, Oxford
December 6, 1880

Dear Madam,

Accept my sincere thanks for your kindness in the matter of the Dictionary of Pseudonyms. I am sorry you had the trouble and expense of telegraphing the result. I by no means intended by telegraphing to you to suggest that the reply should also be a telegram: it was simply to save time, as I do not like, without real necessity, to send letters entailing Sunday-work on the hard-worked Post-office employees.

You have relieved me from what would have been a constant source of annoyance. Again thanking you, I am

Truly yours,
C. L. Dodgson

I am applying to the Bodleian Library to get the information, of which you have told me, erased.

To Ellen Terry

The Chestnuts, Guildford
January 16, 1881

Dear Mrs. Wardell,*

Thanks for writing. I shall have Agnes Hull with me tomorrow – the same lovely child whom I brought to see you play Portia. Like the washer-woman in the *Bab Ballads*, "she long has loved you from afar," and is now "dying to see Camma" as her sister reports. I think I will give that *Corsican Brothers* you so kindly sent me to the said sister, as she has seen the play, but I fear no more of my child-friends have, so I should not know what to do with the further copies you offer: but many thanks all the same: and it encourages me to ask a favour for Agnes Hull. For I am sure you like giving pleasure, and in this case you would raise the child into the seventh heaven of delight, if there is such a thing as a book of the words of *The Cup*, and if you would write her name in a copy ("To Agnes from Camma" or any other inscription you like) and send it round to us (in Stalls 42, 43). To a child's imagination, the actress of a beautiful part (such as I feel sure Camma must be) is a fairy-like and unapproachable being, and to have such a gift from you at such a moment would make it a memorable night for the rest of her life! But I shall not give her any hint that I have suggested this, so there will be no disappointment if it doesn't come.

How *can* you expect me to give my opinion on *The Cup* if you won't give yours? And on the ground that I "know" so much! I don't feel as if I knew *anything* – worth speaking of – about acting. But to pretend that

---

* In 1877 Ellen Terry had married Charles Wardell (Charles Kelly on the stage). Edie and Eddie, mentioned towards the end of the letter, were Edith and Edward Craig, Ellen Terry's children by E. W. Godwin. The second sentence of the postscript refers to a pamphlet entitled *On Catching Cold*.

you know nothing about it is on a par with my saying (for instance), "Don't ask me anything about Euclid" when I have been teaching it for 20 years!

However, I'll give you the opinion of an amateur outsider, as you pay me the compliment of asking for it.

I hope the cards reached E[die] and E[ddie] undamaged, and that they did not prove to be duplicates of any they had already.

Always sincerely yours,
C. L. Dodgson

If there isn't a book of *The Cup* would you send her the "Corsicans"? I have printed the enclosed for friends.

To Edith Blakemore

Christ Church, Oxford
February 1, 1881

My dear little friend,

I have waited since January 27 to thank you for your letter and present, that I might be able to say the "scales" had come. But as they still don't come, I will wait no longer. Thank you very much for all your birthday-wishes, and for the "scales," whatever they are. Oh, how puzzled I am to guess what they will be like. First I think "Dear little thoughtful Edith! She knew I was always an invalid, taking heaps of medicine – and she was afraid I should take too much. So she is sending me a nice pair of medicine-scales to weigh it out grain by grain." Then I think "Oh no, she knows I am fond of music: so she is sending me a set of 'scales' to practise on the piano-forte or the orguinette." Then again I say "Oh, how stupid I am! Why, of course it's a *fish* she's sending me. A nice scaly salmon, just to remind me of Eastbourne, wrapped up in seaweed, and sprinkled with sand." When it comes, I wonder which of these guesses will turn out to be right!

Give my kindest regards to your father (who I hope is better than when I saw him last) and your mother, and believe me

Yours ever affectionately,
C. L. Dodgson

Something fails –
Perhaps the gales –
Still, there *are* scales

> On the rails,
> Packed in bales
> With the mails,
> Coming to a writer who regales
> Little friends of his with fairy-tales.

To Agnes Hull

Christ Church, Oxford
March 25, 1881

My own Aggie,

(Though, when I think of all the pain you have given me, I feel inclined to put the syllables in *another* order and say, "My Agg own ie!") Of course I guessed at once, when I heard that you knew I had been delayed by the snow in getting from London to Oxford, that you had read the paragraph in *The Times* beginning "One of the passengers delayed on this occasion we need not name: it will be enough to tell our readers that he was *the most distinguished man in England.* Not only the tallest, the strongest, the most beautiful – he *is* all that, but that would be little. He is also the wisest, the most amiable, the most, etc., etc., etc.," and I was going to write to you to say how vexed I was that the Editor had made the description so plain, and that I had *begged* him not to let any one know I had been in that train – but on second thoughts, I decided that the most truly modest course would be *not to write about myself*: so I say no more.

Do you know Tennyson's poem beginning:

> It is the miller's daughter,
>   And she is grown so dear, so dear,
> That I would be the jewel
>   That sparkles in her ear?

Well, you will be interested to hear that I have luckily found (among some old papers of Mr. Tennyson's) *the original manuscript.* It is very much torn. I will give you an exact copy over the page. He has altered it very much since. The first title was "How an Elderly Person took a Young Person to the Play, but could not get her away again." And he had begun it in quite a different metre:

Two went one day
To visit the play:
One came away:
The other would stay.

And then he seems to have changed his mind, and written it as I now give it you.

Your ever loving,
Lewis Carroll

It is the lawyer's daughter
And she is grown so dear, so dear
She costs me, in one evening,
The income of a year!
"You can't have *children's* love," she cried
"Unless you choose to fee 'em!"
"And what's *your* fee, Child?" I replied.
She simply said "Lyceum."

———

We saw The Cup. I *hoped* she'd say
"I'm grateful to you – very."
She murmured, as she turned away,
"That lovely Ellen Terry.
Compared with *her*, the rest," she cried
"Are just like two or three um-
berellas standing side by side!
O gem of the Lyceum."

———

We saw Two Brothers: I confess
To *me* they seemed one man.
"Now which is which, Child? Can you guess?"
She cried "A-course I can!"
Bad puns like this I *always* dread,
And am resolved to flee 'em:
And so I left her there, and fled;
She *lives* at the Lyceum.

It is the lawyer's daugh[ter]
    And she is grown so dear, so d[ear]
She costs me, in one evening,
    The income of a year!
"You can't have children's love," she cr[ied]
    "Unless you choose to fee 'em!"
"And what's your fee, Child?" I replied.
    She simply said "[

We saw The Cup. I hoped she'd say
    "I'm grateful to you — very".
She murmured, as she turned aw[ay]
    "That lovely [
Compared with her, the rest," she cri[ed]
    "Are just like two or three um-
-berellas standing side by side!
    O gem of th[e

We saw Two Brothers: I confess
    To me they seemed one man.
"Now which is which, Child? Can you—"
    She cried "A-course I can!"
Bad puns like this I always dread,
    And am resolved to flee 'em:
And so I left her there, & fl[ed]
    She lives at [

"It is the lawyer's daughter" – poem to Agnes Hull;
the missing words are supplied in the printed text opposite.

To Helen Feilden

Christ Church, Oxford
April 12, 1881

My dear Helen,

I have behaved very badly to you in leaving your two interesting (they are always *that*) letters, the first of them dated December 4, 1880, so long unanswered. So, before saying anything out of my own head, I will try to make some appropriate remarks on them.

And first, many thanks for your history of the "Ober-Ammergau Passion-Play." I am very much interested in reading accounts of that play: and I thoroughly believe in the deep religious feeling with which the actors go through it: but would not like to see it myself. I should fear that for the rest of one's life the Gospel History and the accessories of a theatre would be associated in the most uncomfortable way. I am very fond of the theatre, but I had rather keep my ideas and recollections of it *quite* distinct from those about the Gospels.

Next in your letter come many questions about the Terrys. I have not seen any of them, to speak to, for a long time: but I went to the Haymarket and the Lyceum last vacation. At the Haymarket I saw *School*, in which Marion plays charmingly. It was the 18th of January, the day of that fearful storm in London, and the streets were all snow: but I had got tickets for 3, so we braved it, two young ladies (I hardly care to go to a theatre alone now) and self. The theatre was nearly empty: about 100 stalls being empty out of (116 I think it was). Besides the 16 or so in the stalls, there were 20 or 30 other people dotted about. I never saw so curious a sight. The company seemed to think it rather fun than otherwise: or perhaps they wanted to reward the few who had been brave enough to come. At any rate they seemed to act their best.

At the Lyceum (to which I took one of the loveliest children in London – aged 13 – I wish I could show her to you) we saw *The Cup* and *The Corsican Brothers*. *The Cup* is a lovely poem, and the scenery, grouping, etc., are beyond all praise: but really as a *play* there is nothing in it. There are just *two* events in it. The villain (Mr. Irving) tries to carry off Camma and kills her husband – and afterwards wants her to marry him and share his throne. Whereupon she does the (dramatically) obvious thing, accepts him, and makes a poisoned cup a very early ingredient of the marriage-ceremony. Both drink it, so *both* die. Why *she* should die, Mr. Tennyson only knows! I suppose he would say, "It gives a roundness and finish to the thing." So it may; but a heroine who would poison herself for *that* must have an almost

morbid fondness for roundness and finish. I must tell you, I think, of a graceful act of kindness on the part of Miss Ellen Terry. I had happened to be
writing to her a few days before, and told her I was going to bring a child
who was an enthusiastic admirer of hers ("She is like the washerwoman in
the *Bab Ballads*," I said: "she long has loved you from afar") and that we
should be in the centre of the stalls. So, after the 1st Act of *The Corsican
Brothers* the box-keeper came along our row of stalls, and presented "with
Miss Ellen Terry's compliments" a roll of paper and a lovely bouquet of
violets. The roll we found contained one of the illustrated books of *The
Corsican Brothers*, inscribed in some such words as these: "Camma would
have sent the words of *The Cup*, but they are not printed. So she begs Agnes
Hull to accept this with her love. Given at our Temple of Artemis – signed,
Camma." Wasn't it pretty of her? The child was in ecstasies of delight, and
nursed the bouquet all the way home. "And you must send her *heaps* of
love!" she said: "you know she sent me *her* love!" I don't think I ever saw
her look so graceful as she does in the long trailing silk robe (a light sea-
green) which she wears as Camma.

Miss F. Terry *was* engaged to Mr. Cox, but it is broken off.

I haven't ever seen Mdme. Modjeska: but every one, that *has*, praises her.
I am charmed with your neighbours in the theatre, who supposed her to
be playing Marie Stuart *ex tempore*! ("Gagging the part," to use stage-slang.)

And now what can I say on my own account? Shall I send you a Dutch
version of *Alice* with about 8 of the pictures done large in colours! It would
do well to show to little children. I think of trying a coloured *Alice* myself
– a "nursery edition." What do you think of it?

If you won't think me *very* vain, I will add the verses I sent Agnes to
commemorate our visit to the Lyceum. I told her they had been found on a
torn piece of paper, of which I sent a facsimile.

Kindest regards to your mother.

Always yours affectionately,
C. L. Dodgson

To Agnes Hull

Christ Church, Oxford
April 21, 1881

My darling Aggie,

(Oh yes, I know quite well what you're saying – "Why can't the man
take a *hint*? He might have *seen* that the beginning of my last letter was

meant to show that my affection was cooling down!" Why, of course I saw it! But is that any reason why *mine* should cool down, to match? I put it to you as a reasonable young person – one who, from always arguing with Alice for an hour before getting up, has had good practice in Logic – haven't I a right to be affectionate if I like? Surely, just as much as *you* have to be as unaffectionate as *you* like. And of course you mustn't think of *writing* a bit more than you *feel*: no, no, *truth* before all things!) (Cheers. Ten minutes allowed for refreshment.) I came up to town on Monday with Mr. Sampson (some of you have met him at Eastbourne) to see *The Cup* and *The Belle's Stratagem*, and on Tuesday I made a call or two before going back to Guildford, and passed High Street, Kensington. I had turned it (half) over in (half of) my mind, the idea of calling at 55. But Common Sense said, "No. Aggie will only tease you by offering you the extremity of her left ear to kiss, and will say, 'This is for the *last* time, Mr. Dodgson, because I'm going to be sixteen next month!'" "Don't you know," said Common Sense, "that *last times* of anything are very unpleasant? Better avoid it, and wait till her sixteenth birthday is over: then you'll be on shaking-hands terms, which will be calm and comfortable." "You are right, Common Sense," said I. "I'll go and call on other young ladies."

Now, you needn't yawn so, and say, "What a tiresome letter this is!" I'm going to tell you something about *The Cup*, that will interest you. A lady (a cousin of mine) wrote to me that she wished very much to read it – and could I get her a sight of it? (as it isn't published). So I wrote to ask the gem of the Lyceum if she could help us. Immediately there came a parcel by book-post, containing, first, her own printed copy, inscribed "Ellen Terry, from A. Tennyson," with corrections in *Tennyson's* hand, and memoranda of *hers* about attitudes and expression of face, etc. (what they call "business" on the stage) all of which made it extremely interesting, so that, though I found afterwards that *this* copy had been packed by mistake, I'm very glad the mistake was made. The other book was a written copy of the first, in an album, beautifully written out by a young lady, a friend of hers. I sent back the printed one, and I've sent the other to my cousin to read. If Miss Terry allows me, I think of copying it out before I return it to her. And if I do, perhaps *some* day, when you're a *very* good girl indeed, and haven't been cross that day, I may let you look at it – with one eye. What! Won't *that* content you? What a greedy thing you are! Well then, you may use *both* eyes.

The Belle's Stratagem I don't much care for. But it has two *very* funny scenes. One where "Letitia Hardy" (Miss E. Terry), in order to play a trick on "Doricourt" (Mr. Irving), who has been ordered (in some will or other) to marry her, pretends to be a boisterous country-girl: the other where Doricourt, in order to avoid marrying her, pretends to be mad. Mr. Irving can be *very* funny when he likes: and as for *her* comic acting, no words will describe it! You had better try and imagine it.

Well, I expect you'll say, "This letter is *quite* long enough, Mr. Dodgson!" So I'll leave off.

With best love *à vos sœurs* (I hope that's good French), I am

Your loving friend,
C.L.D.

To Lord Salisbury

Christ Church, Oxford
May 19, 1881

Dear Lord Salisbury,

In venturing to send you the enclosed paper,* I hope you will acquit me of motives of personal vanity. Most gladly would I have left it to some abler writer to ventilate the subject: but I have not seen it treated of in print *at all*: and it appears to me to be a matter of really national importance: and I feel that, in urging a change, I am writing neither in Conservative nor Liberal, but in British interests.

Yours very truly,
C. L. Dodgson

Please give my thanks to Lady Salisbury for her kind letter, and my kindest regards to her and your daughters.

To Mrs. P. A. W. Henderson

The Chestnuts, Guildford
June 21, 1881

Dear Mrs. Henderson,

I have run away for a week's change, and to escape the Oxford festivities, but expect to return about the 28th and shall probably not get away finally

---

* Dodgson's letter on "The Purity of Election" appeared in the *St. James's Gazette* on May 4. In it, he asks for more than the secret ballot (a recent innovation); he requires the votes to be sealed up until the voting, which lasted several days, was over, to avoid early returns influencing later voters.

till the middle of July. Today I write to ask if you would like to have any more copies of the full-front photographs of the children. I have 2 or 3 prints of each, but I intend to destroy all but one of each. That is all I want for myself, and (though I consider them perfectly innocent in themselves) there is really *no* friend to whom I should wish to give photographs which so entirely defy conventional rules. Miss Thomson is the only friend who has even *seen* them, and even to *her* I should not think of giving copies. But *you* may have friends to whom you would like to give copies. If you are *quite* sure you would have no use of them, I may as well destroy them: otherwise, I think the best plan will be for me simply to retain one of each, and bring you all the rest. The negatives are already destroyed: so, as no more can be printed, you had better keep them as long as there is *any* chance of your wanting them. There are only 3 kinds, I think:

(1) Annie alone, arms hanging straight;
(2) large group of the two, arms ditto;
(3) small group of the two, Annie with her hands clasped in front.

I wish, now, I had done one of Annie asleep, of the same unconventional type, but I fear from what you said last year it is too late to think of it now. And I also fear it is too late to suggest what a privilege it would be to have Annie as a model for pencil-drawing. From long practice on the sea-beach with little friends who never will keep still more than a few minutes, I have got to be able to sketch a complete figure (such as it is – *all* my work is very poor, I fear) in about 5 minutes. I get plenty of *draped* models to sketch from, but never a real "nude study." However, I ought to have thought of this last year.

I quite hope that picture on your drawing-room table will serve as a sort of "decoy-duck" and reveal to you (and through you to me) other parents who possess well-made children who have a taste for being taken without the encumbrances of dress. But they *must* be well-made. I should decline the offer of others, as I think such pictures would be unpleasant. Ill-made children should be taken in full-dress.

With love to the bairnies, I am

Sincerely yours,
C. L. Dodgson

To Mrs. P. A. W. Henderson

Christ Church, Oxford
June 30 [1881]

Dear Mrs. Henderson,

I write this, to leave with the photos for your brother-in-law, to thank you for your most kind note and to say that I entirely agree with every word of it.

If the remarks that have been made have caused *you* any annoyance, I am indeed sorry to have (indirectly) caused them; otherwise, for *my* part, I am not only indifferent to being thus gossiped about, but even regard it as being possibly useful as an advertisement!

Many thanks for your promise of another model in the future – 4 or 5 years hence will be time enough. I shall trust it to you to bring her a year before she reaches the outside limit of age, within which she is available.

Sincerely yours,
C. L. Dodgson

P.S. After all, I haven't destroyed the other prints. Perhaps *you* may be wanting more some day. I have put them all into an envelope, marked (as I have several packets of letters already marked) "to be burned unopened" – a direction which I can trust my Executors to carry out.

To Mrs. P. A. W. Henderson

Christ Church, Oxford
July 1, 1881

Dear Mrs. Henderson,

I would have gladly stayed yesterday for a little chat, but that I fancied etiquette required I should not, by sitting down, drive away your lady-guest before she had said all she wanted to say: I pictured to myself that you were in the middle of a long confidential chat. Of course I didn't catch her name: one never does, I think, in introductions.

However I think I said in my note all that *I* had to say. But I would have been glad to hear from you (if you don't object to repeating it) what the terrible remark was which *somebody* made in Annie's hearing. Possibly it may be easier to write than to repeat viva voce. Her *name* I don't the least desire to know: I don't think it is good for one to know the *name* of anyone who has said anything against one. But it might be useful to know *what* is said – as a warning of the risk incurred by transgressing the conventional rules of Society.

One thing I will add to the note I left – that your remark that you would even now, but for what has been said by others, have lent me Annie as a model, has gratified me very nearly as much as if you were actually to do it. It is a mark of confidence which I sincerely value.

Very sincerely yours,
C. L. Dodgson

To Agnes Hull

Christ Church, Oxford
December 2, 1881

Dearest Aggie,

I wish the Lord Chamberlain wouldn't be *quite* so interfering in the theatres. When I made the usual formal application for leave for me and Mr. Sampson to go to the "Court" to see *Engaged*, taking Alice with us, he quietly said it was contrary to the new regulations –"the number of ladies and gentlemen in a party must be equal." "But," I pleaded (it was a personal interview), "she would quarrel desperately with *any* other lady I could possibly bring!" "Try one of her *sisters*," said he. "Oh, that would be worse than anything," I said: "they would most likely *fight*!" He smiled and said, "In that case, you can appeal to the police: by the new regulations, every tenth person in the audience is a policeman, and they have strict orders to take into custody every one who gets the least excited." I *couldn't* get him to alter the rule: so I'm afraid there is no help for it: *you* will have to come too. (I suppose neither of you will object to Mr. Sampson being of the party?) Here is a choice of 3 days – the 14th, the 15th, the 20th. Will any one of them do? If so, or if not, *write*! – with even more than your usual fiery activity! And believe me ever

Lovingly yours,
C. L. Dodgson

To F. H. Atkinson

Christ Church, Oxford
December 10, 1881

Dear Mr. Atkinson,

First, will you kindly write my name in the little book, and so add to it a tenfold value in my eyes. I return you many thanks for it. But as to my photo, I must still beg to be excused. Possibly your book of poetry has not brought on you all the annoyances of one who, having been unlucky enough to perpetrate two small books for children, has been bullied ever since by the herd of lion-hunters who seek to drag him out of the privacy he hoped an "anonym" would give him. I have really had *much* persecution of that sort, since I wrote *Alice's Adventures in Wonderland* and *Through the Looking-Glass*, and I so much *hate* the idea of strangers being able to know me by sight that I refuse to give my photo, even for the albums of relations. I have just refused one to a lady, a cousin by marriage. Let me somewhat atone for my discourtesy by asking if you have any girl (between 8 and 16 say) who does not own, and would like to have, one of the above-named books – and if I may present her with a copy. If you will send her name (to which age and birthday would be an interesting addition) I will write it in the book.

In haste, to catch the post,

Yours most truly,
C. L. Dodgson

When I named those limits of age I quite forgot date of marriage! I remember now you said there *is* a girl.

To Edith ?Blakemore

The Chestnuts, Guildford
December 27, 1881

My dear Edith,

Thank you very much for your drawing. I think a Christmas-card, drawn by the child herself who sends it, is worth ever so much more than a bought one. But how much *is* "ever so much more"? you will want to know. Well, it is very easy to find out. Go to the bookseller's and take up any book, and say "how much is it?" Perhaps he will say "two shillings." Then *you* will say "very well. Now bring me one that costs ever so much more." And when he brings it, you will say "Now then, stupid, why didn't you bring it quicker? Well, how much is it?" Perhaps he will say "Eighty-eight pounds, four and sixpence." Then you will take pencil and paper and do a subtraction-sum something like this

	£	s.	d.
big book	88	4	6
little book		2	0
	88	2	6

and when you have done it, you will know what "ever so much more" means.

I am very sorry to hear that your father has been so ill, and is still suffering so much. Give him my kindest regards, and my best wishes that he may leave his gout behind him in the Old Year, and only take with him into the New Year things he really likes, such as Edith, and little things of *that* kind. Also give my kindest regards to your mother, and best New Year hopes for you all. Good-bye, dear little friend.

Yours affectionately,
C. L. Dodgson

To Edith Blakemore

Christ Church, Oxford
January 27, 1882

My dear Edith,

Many thanks for your letter, and painted crocus, and paper-rack. I am very sorry your father is no better: when the summer comes, I think it will be a good thing if you advise him (you know how much he depends on your advice) to come to Eastbourne. Then sometimes I shall have the plea-

sure of seeing you, with my opera-glass, at the other end of the beach: and I shall be able to say "There's Edith: I can see *her*: but I shall go home again if she looks this way, for fear of her seeing *me*." And what do you think I am going to have for my birthday treat? *A whole plum-pudding*! It is to be about the size for four people to eat: and I shall eat it in my room, *all by myself*! The doctor says he is "afraid I shall be ill": but *I* simply say "Nonsense!"

> Your loving friend,
> C. L. Dodgson

Dodgson's sketch of Edith Blakemore at Eastbourne

To Jessie Hull

Christ Church, Oxford
February 1, 1882

My darling Jessie,

And how do you get on with Miss Heaphy? Any "scenes" yet? Any sulks? Any tears? I hope Miss Heaphy will not be offended at my copying out a few sentences from *her* letter about *you*.

Dear Mr. Dodgson,

. . . I am afraid your idea about joining Agnes and Jessie, so as to make a class of three, is quite out of the question. . . . Another reason against it is that your *style* of drawing would never suit the class: it would simply hinder them in making progress. When I tell you that Agnes is already decidedly better than Tintoret and Turner, and is *nearly* equal to Millais – and that Jessie (the pet!) now draws in a way that would make Raphael (if he were now alive) shake in his shoes – do you think, dear Mr. Dodgson, that *your* twopenny-halfpenny scrawls can be endured in the same room with *their* unapproachable pictures? The idea is simply absurd. . . . Yes, I assure you that neither Turner's, nor Raphael's, nor Titian's, nor Rubens' pictures are *the least like* what Agnes and Jessie can do! . . . The sweet Agnes at present inclines chiefly to houses. When I say "inclines," I write thoughtfully, for her houses *do* incline, it must be confessed, rather to one side: and the smoke from the chimnies is certainly *rather* solid: also her idea of a tree is at present slightly liable to be taken for a ball of worsted: but these are trifles. . . . Dear little Jessie prefers figures – children and animals: she nearly always gets the number of fingers and toes *quite* right: and as to the animals, when once you have learned to distinguish which are cows and which are ducks, they are lovely, quite lovely!

There! Now I've given you a good idea what Miss Heaphy thinks of *you*. Now please (you or Aggie) tell me, with equal candour (I *do* like candid children – and sugar) what *you* think of *her*.

Give my dearest love to Aggie, and I *hope* she won't be *too* much set-up at Miss Heaphy's high opinion of her – also love and kisses to Evie, and Alice – also accept many of the same yourself – also believe me

Your loving friend,
Charles Lutwidge also Dodgson

To Florence Balfour

Christ Church, Oxford
February 10, 1882

My dear Birdie,

As are the feelings of the old lady who, after feeding her canary and going out for a walk, finds the cage entirely filled, on her return, with a live turkey – or of the old gentleman who, after chaining up a small terrier overnight, finds a hippopotamus raging around the kennel in the morning – such are my feelings when, trying to recall the memory of a small child who used to wade in the sea at Sandown, I meet with the astonishing photograph of the same microcosm suddenly expanded into a tall young person, whom I should be too shy to look at, even with a telescope which would no doubt be necessary to get any distinct idea of her smile, or at any rate, to satisfy oneself whether she has eyebrows or not!

There! that long sentence has exhausted me, and I have only strength to say "thank you" very sincerely, for the 2 photographs. They are terribly lifelike! Are you going to be at Sandown next summer? It is just *possible* I may be running over there for 2 or 3 days: but Eastbourne is always my headquarters now. Believe me

Yours affectionately,
C. L. Dodgson

To Kate Terry Lewis*

Christ Church, Oxford
June 5, 1882

My dear Katie,

I wonder if you could find a minute to write me a post-card, just to tell me how your mother is going on? Dr. Giraud gave but a bad account of her last time he wrote: and I suppose he has left you by this time. I shall be *very* glad to hear she is getting better again. Next time I call I hope *you'll* be at home: you had gone to the Dentist when I called the other day. Oh, how I envied you when I heard it! A good play, or a gallery of good pictures, is

* Daughter of the actress Kate Terry, niece of Ellen Terry, and, later, mother of John Gielgud.

a very delightful thing to go to – but a *Dentist*, oh, there are not words (are there?) to describe the delight! In fact, Dr. Giraud was quite alarmed when he saw the effect the news had on me. "Is it a sudden attack of jaundice?" he asked anxiously. "No!" I said. "Why should you think so?" "Because your eyes have turned quite green, all in a moment!" "Oh, that's nothing," I said: "it's only green-eyed jealousy, at hearing of dear Katie's happiness!" Is not that a curious and interesting anecdote?

Kindest regards to your parents, and best love to your sisters, from

> Yours very affectionately,
> C. L. Dodgson

To an unidentified recipient

[? Mid-1882]

...I am a member of the English Church, and have taken Deacon's Orders, but did not think fit (for reasons I need not go into) to take Priest's Orders. My dear father was what is called a "High Churchman," and I naturally adopted those views, but have always felt repelled by the yet higher development called "Ritualism."

But I doubt if I am fully a "High Churchman" now. I find that as life slips away (I am over fifty now), and the life on the other side of the great river becomes more and more the reality, of which *this* is only a shadow, that the petty distinctions of the many creeds of Christendom tend to slip away as well – leaving only the great truths which all Christians believe alike. More and more, as I read of the Christian religion, as Christ preached it, I stand amazed at the forms men have given to it, and the fictitious barriers they have built up between themselves and their brethren. I believe that when you and I come to lie down for the last time, if only we can keep firm hold of the great truths Christ taught us – our own utter worthlessness and His infinite worth; and that He has brought us back to our one Father, and made us His brethren, and so brethren to one another – we shall have all we need to guide us through the shadows.

Most assuredly I accept to the full the doctrines you refer to – that Christ died to save us, that we have no other way of salvation open to us but through His death, and that it is by faith in Him, and through no merit of ours, that we are reconciled to God; and most assuredly I can cordially say, "I owe all to Him who loved me, and died on the Cross of Calvary."...

To Christina Rossetti

7 Lushington Road, Eastbourne
August 16, 1882

Dear Miss Rossetti,

I had learned from the newspapers the sorrow that has fallen on you,* and beg to offer, to you and your family, my sincere sympathy. My photographic negatives are all locked up at Oxford, and I fear I can do nothing in the matter till I return there about the middle of October, when I will send you word what negatives and prints still exist. I am very sorry you should have to wait so long.

This is a favorite haunt of mine, and I am enjoying it much. When I add that this is the 13th letter I have had to write today, you will I hope excuse its brevity. With very kind regards to your Mother, I am

Yours sincerely,
C. L. Dodgson

To Edith Blakemore

Christ Church, Oxford
November 7, 1882

My dear Edith,

How often you must find yourself in want of a pin! For instance, you go into a shop, and you say to the man, "I want the largest penny-bun you can let me have for a half penny." And perhaps the man looks stupid and doesn't quite understand what you mean. Then how convenient it is to have a pin ready to stick into the back of his hand, while you say, "Now then! Look sharp, stupid!" Then again, when you are walking in the street, and a large dog gets in your way: how *can* you get on, unless you have a pin to prick it with! Then of course it runs off, howling: and you walk off, with a quiet smile.

And even when you don't happen to want a pin, how often you must think to yourself, "They say Interlaken is a very pretty place. I wonder what it looks like!" (That is the place that is painted on this pincushion.)

When you don't happen to want either pins or pictures, it may just remind you of a friend who sometimes thinks of his dear little friend Edith, and who

---

* Her brother, Dante Gabriel Rossetti, died on April 9.

is just now thinking of the day he met her on the parade, the first time she had been allowed to come out alone, to look for him.

I hope your Papa is better. Give my kindest regards to him and your Mama.

Always affectionately yours,
C. L. Dodgson

The pincushion was painted by a lady, a friend of mine.

C. L. Dodgson as a young man

Lewis Carroll's father,
Archdeacon Charles
Dodgson: "The
greatest blow that has
ever fallen on *my* life
was the death...of my
own dear father"

Dodgson's seven sisters in
the garden at Croft Rectory

Dodgson's sitting-room at Christ Church, Oxford

The Chestnuts, Dodgson's home at Guildford

Arthur Hatch as Cupid,
taken by Dodgson

Maud and Isabel Standen
by Dodgson

Alice Liddell
all taken by Dodgson

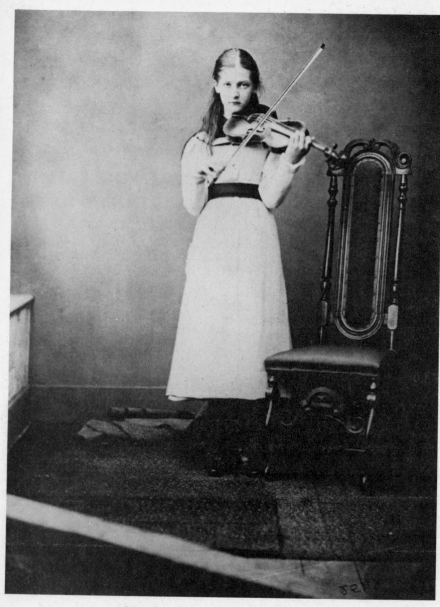

Alexandra ("Xie") Kitchin by Dodgson
"the best way to secure *Excellence* in a photograph"

John Ruskin

The Rossettis in the garden at Cheyne Walk: Dante Gabriel, Christina,
Mrs. Rossetti, and William Michael. "If you take good photographs
of people, you know you cannot help them wanting to see them"
(D. G. Rossetti to Dodgson).

Hallam Tennyson sitting in the poet's lap on the left, Mr. and Mrs. John Marshall and their daughter Julia on the right, taken by Dodgson

Dodgson's portrait of the Terry family. From left to right: Tom, Benjamin (father), Florence, Ellen, Kate, Charles, Marion, and Sarah (mother).

IV. Curator of Senior Common Room, Christ Church

Carroll was elected Curator of the Senior Common Room, Christ Church, on December 8, 1882. "I . . . accepted office with no light heart," he wrote in his diary; "there will be much trouble and thought needed to work it satisfactorily: but it will take me out of myself a little, and so may be a real good. My life was tending too much to become that of a selfish recluse." In fact, Carroll took great pains with the job, and the job was formidable for even so systematic and well-organized a person as he. It meant stocking and running a large private gentleman's club. Carroll paid particular attention to the wine cellars (he even had them extended), and generations of Christ Church members who followed him should have toasted his memory for his prudence in laying down such excellent and ample supplies. He began a Complaint Book for members' comments, and he dealt with all matters efficiently and effectively, even, some people thought, abrasively. But he never lost his sense of the ridiculous. At the end of his first year as Curator, he published a pamphlet entitled *Twelve Months in a Curatorship by One Who Has Tried It* and two years later another entitled *Three Years in a Curatorship by One Whom It Has Tried*. They are both light and breezy reports to his colleagues. The second one begins by dealing with ventilation, lighting, and furniture, or, as he designates the section, "Of Airs, Glares, and Chairs."

To Messrs. Barrett & Clay

Christ Church, Oxford
January 25, 1883

The Curator of the Common Room (the Rev. C. L. Dodgson) will be much obliged if Messrs. Barrett & Clay would give him the benefit of their advice on 2 or 3 points in the treatment of wine, about which he finds much difference of opinion to exist.

(1) What amount of damp is desirable in a wine-cellar?

(2) Is ventilation desirable?

(3) Should light be admitted?

He would also thank them if they would fill in the enclosed paper, as to particular temperatures needed, etc.

Mr. Dodgson takes this opportunity of mentioning that he understands from the previous Curator, Mr. Bayne, that the wine-merchants, or representatives of them, are in the habit of calling periodically on the Curator. This practice he hopes he may, without giving offence, request may be discontinued. He cannot undertake to remember accurately any information given by word of mouth, to lay it before the committee who manage the details of the wine. It would be necessary to have it all in writing, and any such information, in the form of letters, price-lists, etc., will be very acceptable.

Moreover Mr. Dodgson has his time very fully occupied, and such interviews, without giving him any information he could use, would be a serious tax on time already wanted for other purposes.

To Agnes Hull

Christ Church, Oxford
January 26, 1883

My dearest Aggie,

(It's no good. I really *can't* go on writing letters without heads and tails – and I can't call a child "dear" who isn't – so please bear it as well as you can: I will thankfully accept *whatever* heads and tails you choose to attach to *your* letters. Not only your last letter was very welcome, but even its envelope, as its predecessor was getting quite shabby and worn-out. Do you want that explained? Well, you're sure it won't make you vain? I keep stamps of different values in old envelopes, and, as I'm constantly referring to them, it is pleasant to have handwriting on them which one likes to see, outside: *one* is generally an "Edith Denman" envelope – and *one* is generally – has been always I think, since first I heard from you – an "Agnes Hull" envelope. Very weak and foolish, I fear: but I am old, child, I am old. Here ends this parenthesis. Now we shall get on to the real subject of the letter.)

I want to tell you what a Terryble time I have had of it for the last few days. I once knew a young lady who was a frantic admirer of Miss Ellen Terry, and actually treasured up, for some days, some violets given her by that moderately-good actress: but that was nothing compared to the state of mind of my young friend Ethel Arnold*(you saw her with me on Wednesday) when I first started with her from Oxford on Saturday morning. She had a wild love of *all* the Terrys, I believe, but her special idol was Miss Marion Terry, and I had promised to introduce her, if possible. So, when it had been settled that I might take her to my sisters at Guildford, round by London, on Saturday, to return here on Monday, I wrote to Marion to propose calling. She wrote to fix Saturday morning, also telling me that her mother was seriously ill. So I thought it likely that she *might* prefer our *not* calling – especially on so busy a day – and had merely said "come" out of kindness to us: and I wrote to say so, and that we were not coming, but that, if I found she really wished it, we would call on Monday. On Saturday afternoon we went to see *Comrades* at the Court (it is a poor piece, but the acting is first-rate), and Ethel's great hope was that Marion might send a note round to us in the stalls ! And great was her joy when a note came, saying she would be away on Monday morning and asking us to come round to the stage-door for her after the play. *That* was a new experience for both of us: we sat in the entrance room, and saw the players come out in their ordinary dresses. Mr. Clayton, the manager, glared at us and stalked away. Miss Carlotta Addison came through and I think looked at us rather enquiringly (as much as to say, "Who *is* that very distinguished looking young man?"). At last Marion appeared, and she and Ethel rushed into – I mean they shook hands. She took us with her in her brougham to Mrs. Morris (Florence Terry that was) in Campden Hill Road, who was giving a child's party, where the little Lewises and friends were acting a play. But the play was over when we got there. However Mrs. Lewis was there, so that Ethel had now been introduced to 3 of the 4 sisters, Miss Ellen Terry alone remaining unknown. I arranged with Mrs. Lewis that we would come and borrow a child on Monday to take with us to the Avenue Pantomime. (By the way, you are quite right about the banjo. I took an opera-glass on Monday and made out for certain that the child *does* play it herself even while whirling it round.)

On Monday we lunched at Moray Lodge before carrying off Janet for the Pantomime: and Mrs. Lewis invited us to come on Wednesday to see

* One of eight sisters, daughters of Thomas Arnold, granddaughters of Dr. Arnold of Rugby, and nieces of Matthew Arnold.

the little play (*Lady Barbara's Birthday*) which was to be repeated at Moray Lodge. To see so unique a performance, I thought it worth while to bring Ethel over a 2nd time; and that is how you came to meet us that day. The play *was* a treat! Mabel Lewis – the youngest, only about 9 – is simply *wonderful.* I never saw any child's acting to come near it, with the one exception of Miss Ellen Terry when *she* was a child. Mr. Gilbert (the author of *Patience*) was there and I had a little talk with him. But what charmed Ethel most, I think, is that Mrs. Wardell (Miss Ellen Terry) was there. She was constantly being summoned by the children to go round behind the scenes and help, so that she was only about $\frac{1}{2}$ her time among the audience. All the 4 sisters were there: I never met all four at once before. Ethel was actually introduced to Miss E.T. *three* times. She had driven by us as we walked up to the house, and I had bowed to her: so, when she found Ethel in the ladies' cloak-room taking off her walking-things, she shook hands with her, saying, "I don't know *who* you are, but I saw you walking with Mr. Dodgson," and Ethel had to introduce herself. Then in the drawing-room she was sitting just in front of us and began talking, and I had to introduce Ethel again and explain who she was. When the play was over, and we all stood up, Miss E.T. was talking, in a very excited way, to me about *Much Ado,* and all the while (I don't believe she the least knew she was doing it) she was arranging and re-arranging Ethel's bead necklace – pulling it about her neck into all possible positions. Ethel bore it very meekly. Lastly, when we were in the hall, just going off, Marion was talking with Ethel, when up came Miss E.T. and threw her arms round her sister. "Now, Polly," she said, "perhaps *you*'ll enlighten me as to *who* this young lady is!" And when the *third* introduction had been performed, "What a stupid mistake!" she cried, "but I thought Mr. Dodgson had *two* young ladies with him. You look quite different with your hat on, and ever so much taller!" Altogether I think Ethel regards it as a very eventful day, and will probably remember it as long as *somebody* remembered those violets!

There! I've told you all the Terryblé Tale. And you're quite tired of reading it: and my pen is out of breath: so I'll only sign myself

Your (whether loved or not) loving,
C. L. Dodgson

P.S. Edith has just come in, and sends you her love. She is visiting Oxford with her fiancé.

To E. R. Dukes

Christ Church, Oxford
February 27, 1883

My dear Dukes,

My immediate object in writing is to ask you to send back to Common Room the *Illustrated London News* picture of the Manchester Ship Canal, which Telling informs me you have removed, and which members of Common Room wish to see. But I may as well say my say about the pictures, which you have hitherto bought from Common Room. I am not clear yet whether or no to carry on the arrangement which existed under Bayne's regime, but wish to defer settling it till the end of the year, and that till then the pictures shall remain in Common Room. But *in no case* would it do, or be (I think) fair to the other members of Common Room to allow any pictures to be removed during the Term in which they appear. If any other separate pictures have come out this year, and are with you, please return them as well, and believe me

Curatorically but sincerely yours,
C. L. Dodgson

To Charles Rousselet

Christ Church, Oxford
March 3, 1883

Mr. Dodgson is very much obliged to Mr. Rousselet for his letter, which he will submit to the Committee who manage the Wine, and he fully expects that they will accept Mr. Rousselet's very handsome offer. As to Mr. Rousselet's proposal to call and talk over the matter, he does not wish to seem unfriendly, but he really has no spare time whatever for a call: and he must decline any viva voce discussion of business, as everything to be brought before the Committee ought to be *in writing*. Even if Mr. Rousselet lived next door, Mr. Dodgson would still transact *all* the Wine business *in writing*.

To Agnes Hull

The Chestnuts, Guildford
April 6, 1883

My east-red Aggie,

("My!" is an exclamation: "east" is an allusion to your early rising – while the sun is yet in the east: and "red" to the complexion produced by habits of such feverish activity.) On Monday, Tuesday, or Wednesday next, I *may* (though, to be sure, this is only April) be visiting Miss Heaphy at her studio in Newman Street. *If* I do (mark the "if") I *may* (or "Bryant,"* if you think that will throw more light on the subject) be able to take a *single* child with me. ("Single" sometimes means "unmarried," but has another meaning here. I might have said, equally well, "a *singular* child." "Singular" sometimes means "out-of-the-way," but has another meaning here.) Tuesday would be the best day, because then we should find her painting from life: and Aggie would be the best child, because I took Jessie last time. To save you trouble, I shall adopt the simple rule that, if I *don't* hear, I shall *not* call for you. My plan would be to go about noon. Even on Monday or Wednesday you would still see painting going on, though Miss Heaphy would be drawing: the Monday-Wednesday-Friday model is a rather handsome girl dressed in old-fashioned English costume, with a broad-brimmed hat. I forget what the other model is, that *she* paints from: an old man, I think, an aged aged man, a-sitting on a gate. They have to pay him extra, because sitting on a gate, for hours together, is not comfortable.

With "evol" to your sisters ("evol" is short for "evolution"), I remain your vin-log friend ("vin" is a French allusion to my favourite beverage: "log" alludes to my condition after partaking of it),

C. L. Dodgson

To Edith Blakemore

7 Lushington Road, Eastbourne
August 16, 1883

My dear Edith,

It had got into the room, and it couldn't get out again, because the silly thing wouldn't go to the open window where it came in, but *would* try another window, which happened to be shut. Why, actually I've never told you what it was, all this time! Well, it was a very young sparrow: and there were lots more, older ones, in the tree outside, anxiously waiting for it, and wondering where it had got to. So, when I put my hand out to try and catch it, it didn't try to escape, but just huddled itself together and let me take it.

---

* Bryant & May matches, still produced today.

No doubt it said to itself, "Now here is a large wise creature, that understands all about these horrid windows, and knows how to fly through them. I think I'd better let *him* help me." While I was carrying it to the other window, I peeped in to see how it was getting on; but it was shy, and tried to hide its face. Very likely it hadn't been much into society. When I got to the open window, I opened my hand, but it wouldn't go just at first: it held on tight to my thumb, and seemed to be saying, "Why, you don't mean to say I may really *go*? And just where I like?" And then all in a moment it found out it was free, and went straight into the tree like an arrow. But the most curious part was the conversation of the birds afterwards. They all crowded round it, and all began talking at once. I suppose they made it tell its adventures, but I couldn't hear its little squeaky voice in such a fuss. Every one of them was asking it questions the *whole* time, and I don't believe they heard a word of its adventures: how could they? When it had finished, they all explained what *they* would have done if it had happened to *them*: but they all explained at once, so I don't think *that* was any use. And after that (I guessed all this by the voices) they gave the young sparrow good advice. I think it was the *old* birds did this, they had such deep voices: but they spoiled it all, as usual, by all speaking together. That was the last I heard: the young one didn't speak again: I think it must have gone to bed while they were all busy advising it.

Let me see. Was that what I meant to write to you about? No, it wasn't: so please just *un*read all that. What I really want to talk about is birthday-presents – the presents you are so fond of giving me. As I see there's no stopping you from giving them, I want to tell you a few things that really would be useful to me, next time you think of giving anything. Well, first, anything that is *made for me* by a child, I like ever so much better than bought presents. I haven't had many such, but they are *very* nice when they come. Now, little brown holland bags are things that always come in useful: 4 inches square, or 6 inches square, are very good sizes: with double strings, to pull *both* ways – then they keep safe shut. Or, if you like worsted-work better, a kettle-holder would be *very* welcome. I've got two, but they are nearly worn out. I'm afraid all this sounds very greedy: but I only tell you because I know you're so dreadfully fond of sending me presents! So now I've told you enough things to last for 3 or 4 birthdays. But if ever you *do* make me anything, *please* remember to put "E.B.," or else "Edith" in one corner, so that I may always know who it came from.

I wish there was any chance of seeing you on the beach sometimes! Nearly all the children I used to know are gone, and I have very few friends indeed: and it's not so easy to make new friends: besides, they might turn out horrid, instead of nice. Children do that, sometimes.

I hope your father is going on well now. Give him, and your mother, and sister, my kindest regards.

I *hope* I've thanked you for the dear little Christmas card, of your own drawing, and the envelope-case, and the letter you wrote me in January. I'm afraid it was only in a message: so now I thank you, ever so much, from myself.

Excuse this short note: but you see, when one has only *two* minutes to write in, envelope and all, one *has* to put things rather shortly: don't you find it so?

Your loving friend,
C. L. Dodgson

To Alice J. Cooper*

Christ Church, Oxford
November 14, 1883

Dear Madam,

I thank you sincerely for your kind offer of assistance in preparing a "Shakespeare for girls." I had given up the idea, believing that Miss Yonge was doing the very thing: but, on receiving your letter, I wrote to ask her if this was so; and this morning I hear from her that she does not expect to do more than a few of the historical plays, which she is preparing definitely to meet the requirements of the new Code, for "the 6th Standard." So the field is still open, and *when* I can find leisure for it (but I have a bewildering number of "irons in the fire") I will gladly avail myself of your kind co-operation. My notion is to bring out the plays one by one (at 4*d*. or 6*d*. each), and then everybody can select which they please to make a volume of. I have begun on *Tempest*, but done very little as yet.

I will write again more fully. We shall probably agree as to "the kind of expurgation" needed. At any rate, *my* principle is, that it will not be worth doing at all unless it is *thorough*. And the method I propose to myself is to erase ruthlessly every word in the play that is in any degree profane, or coarse, or in any sense unsuited for a girl of from 10 to 15; and then to make the best I can of what is left.

* Headmistress of the Edgbaston High School for Girls, Birmingham.

I wonder if you know my friends the Blakemores, and their little Edith, an old child-friend of mine?

I drop the name "Lewis Carroll" in writing this: but please don't give any publicity to my real name in connection with it.

Very truly yours,
C. L. Dodgson

P.S. I taught the enclosed game to a young ladies' school the other day: and they seemed to like it.*

To Margaret Brough

Christ Church, Oxford
November 24, 1883

My dear Daisy,

I enclose you the Rules for that game I taught you. Also the puzzle of *Doublets* for your sister. I was very nearly writing on it "for Polly," when luckily I remembered that she is probably *very* old, and would be *very* much offended. Would you give me a list of your names, ages, and birthdays?

Yours affectionately,
Lewis Carroll

To William De Morgan

Christ Church, Oxford
December 14, 1883

Dear Mr. De Morgan,

I think we are all well satisfied, now, with the tiles, and that it is a good thing we tried no further change. The desideratum is, it seems clear, tiles at the *back*: the contrast between the tiles at the sides and the black chimney-back is painfully sudden. So I wish to carry out your suggestion. Was your idea to have them right across, or with a black strip up the middle for a smoke-channel? The first half of January would be a very good opportunity for putting them in, if you could supply the tiles, and if you could give us full instructions how to do it. If you think it would be desirable to come over and arrange it all, by personal inspection, I will stand the expense

* Mischmasch.

Ch. Ch.
Oxford
Nov. 24/83

My dear Daisy,

I enclose you the Rules for that game I taught you – also the puzzle of "Outlets" for your letter. I was very nearly writing it "for Polly", when luckily I remembered that it is probably very old, & would be very much offended. Would you give me a list of your names, etc, & kindly say?

Yours affectionately,
Lewis Carroll.

Looking-glass letter to Daisy Brough, November 24, 1883

of journey, and will give you bed and board: I expect to be here till Saturday the 22nd inst.

Yours very truly,
C. L. Dodgson

Please send bill for tiles.*

To Alice (Liddell) Hargreaves

Christ Church, Oxford
December 21, 1883

Dear Mrs. Hargreaves,

Perhaps the shortest day in the year is not *quite* the most appropriate time for recalling the long dreamy summer afternoons of ancient times: but anyhow if this book gives you half as much pleasure to receive as it does me to send, it will be a success indeed.

Wishing you all happiness at this happy season, I am

Sincerely yours,
C. L. Dodgson

To Cecil Alderson[†]

The Chestnuts, Guildford
January 7, 1884

Dear Mr. Alderson,

I am going to the afternoon performance of *Claudian* on Saturday the 12th, and *if* Nellie should happen to be then in town, and *if* you sanctioned it, I should much like taking her to it. As yet I do not know if you would sanction any such expedition, without other chaperon: but let me give you the same explanation of my position, which I have already found it advisable to give to parents of other child-friends of mine who have grown up. And that is, that I am an entirely *confirmed* old bachelor, who is now well over 50, and has not the slightest idea of ever changing his state of life. So, why should Mrs. Grundy object to my having, what is so pleasant to me, the *friendship* of my old child-friends? So many of my friends have now accepted that

---

* As a result of these negotiations, the artist, inventor, and novelist William De Morgan installed tiles of his design in the fireplaces in Dodgson's own large sitting room and in the Senior Common Room. Both sets survive, the ones from Dodgson's room having been removed and made into a fire screen.

† Lady Salisbury's brother.

view, and have allowed me to chaperon my quondam child-friends – at all ages from 15 to 25 and upwards – that I hope *you* will be willing to do the same. But I need hardly say that if you take a different view, I shall not feel hurt at so natural a course of thought.

If you approve of my theatrical ideas in the *abstract*, but say that it cannot be on this occasion realised in the *concrete*, then I hope I shall be informed, if at any time she *should* be staying in town. For Oxford is now very handy for town, and it is no uncommon thing with me to run up to see a new play. Believe me

Sincerely yours,
C. L. Dodgson

To *? Adelaide Paine*

The Chestnuts, Guildford
January 9, 1884

My dear Ada,

Let me assure you, lest you should think I was feeling aggrieved by what seemed "a new departure" in the terms of our friendship, that I was not so: it is a change that is very usual with my young friends. To speak the truth (a course that is often advisable and that has several advantages) the *majority* (say 60 p.c.) of my child-friends cease to be friends *at all* after they grow up: about 30 p.c. develop "yours affectionately" into "yours truly": only about 10 p.c. keep up the old relationship unchanged. It is a satisfaction to know that *you* are one of the 10.

The enclosed is illustrated by a friend of mine. I trust you won't think it too juvenile for your acceptance !

Yours affectionately,
C. L. Dodgson

To *Wilson Barrett*

Christ Church, Oxford
January 15, 1884

Dear Sir,

I am much obliged by the trouble you have kindly taken in sending the tickets. It being a business-transaction, I ought to have enclosed the postage: I do it now. We (I and the young friend I brought) thoroughly enjoyed

Claudian: and a good deal more than I had expected, as I thought it would be difficult to give anything like a *living* interest to such ancient history: but I think Mr. Wills and you have done it to a marvellous extent.

This time I have not even such an emendation to suggest as the omission of a single sentence. But I think I may venture to say, in the interest of all play-goers, that I feel sure that a short sketch of the *plot* would be a most welcome addition to the play-bill. The effort to make out, from the action and dialogue, the plot, is a piece of mental *work*; and, for *my* part, I am always glad to be saved that work – and also glad to have a general idea of what is coming.

Are you not going to print a book of the words? I should much like to be able to read the play before coming again, as I am sure I have not as yet half entered into its beauties. I should like to see it several times more, but doubt if I shall be able to manage so much.

One feels, in praising anything in the play, that you must be already weary of hearing its praises; but I must just name the earthquake, which I thought one of the most effective things of that kind I had ever seen.

Perhaps I might also venture to suggest, with all possible respect to the young lady, that Miss Mary Dickens is *scarcely* audible in the 6th row of the stalls, and I doubt if she can be heard at all beyond that distance. Believe me

Very truly yours,
C. L. Dodgson

To Beatrice Earle

Christ Church, Oxford
February 3, 1884

My dear B,

You were so gracious the other day that I have nearly got over my fear of you. The slight tremulousness, which you may observe in my writing, produced by the thought that it is *you* I am writing to, will soon pass off. Next time I borrow you, I shall venture on having you *alone*: I like my child-friends best *one by one*: and I'll have Maggie alone another day, *if she'll come* (*that* is the *great* difficulty!). But first I want to borrow (I can *scarcely* muster courage to say it!) your *eldest* sister. Oh, how the very thought of it frightens me! Do you think she would come? I don't mean alone: I think Maggie might come too, to make it all proper.

When is school over in the afternoon? It wouldn't be too late, would it, to fetch "Miss Earle" (I suppose that is what she expects to be called) and Maggie down to have tea here: and if we're *very* lucky, we might have a rather finer evening to come back in! If that plan would do, I could come any day she likes to fix: otherwise I could come next Saturday at (say) 3½. One thing more I have to ask you. Either I never got, or have lost the memorandum, the names, ages, and birthdays of you and your sisters. Could you write them down for me?

Always yours affectionately,
C. L. Dodgson

Love to Maggie.

The first page of a tremulous letter to Beatrice Earle, February 3, 1884

To Wilson Barrett

Christ Church, Oxford
May 12, 1884

Dear Sir,

Having become a periodical visitant at your delightful play of *Claudian*, I venture to make a little suggestion on the "business" of the piece, which  I hope may prove of service. When the unfortunate blacksmith is thrown over the bridge – apparently into a roaring torrent – not only do we *not* hear any splash, but I *did* hear (the other day) the sound of his feet lighting on the floor. A little bit of realism here would be very welcome, if you would treat your audience to it. A barrel half full of water, and a stick ending like that in a churn, plunged into the water at the right moment, would I think produce the effect, and add much to the thrilling nature of the incident.

With sincere congratulations on the well-deserved success of the play, I am

Truly yours,
C. L. Dodgson

To Ethel Arnold

Christ Church, Oxford
May 12, 1884

Dear Ethel,

Are you up to about 6 miles (altogether) of walking? If so, I should much like to have your society in going to Hampton Poyle to call on an old "child-friend," Mrs. Kidston that is, Mona Paton (daughter of Sir Noël Paton) that was. The train to Woodstock Road goes at 3, and I would meet you at ¼ to 3, punctually, on the shady side of Beaumont St. We should reach W. Road at 3.12, and (after a mile's walking) H. Poyle about 3½. We might stay about ½ an hour, and we must then walk home (about 5 m.) as there is no train handy. We ought to be home about 6. I would go almost any day except Saturdays that suited you: but the more choice of days you can give me, the better.

Ever affectionately yours,
C. L. Dodgson

There is a baby-boy there, to be admired – about 2 years old, I think: and in this matter you will be of *incalculable* service to me, and relieve me of all responsibility as to saying the proper thing when animals of that kind are offered for inspection.

To the Lowrie children

Care of Messrs. Macmillan
29 Bedford Street, Covent Garden, London
August 18, 1884

My dear Children,

It was a real pleasure to me to get your letter; but, before I answer it, I have two humble requests to make: One is, please don't make it generally known that I have written to you, so as to bring on me a flood of letters from all the American children who have read *Alice*, and who would all expect answers! I *don't* want to spend all the rest of my life (being close on the age when Dr. O. W. Holmes says "old age" begins) in writing letters! (I wonder if you know his *Autocrat of the Breakfast Table?* I delight in it.) And my other request is, please never again *praise* me at all, as if any powers I may have, in writing books for children, were my own doing. I just feel myself a trustee, that is all – you would not take much credit to yourselves, I suppose, if a sum of money had been put into your hands and you had been told "spend all this for the good of the little ones"? And besides *praise* isn't good for any of us; love is, and it would be a good thing if all the world were full of it: I like my books to be loved, and I like to think some children love me for the books, but I don't like them *praised*. I'll tell you what I like to think of best, about the *Alice* books. I've had a lot printed on cheaper paper, in plain bindings, and given them to hospitals and Convalescent Homes – for poor, sick children: and it's ever so much pleasanter to think of one child being saved some weary hours, than if all the town followed at my heels crying, "How clever he is!" I'm sure you would think so too.

Some rather droll things happened about those hospitals: I sent round a printed letter, to offer the books, with a list of the Hospitals, and asking people to add to the list any I had left out. And one manager wrote that he knew of a place where there were a number of sick children, but he was afraid I wouldn't like to give them any books – and why, do you think? "Because they are Jews!" I wrote to say, of course I would give them some: why in the world shouldn't little Israelites read *Alice's Adventures* as well as other children!

Another – a "Lady Superior" – wrote to ask to see a copy of *Alice* before accepting it: for she had to be very careful, all the children being Roman Catholics, as to what "religious reading" they got! I wrote to say, "You shall certainly see it first, if you like: but I can guarantee that the books have no religious teaching whatever in them – in fact, they do not teach anything at all." She said she was quite satisfied, and would accept the books.

But, while I am running on in this way, I'm leaving your letter unanswered. As to the meaning of the Snark? I'm very much afraid I didn't mean anything but nonsense! Still, you know, words mean more than we mean to express when we use them: so a whole book ought to mean a great deal more than the writer meant. So, whatever good meanings are in the book, I'm very glad to accept as the meaning of the book. The best that I've seen is by a lady (she published it in a letter to a newspaper) – that the whole book is an allegory on the search after happiness. I think this fits beautifully in many ways – particularly, about the bathing-machines: when the people get weary of life, and can't find happiness in town or in books, then they rush off to the seaside, to see what bathing-machines will do for them.

Would you mind giving me a more definite idea of who I am writing to, by sending me your names and your ages? I feel as if we were kind of friends already, but the one idea of "The Lowrie Children" is too shadowy to get hold of fairly. It is like making friends with a will-o'-the-wisp. I believe nobody ever succeeded in making an intimate friend of one of those things. Read up your ancient history, and you won't find a single instance of it. I would have added, to "names and ages" "and your cartes," only I'm afraid you'd then expect mine, and that I never give away (my reason is that I want to be personally unknown: to be known by sight, by strangers, would be intolerable to me), so I'm afraid I can't, with a good grace, ask for yours.

I'm very fond of inventing games; and I enclose you the rules of one, *Mischmasch*: see how you like it. One advantage is that it needs no counters or anything: so you can play it out walking, or up in a balloon, or down in a diving-bell, or anywhere!

Your loving friend,
Lewis Carroll

After posting the letter, I remembered I had never said a word about Jabberwocky and *Der Tyroler und sein Kind*. Thank you very much for it: it is one of the loveliest airs I know – and oh, so much too good for such words! Once more, your loving friend (your twopenny-halfpenny friend this time),

Lewis Carroll

To Ethel Hatch

7 Lushington Road, Eastbourne
August 19, 1884

My dear Ethel,

Miss Thomson told me I might read this note before sending it on to you. It is very interesting, but it filled me with green-eyed jealousy! To think of *you*, having (as most likely you will have in years to come) heaps of leisure time to practise figure-drawing, and then of poor *me*, who would like to do it of all things, but never can find the time: always there is something turns up that says "do me," and then another thing "and now do *me*": so that it's as much as I can do to find time to draw the corks of the bottles of beer I consume – and as for drawing *children*, it's out of the question! Yesterday I tried to draw a pretty little girl, who was building a sand-castle: but, as she didn't keep in the same position for 2 moments together, I had to invent every line of it: and the result is awful – worse than *you* would draw, with your left foot, and both eyes shut!

LOVE TO BE

(This doesn't mean "future love" – nor does it mean "lavish all your affection on the verb 'To be' " – and BE *isn't* short for "Beatrice.") So I remain

Your loving friend,
C.L.D.

To Mrs. C. H. M. Mileham

7 Lushington Road, Eastbourne
September 5, 1884

Dear Mrs. Mileham,

Not all of life is bright and happy, like the 4 days when I had May in charge: the very afternoon I left you, my dear old Uncle died – one of the kindest friends I ever had, from early childhood till now – and I am heavy-hearted, and out of harmony with this lovely weather. And I suppose I must go to what we make such a gloomy scene, the funeral. Why should we not, at least when an aged Christian is taken, show signs of rejoicing instead of sorrow? I think we treat Death far too much as the end of all things.

I am glad it did not cut short the sweet little episode of May's visit. If her friendship for me (you would think I was talking nonsense if I tried to say

how unworthy I feel of being loved by her) survives the winter-frosts,
I shall be wishing next year to emulate the achievement of an (elderly I presume) gentleman I know of, who, wishing to make a little tour, and to have
a companion for it, took with him a friend's child, a little girl of 12. However,
that can be discussed hereafter: I need not ask you just now to nerve yourself
for *another* great effort of trustfulness!

If Mrs. F. Holiday is still with you, would you tell her I *don't* want
Climène to be bothered to write to me, in case she gets anything by post:
a *message* of thanks would be amply sufficient.

Best love to May.

Sincerely always,
C. L. Dodgson

To his cousin James Hume Dodgson

7 Lushington Road, Eastbourne
September 8, 1884

My dear Hume,

I could not well explain to you in my telegram, and had not the opportunity of doing so when we met, my reason for not undertaking, as you
wished, to read the service. If I could have trusted myself to command my
feelings and my voice, I should much have wished to read the service over
the remains of my dear old uncle, whom I can never think of without the
deepest affection and gratitude for his life-long kindness: but I did not feel
I could safely do so. Otherwise, you may be sure I would have attempted it.

I hope your sisters and you are not suffering in health from this trial, and
the sad blank you must feel after such a loss.

Yours affectionately,
C. L. Dodgson

To Ethel Arnold

[Christ Church, Oxford]
Tuesday [February 24, 1885]

My dear Ethel,

To save the few surviving fragments of our friendship (blighted as it is by
the transference of *all* your capabilities of affection to one single individual

in London) from drifting away into oblivion, I will, if Thursday afternoon be fine, be at our usual rendezvous at 3½, and, if you are there, we will take a walk and then come round here to partake of the cup that does not inebriate: and you shall tell me your experiences in the society of one who was once *my* friend!

You will be kind enough to tell Judy (with my love, which I send *most* reluctantly) that I *may* forget, but *cannot* forgive, her utterly heartless behaviour in my rooms yesterday. You were not present, and I will not pain your sensitive nature by describing it. But I will be even with her some day: some sultry afternoon, when she is here, half fainting with thirst, I will produce a bottle of delicious cool lemonade. This I will uncork, and pour it foaming into a large tumbler: and then, after putting the tumbler well within her reach, *she shall have the satisfaction of seeing me drink it myself*! Not a drop of it shall reach *her* lips!

I was very glad to see your mother looking so well and so much up to joining in the dissipations of the day.

Yours always affectionately,
C. L. Dodgson

However it *was* very nice of you to bring my dear old friend to see me: and, when she had vanished from my gaze, what had I but mathematical considerations to console me? "She may be limited and superficial," I said to myself. "She may even be without depth. But she is at least equilateral and equiangular: in one word, what else is she but a Polygon!"

To Alice (Liddell) Hargreaves

Christ Church, Oxford
March 1, 1885

My dear Mrs. Hargreaves,

I fancy this will come to you almost like a voice from the dead, after so many years of silence – and yet those years have made no difference, that I can perceive, in *my* clearness of memory of the days when we *did* correspond. I am getting to feel what an old man's failing memory is, as to recent events and new friends (for instance, I made friends, only a few weeks ago, with a very nice little maid of about 12, and had a walk with her – and now I can't recall either of her names!) but my mental picture is as vivid as ever, of one who was, through so many years, my ideal child-friend. I have had scores of child-friends since your time: but they have been quite a different thing.

However, I did not begin this letter to say all *that*. What I want to ask is – would you have any objection to the original MS book of *Alice's Adventures* (which I suppose you still possess) being published in facsimile? The idea of doing so occurred to me only the other day. If, on consideration, you come to the conclusion that you would rather *not* have it done, there is an end of the matter. If, however, you give a favorable reply, I would be much obliged if you would lend it me (registered post I should think would be safest) that I may consider the possibilities. I have not seen it for about 20 years: so am by no means sure that the illustrations may not prove to be so awfully bad, that to reproduce them would be absurd.

There can be no doubt that I should incur the charge of gross egoism in publishing it. But I don't care for that in the least: knowing that I have no such motive: only I think, considering the extraordinary popularity the books have had (we have sold more than 120,000 of the two) there must be many who would like to see the original form.

> Always your friend,
> C. L. Dodgson

To Alice (Liddell) Hargreaves

> Christ Church, Oxford
> March 7, 1885

My dear Mrs. Hargreaves,
Many thanks for your permission. The greatest care shall be taken of the MS (I am gratified at your making *that* a condition!). My own wishes would be distinctly *against* reproducing the photograph.

> Always your friend,
> C. L. Dodgson

To Mrs. F. S. Rix

> Christ Church, Oxford
> March 9, 1885

Dear Madam,
My delay in answering the letters received from you and your daughter on February 16 has not been caused by any want of interest or sympathy, for I have thought of them many times since: but it is difficult to find time for letter-writing, my life is (I am thankful to say) so full of various kinds of work. In response to the friendly tone in which you and she write, I can

only say "please accept me as a friend": and, to bring us a little nearer together, I will drop my *nom de plume*, only asking you *not* to make my name known to your ordinary acquaintances. The fewer strangers there are, who know my real name, the more comfortable for me: I *hate* all personal publicity.

I feel no doubt, from what you tell me, as well as from what I have seen of her work, that your daughter *does* work too hard, and is in danger of defeating her own object. As one who has lectured for 26 years on Mathematics, I may perhaps make bold to say that the amount of work you tell me she went through in 5 months is simply absurd. Thorough mastery, of so much in so short a time, would be (even if she were a female Isaac Newton) out of the question: and if there is one subject less adapted than another to be got up by "cram," it is Mathematics. And again, if there is one subject more than another, where it is absolutely fatal to success to attack higher parts of the subject, while lower parts are still only half-understood, it is Mathematics. That she "passed" an examination in those subjects is no real criterion of her having *mastered* them.

That she should be "insatiable in work" is an excellent thing, and promises well, if only she knows how to be idle *too*, at fitting times: otherwise her working years will very soon come to an end. I am no great advocate for *regular* work – i.e. so many hours a day all the year round. I believe in periods of *intense* work followed by periods of *perfect* idleness: I think your daughter needs to be driven to the latter more than the former!

I am sorry there is a prospect of your daughter (I use this phrase as shorter than "Miss Edith Rix," since I dare not, so soon in our acquaintance, say "Edith" only, even though I *am* 34 years older than she is!) going to Girton. There is not a nice *tone* about "Girton Girls." They have an uncomfortable reputation for being fast and "mannish." I believe Newnham is much better. But why not Oxford? There is I believe *no* ground for thinking that, because her turn is for Mathematics, she ought to go to Cambridge. Oxford teaching is, I am sure, all that she can *possibly* need, for a great many years to come. Also (but this I admit is a smaller consideration), *I* can hardly befriend her so well at Cambridge as here! I *hope* you will reconsider the matter.

Only last Saturday, I had a talk with Miss Wordsworth, principal of Lady Margaret Hall, about some young friends of mine who wish to earn money by teaching, and took the opportunity of naming your daughter, and I got her to give me the enclosed papers to send you. Miss W. advises, if she should think of coming here, that she should offer herself for "The First Examination," on the 8th of June.

Lady Margaret Hall is the one conducted on Church principles: Somerville Hall professes no particular form of religious persuasion. Do not however suppose that, because I am a clergyman, and recommend the former of the two, that it would make any abatement in the friendship, which I hope has begun between us, if you were to tell me you were not "Church people." Among my many "child-friends" (ages varying from 7 to 27) I have some, *very* nice ones, who are Wesleyans: and one dear little friend who is a "Plymouth Sister" (if that is a correct phrase: "Plymouth Grand-daughter" would be nearer the mark, she is so *very* young).

The "Honour Mathematics" at Lady Margaret Hall are taught by a Christ Church man. I don't know him well, but he seems a very pleasant gentlemanly fellow.

You will see that there are "Exhibitions" to be had, for students whose means are limited.

I will give myself the pleasure of answering your daughter's letter another day. Believe me, with kindest regards to her,

Yours very sincerely,
C. L. Dodgson
(alias "Lewis Carroll")

To Alice (Liddell) Hargreaves

Christ Church, Oxford
March 21, 1885

Dear Mrs. Hargreaves,

I am indeed grateful to you for sending the MS book, which has just arrived. The greatest care shall be taken of it. Believe me

Always yours sincerely,
C. L. Dodgson

To Edith Rix

[Christ Church, Oxford]
[Before April 9, 1885]

My dear Edith,

Would you tell your mother I was aghast at seeing the address of her letter to me: and I would much prefer "Rev. C. L. Dodgson, Christ Church,

Oxford." When a letter comes addressed "Lewis Carroll, Christ Church," it either goes to the Dead Letter Office, or it impresses on the minds of all letter-carriers, etc., through whose hands it goes, the very fact I least want them to know.

Please offer to your sister all the necessary apologies for the liberty I have taken with her name. My only excuse is, that I know no other; and how *am* I to guess what the full name is? It *may* be Carlotta, or Zealot, or Ballot, or Lotus-blossom (a very pretty name), or even Charlotte. Never have I sent anything to a young lady of whom I have a more shadowy idea. Name, an enigma; age, somewhere between 1 and 19 (you've no idea how bewildering it is, alternately picturing her as a little toddling thing of 5, and a tall girl of 15 !); disposition – well, I *have* a fragment of information on *that* question – your mother says, as to my coming, "It must be when Lottie is at home, or she would never forgive us." Still, I *cannot* consider the mere fact that she is of an unforgiving disposition as a complete view of her character. I feel sure she has some other qualities besides. Believe me

Yours affectionately,
C. L. Dodgson

To Wilton Rix

[Christ Church, Oxford]
May 20, 1885

Honoured Sir,

Understanding you to be a distinguished algebraist (i.e. distinguished from other algebraists by different face, different height, etc.) I beg to submit to you a difficulty which distresses me much.

If x and y are each equal to "1," it is plain that $2 \times (x^2 - y^2) = 0$, and also that $5 \times (x - y) = 0$. Hence $2 \times (x^2 - y^2) = 5 \times (x - y)$.

Now divide each side of this equation by $(x - y)$.

Then $2 \times (x + y) = 5$.

But $(x + y) = (1 + 1)$, i.e. $= 2$.

So that $2 \times 2 = 5$.

Ever since this painful fact has been forced upon me, I have not slept more than 8 hours a night, and have not been able to eat more than 3 meals a day.

I trust you will pity me and will kindly explain the difficulty to

Your obliged,
Lewis Carroll

To Mrs. F. S. Rix

Christ Church, Oxford
June 7, 1885

Dear Mrs Rix,

Many thanks for your long and interesting letter. I like *getting* long letters – and all the more, if the writers will sometimes excuse short replies! And you write with so much openness and confidence that I cannot well write otherwise to *you*. So let me confess, in confidence, that I don't think I *did* succeed, as you think, in setting Lottie "at her ease." I feel no doubt that, if she had *quite* felt that, she would have talked more, and not merely *replied*. (She *did* talk a little.) The pictures were a resource, and helped us out a bit, but I shouldn't dare, at present, to ask her over here for a day. She would feel constrained, and the hours would drag: for, if people are shy with me, I generally feel so too. Now, if *Edith* were in her place, I would ask *her* at once, though I've never seen her: but I know her from her letters now, and can't believe we should be a bit constrained, though you *do* credit her with "the manners of an ill-assured baby"! "Ill-assured" I can't believe in, and as to "baby," she'd better not look *that* too truthfully, when she comes – unless she wants to plunge me into a *fresh* problem of casuistical doubt as to "greetings"! (Many thanks, by the way, for your kind acceptance of my (tentative) solution of the problem in Lottie's case.) And please what am I to do when a young lady of 19, whom I have never seen, sends me her "love"! I despair of a correct solution, so I send my love in return: please deliver it, or not, as you think fit.

I did, yesterday, what I should *not* have ventured on with Lottie – I borrowed a young friend (only seen *once* before) at 8 a.m. to go to the R.A., and took her home at 6 p.m. True, she hasn't yet reached the shy age: being not quite 10: she is a little actress (I may have mentioned her in writing to Edith: I don't know), and, though her parents are "only working people" (as she took care to write me word before I had met her), she has very nice manners, and was a charming companion to take about among my friends. Some of her talk was almost thinking aloud: before one of the pictures I had said something (I forget why) about worshipping idols, and she broke out almost indignantly "I'd *never* be so silly as *that*! I'd *always* worship God!" Her mother seems to be a good woman, who is trying to bring up her child to be so too.

I shall very likely be in town on the 26th and 27th: but please bring Edith *here* on the 25th. Come as early, and stay as long, as you can.

I'll write to Edith. Please give her the enclosed, which I've copied out (from Robertson's Sermons II. 117) for her friend. I send it with an earnest prayer that it may be of use.

Very sincerely yours,
C. L. Dodgson

To Mrs. F. S. Rix

Christ Church, Oxford
July 7, 1885

Dear Mrs. Rix,

Many thanks for your letter, one or two points in which will be all the better, I think, for an immediate reply.

I am quite content to be regarded as an Oliver Twist, if you like to do so! But I can assure you that, so far as any obligations to *me* are concerned, the pleasure of having Edith at Eastbourne will *quite* "make us quits"! My tenancy of my lodgings there (I always have the same, 7 Lushington Road) begins tomorrow (though I shall not be able to go for some days yet: please address "Christ Church" till I notify any change) and lasts, according to present plans, till the end of September: so there will be plenty of choice of times.

You will pardon my being a little amused at your thinking it possible I should wish to argue with Edith about her "High Church" views. First, I *hate* all theological controversy: it is wearing to the temper, and is I believe (at all events when viva voce) worse than useless. Secondly, I myself belong to the "High Church" school. My dear father was a "High Church" man, though *not* a "Ritualist," and I have seen little cause to modify the views I learned from him, though perhaps I regard the holding of different views as a less important matter than he did. As life draws nearer to its end, I feel more and more clearly that it will not matter *in the least*, at the last day, what *form* of religion a man has professed – nay, that many who have never even *heard of* Christ, will in that day find themselves saved by His blood. You may be sure that, whether Edith were a Roman Catholic, or Wesleyan, or Baptist, or "Plymouth Sister," it would be all one to me, so far as making *any* attempt to disturb her views is concerned. And I would escort her, with pleasure, to (the door of) *any* place of worship she liked to attend! But I would not go *in* (in the above 4 cases) unless it were the first: I should not object to attending a Roman Catholic service. I have done so, when abroad.

There is no *extreme* Ritualistic church in Eastbourne: but she shall go to the most advanced that can be found – or to the Roman Catholic Chapel, if you prefer it. I fancy many Ritualists regard the differences, in the services, as quite unimportant. I hope all this will be reassuring to you, and that you will forgive my having disobeyed you so far as to enter on the subject.

I would advise your *not* giving Phoebe any present for some time to come. I am giving her a handsome doll, and, as she belongs to poor people, I think more presents, just now, would not be good for her.

Always very sincerely yours,

C. L. Dodgson

To Lord Salisbury

Christ Church, Oxford

July 7, 1885

Dear Lord Salisbury,

I venture to utilise the fact that you have honoured me with your personal friendship, to call your attention, even at a moment when you must be overwhelmed with the gravest matters, to a matter that seems of great national importance, and to need *immediate* attention, if any. I would ask you to look at the *Pall Mall* of last night, and see if it seems to you that the publication, in a daily paper sure to be seen by thousands of boys and young men, of the most loathsome details of prostitution, is or is not conducive to public morality. If not, *the sooner* legal steps are taken, *the better*. Possibly some Society will try to set the machinery of the law to work, *from below*: but I believe much in the leverage gained by working *from above*; and that *you* could effect more in an hour than a Society could in a week. The *Pall Mall* announces it as "to be continued." Believe me always

Sincerely yours,

C. L. Dodgson

To Alice (Liddell) Hargreaves

Christ Church, Oxford

July 15, 1885

Dear Mrs. Hargreaves,

After a good deal of casting about among various photographers and photo-zincographers, I seem at last to have found out *the* man who will reproduce

Alice's Adventures Under Ground in really first-rate style. He has brought his things to Oxford, and I am having all the photographs taken in my own studio, so that no one touches the MS book except myself. By this method I hope to be able to return it to you in as good a condition as when you so kindly lent it me – or even better, if you will allow me to have it rebound before returning it. May I?

Whether the publication will be a source of gain, or not, it is impossible to say: but if it is, I hardly like the idea of taking the whole profits, considering that the book is now *your* property, and I was thinking of proposing to send half of them to *you*. But a better idea has now occurred to me, which I now submit for your approval: it is to hand over the profits to Hospitals, and Homes, *for Sick Children.*

The following is the announcement which I propose to make (if you approve) at the beginning of the book, and also at the end of all advertisements of it:

"The profits, if any, of this book will be devoted to Hospitals, and Homes, *for Sick Children*: and the accounts, up to June 30 in each year, will be published in the *St. James's Gazette* on the second Tuesday in the following December."

I hope to be able to return the book to you (or to send it to the binder, as you prefer) in about a week. Believe me

Very sincerely yours,
C. L. Dodgson

To E. Gertrude Thomson

Christ Church, Oxford
July 16, 1885

Dear Miss Thomson,

I haven't yet said a word to Mr. Furniss about the "serious poems." First, it would be quite premature, as we shall probably be 2 years over our present job: secondly, because I still cherish the hope of your finding yourself well enough to undertake them. Half of them, at least, ought to be landscapes, and *these* I believe you would do altogether better than he would: and even the figure-ones – the more I look at *Fairies*, the more I am inclined to think you would do *them* beautifully, if only you would study a few *different* faces from real life, so as to avoid the family-likeness, which seems so entirely inevitable, when an artist draws out of his own head.

Don't you think you could draw me just a few landscapes, which I would get reduced to the *Alice* size, and cut on wood, and I would use them, even if Mr. Furniss did the other pictures?

If you think favorably of this, and do not possess *Phantasmagoria*, I will lend it you (or rather a fragment of it, containing the serious poems), and you could try a sketch now and then, when you feel in the vein. It would give you some out-of-door work – ever so much healthier than indoors. You might draw as *large* as you like: the only thing to observe would be the *proportionate* height and width. We might try 3 kinds:

$3\frac{1}{2}$ $3\frac{1}{2}$ $3\frac{1}{2}$

$5\frac{1}{4}$ *full page* $2\frac{3}{4}$ *half page*   *vign.* $2\frac{1}{4}$

The first would want the proportion of 2 wide to 3 high: the second 14 to 11: the third 14 to 9. You might draw the third oval, and draw up to the limit: the photographer would vignette it off, by printing it through a "vignette-glass." This kind would make a lovely tail-piece for a poem. If you don't think the proportions of No. 2 and No. 3 pretty, you can alter them: but for a *full-page* picture we have no choice.

My original plan for this Long Vacation, was to go to Eastbourne as soon after July 1 as my rooms (I always go to the same) should be vacant. This, however, did not happen till July 9th, so I took them from that day, and have been paying for the empty rooms for a week now, not being able to go myself, or to find a couple of lady-friends (or even a single one) to put in as my guests. What keeps me here is a grand piece of photo-zincography which is being done (at least the photography-part) in my studio, by a man who has come, with assistant and a mass of boxes of chemicals, etc., all the way from Essex. It has taken some time and trouble to find a really good man for this: and I was resolved to have the thing done in first-rate style, or not at all. But you will be wondering, all this while, what this important work can be! The germ of *Alice's Adventures in Wonderland* was an extempore story, told in a boat to the 3 children of Dean Liddell: it was afterwards, at the request of Miss Alice Liddell, written out for her, in MS print, with pen-and-ink pictures (*such* pictures!) of my own devising: without the least idea, at the time, that it would ever be published. But friends urged me to print it, so it was re-written, and enlarged, and published. Now that we have sold some 70,000 copies, it occurred to me that there must be a good many people, to whom a facsimile of the MS book would be interesting: and that is my present task. There are 92 pages, and, though we do them 2 at a time, it is a tedious business: and I have to stay in all day for it, as I allow no hands but mine to touch the MS book. Workmen's hands would soon spoil it, and it is not my property now, so I feel a terrible responsibility in having it lent me by the owner, who (I am happy to believe) sets a certain value on it as something unique. Luckily (as it will avoid confusion) the name is different from the published book, and is *Alice's Adventures Under Ground*. In another month, or two, I hope to have the pleasure of sending to you (and also to two or three other friends!) the facsimile.

The other day I had quite a new form of artistic treat. You remember those 2 little Henderson girls, whom I have so often photographed naked? (I think you have photographs of both.) It is 3 or 4 years now since I have photographed – I have been too busy: but I borrowed their little sister (aged 5½) to *draw* as a nude model. (There was never time, in photographic days, to try *drawings*.) The 2 elder ones brought her, and I gave an hour to making 4 sketches, and a second hour (after dressing her up again) to showing the trio my albums, musical-boxes, etc. She *is* such a sweet little figure! If only you, or some other person who *can* draw, had been here! *Then* there would have been some result worth showing. I could have had her here again and again, but did not like to tax the patience of so young a sitter any more. Next year, they say she may come again: and then I shall venture on a rather longer sitting. Even this time she sat nearly 15 minutes, I think, for one of the drawings. The results were, I think, about 10 times as good as I ever draw out of my own head: but what good is it to multiply zero by 10? The mathematical result is zero!

And I have a further treat in prospect. A Mr. Paget, a London artist, kindly says that, whenever I can come to his studio and he happens to have a nude model sitting, I may draw her too (of course the model's consent must first be asked). I *hope* it will be a child, if ever I do go: but I would try an adult rather than lose the chance of such splendid practice, with an artist sitting by who could correct my mistakes for me. So no more at present from

Yours very sincerely,
C. L. Dodgson

To Edith Rix

[7 Lushington Road, Eastbourne]
[July 29?, 1885]

My dear Child,

It seems quite within the bounds of possibility, if we go on long in this style, that our correspondence may at last assume a really friendly tone. I don't of course say it will actually do so – that would be too bold a prophecy – but only that it may tend to shape itself in that direction.

Your remark, that slippers for elephants *could* be made, only they would not be slippers, but boots, convinces me that there is a branch of your family in *Ireland*. Who are (oh dear, oh dear, I am going distracted! There's a lady in the opposite house who simply sings *all* day. All her songs are wails, and their tunes, such as they have, are much the same. She has one strong note in her voice, and she knows it! I *think* it's "A natural," but I haven't much ear. And when she gets to that note, she howls!) they? The O'Rixes, I suppose?

About your uninteresting neighbours, I sympathise with you much; but oh, I wish I had you here, that I might teach you *not* to say "It is difficult to visit one's district regularly, like every one else does!"

And now I come to the most interesting part of your letter – May you treat me as a perfect friend, and write anything you like to me, and ask my advice? Why, *of course* you may, my child! What else am I good for? But oh, my dear child-friend, you cannot guess how such words sound to *me*! That any one should look up to *me*, or think of asking *my* advice – well, it makes one feel humble, I think, rather than proud – humble to remember, while others think so well of me, what I really *am*, in myself. "Thou, that teachest another, teachest thou not thyself?" Well, I won't talk about myself, it is not a healthy topic. Perhaps it may be true of *any* two people, that, if one could see the other through and through, love would perish. I don't know. Anyhow, I like to *have* the love of my child-friends, though I know I don't deserve it. Please write as freely as *ever* you like.

I went up to town and fetched Phoebe down here on Friday in last week; and we spent *most* of Saturday upon the beach – Phoebe wading and digging, and "as happy as a bird upon the wing" (to quote the song she sang when first I saw her). Tuesday evening brought a telegram to say she was wanted at the theatre next morning. So, instead of going to bed, Phoebe packed her things, and we left by the last train, reaching her home by a quarter to 1 a.m. However, even four days of sea-air, and a new kind of happiness, did her good, I think. I am rather lonely now she is gone. She is a very sweet child, and a thoughtful child, too. It was very touching to see (we had a little Bible-reading every day: I tried to remember that my little friend had a soul to be cared for, as well as a body) the far-away look in her eyes, when we talked of God and of heaven – as if her angel, who beholds His face continually, were whispering to her.

Of course, there isn't *much* companionship possible, after all, between an old man's mind and a little child's, but what there is is sweet – and wholesome, I think. . . .

To Isabel Standen

7 Lushington Road, Eastbourne
August 4, 1885

My dear Isabel,

I excuse the egoism! It is a *great* effort, of course, but I can *just* manage it. What is there, I wonder, that I would *not* excuse in you? I always feel specially grateful to friends who, like you, have given me a child-friendship and a woman-friendship too. About 9 out of 10, I think, of my child-friendships get shipwrecked at the critical point "where the stream and river meet" (I must pause to shut the window: there is a woman singing in the road. Her voice may have had some sweetness in it once: but open-air work has made it harsh. It gives me no pleasure. I wish you were here to sing instead! But this is a digression.) and the child-friends, once so affectionate, become uninteresting acquaintances, whom I have no wish to set eyes on again.

I can quite understand, and *much* sympathise with, what you say of your feeling lonely, and not what you can honestly call "happy." Now I am going to give you a bit of philosophy about that. My own experience is, that *every* new form of life we try is, just at first, irksome rather than pleasant. My first day or two at the sea is a little depressing; I miss the Christ Church interests, and haven't taken up the threads of interest here. And, just in the same way, my first day or two, when I get back to Christ Church, I miss the sea-side pleasures, and feel with unusual clearness the bothers of business-routine. In all such cases, the true philosophy, I believe, is "*wait* a bit." Our mental nerves seem to be so adjusted that we feel *first*, and most keenly, the *dis*comforts of any new form of life: but, after a bit, we get used to them, and cease to notice them; and *then* we have time to realise the enjoyable features, which at first we were too much worried to be conscious of.

Suppose you hurt your arm, and had to wear it in a sling for a month. For the first 2 or 3 days, the discomfort of the bandage – the pressure of the sling on the neck and shoulder – the being unable to use the arm – would be a constant worry. You would feel as if all comfort in life were gone. After a couple of days you would be used to the new sensations: after a week you perhaps wouldn't notice them at all: and life would seem just as comfortable as ever.

So my advice is, don't think about loneliness, or happiness, or unhappiness, for a week or two. Then "take stock" again, and compare your feelings with what they were 2 weeks previously. If they have changed, even a little, for the better, you are on the right track: if not, we may begin to suspect the life does not suit you. But what I want *specially* to urge is that there's no use in comparing one's feelings between one day and the next: you must allow a reasonable interval, for the *direction* of change to show itself.

Sit on the beach, and watch the waves for a few seconds: you will say "the tide is coming in": watch half a dozen successive waves, and you may say "the last is the lowest: it is going out": wait a quarter of an hour, and compare its *average* place with what it was at first, and you will say "no, it is coming in, after all."

With love, I am

Always affectionately yours,
C. L. Dodgson

To Charlotte Rix

7 Lushington Road, Eastbourne
September 2, 1885

My dear Lottie,

I know you are thinking all manner of bad things about me – first, because I have got your sister down here, and am taking her to various Larks (which, alliteratively, belong to *you*) – secondly, because I have not sent you a Letter (to which, alliteratively, you are entitled) for many days, if not weeks. But really I am not so bad as you think – or at any rate there are many worse. You know I often send you Love: and I was just thinking how Lucky you are to be so initialled: so that everybody must send Love. If, like me, you had "D" for an initial, things would be Different, and I should send you "Dislike" as soon as Look at you! Your destiny, of course, has other things in store: e.g. to be Long, and Lank, and in disposition Lugubrious.

However Love outweighs all that. Now for *Edith*, I need hardly say, I can only feel Esteem: and Early walks and Education are the only articles I can supply her with: and, in both those respects she is catching it – as she will tell you when you meet. But that can't be helped: one of the deepest motives (as you are aware) in the human breast (so deep that many have failed to detect it) is Alliteration.

That's about all I have to tell you at present, except that I am Enjoying Edith a good deal – or rather, I *should* be doing so, if she were not Enjoying herself so much: but, as you know (for you are *nothing* if not Logical), it is no more possible for two persons to Enjoy the same individual than to Eat the same cherry.

Always affectionately yours,
C. L. Dodgson

To Mary Mileham

7 Lushington Road, Eastbourne
September 6, 1885

Dearest May,

Thank you very much indeed for the peaches. They were *delicious*. Eating one was *almost* as nice as kissing you: of course not *quite*: I think, if I had to give the *exact* measurement, I should say "three-quarters as nice." We *are* having such a lovely time here: and the sands are beautiful. I only wish I could some day come across *you*, washing your pocket-handkerchief in a pool among the rocks! But I wander on the beach, and look for you, in vain: and then I say, "Where is May?" And the stupid boatmen reply, "It isn't May, sir! It's *September*!" But it doesn't comfort me.

Always your loving,
C.L.D.

To his cousin and godson W. M. Wilcox

7 Lushington Road, Eastbourne
September 10, 1885

My dear William,

I find I cannot satisfactorily advise you on the subject of your letter without more information. First, I don't know what the "conditions" are by which you would be bound if you accepted the grant. Secondly, I am puzzled by your phrase "my university career." I didn't know you were going to be a member of a University, but thought it was some Theological College you were trying for.

Meanwhile, I will tell you a few facts about myself, which may be useful to you. When I was about 19, the Studentships at Christ Church were in the gift of the Dean and Chapter – each Canon having a turn: and Dr. Pusey, having a turn, sent for me, and told me he would like to nominate me, but had made a rule to nominate *only* those who were going to take Holy Orders. I told him that was my intention, and he nominated me. That was a sort of "condition," no doubt: but I am quite sure, if I had told him, when the time came to be ordained, that I had changed my mind, he would not have considered it as in any way a breach of contract.

When I reached the age for taking Deacon's Orders, I found myself established as the Mathematical Lecturer, and with no sort of inclination to give it up and take parochial work: and I had grave doubts whether it would not be my duty *not* to take Orders. I took advice on this point (Bishop Wilberforce was one that I applied to), and came to the conclusion that, so far from educational work (even Mathematics) being unfit occupation for a clergyman, it was distinctly a *good* thing that many of our educators should be men in Holy Orders.

And a further doubt occurred. I could not feel sure that I should ever wish to take *Priest's* Orders. And I asked Dr. Liddon*whether he thought I should be justified in taking Deacon's Orders as a sort of experiment, which would enable me to try how the occupations of a clergyman suited me, and *then* decide whether I would take full Orders. He said "most certainly" – and that a Deacon is in a totally different position from a Priest: and much more free to regard himself as *practically* a layman. So I took Deacon's Orders in that spirit. And now, for several reasons, I have given up all idea of taking full Orders, and regard myself (though occasionally doing small clerical acts, such as helping at the Holy Communion) as practically a layman.

Always your affectionate Cousin
("godfather" is a terminable relationship),
C. L. Dodgson

---

* Henry Parry Liddon was one of Dodgson's close associates and friends at Christ Church. They travelled together to France, Germany, and Russia on the only journey Dodgson made abroad. A brilliant preacher, Liddon went on to be Canon and Chancellor of St. Paul's Cathedral.

To Edith Rix

7 Lushington Road, Eastbourne
September 25, 1885

My dear Edith,

One subject you touch on – "the Resurrection of the Body" – is very interesting to me, and I have given it much thought (I mean long ago). *My* conclusion was to give up the *literal* meaning of the *material* body altogether. *Identity*, in some mysterious way, there evidently is; but there is no resisting the scientific fact that the actual *material* usable for *physical* bodies has been used over and over again – so that each atom would have several owners. The mere solitary fact of the existence of *cannibalism* is to my mind a sufficient *reductio ad absurdum* of the theory that the particular set of atoms I shall happen to own at death (changed every seven years, they say) will be mine in the next life – and all the other insuperable difficulties (such as people born with bodily defects) are swept away at once if we accept St. Paul's "spiritual body," and his simile of the grain of corn. I have read very little of *Sartor Resartus*, and don't know the passage you quote: but I accept the idea of the material body being the "dress" of the spiritual – a dress needed for material life. ...

To Charlotte Rix

Christ Church, Oxford
October 30, 1885

My dear Lottie,

You are evidently getting confused between the two meanings of "Letters." The only "letters," to which *you* have a right, are of course merely "L-O-T-T-I-E." But as to *Epistles* – quite another meaning – of course, on all alliterative principles, it is *Edith* who should have them. And a *third* meaning seems to have come over you, and to be too much for your little mind – you seem to think *I* am a "man of Letters": quite a mistake.

I hope you're not so *blasée* as to autographs, as not to care to have the enclosed – which was specially written *for you*. I don't know if you knew I had asked Miss Terry to write her name, for you and Edith: it was Edith's idea, I think: and I told her your names, etc., and knowing you had seen her as "Olivia" is the reason, no doubt, why she had written that quotation for you. She has written one for Edith, with a quotation from Goldsmith – which I am forwarding to her.

I shall be writing soon, to thank Miss Terry for her kindness: but I'll wait a bit, on the chance that you might have some message to send.

I was afraid she had forgotten the matter, and wrote a gentle reminder. Shall I copy you a bit of her answer? It will give you a notion of the sort of letter she writes. I think her letters are *more like speaking* than any I get.

"Oh dear, oh dear! I'm really sorry – and I have no particular excuse to make, except that I'm busy every moment of my time, that *I've an idiotic memory*, and that I'm '*that*' ill – oh! but it *does* go to my heart when I neglect the *little* desires of *little* children, so now I send the *in*valuable autograph."

What stopped her acting was "an acute attack of cold and neuralgia": so she tells me.

You didn't expect to get an answer from me by return of post – now did you? "It is always the unexpected that happens" (Voltaire, or somebody).

With Lotties of

Yours always affectionately,
C. L. Dodgson

I beg to say I *didn't* tell Miss Terry that you were "little children"! That's entirely her own idea! Please let Edith see this letter. I've no time to write it all to her as well.

To an invalid

[Christ Church, Oxford]
November 1885

. . . . About answered and unanswered prayer: we certainly are not authorised to ask that *miracles* should be worked for us. The Apostles were, but it is not a general permission – also (but this of course I need not say), we should only ask *anything* of our own devising, *hypothetically*, i.e. *if* it be good (which we cannot know). I have had prayers answered – most strangely so sometimes – but I think our heavenly Father's loving-kindness has been even more evident in what He has *refused* me. . . .

To Mary E. Manners

[c/o Macmillan & Co.]
29 Bedford Street, Covent Garden, London
December 5, 1885

Dear Madam,

Permit me to offer you my sincere thanks for the very sweet verses you have written about my dream-child (named after a real Alice, but none the less a dream-child) and her Wonderland. That children love the book is a very precious thought to me, and next to their love I value the sympathy of those who come with a child's heart to what I have tried to write about a child's thoughts. Next to what conversing with an angel *might* be – for it is hard to imagine it, comes, I think, the privilege of having a *real* child's thoughts uttered to one. I have known some few *real* children (you have, too, I am sure), and their friendship is a blessing and a help in life.

It will please me much to be allowed to send you (if you will kindly tell me to what address it should go) a copy of a little book I hope to get out this winter – a facsimile of the original MS book (written for a child, with no thoughts of publication) which afterwards became *Alice in Wonderland*.

Meanwhile, wishing you a full share of happiness in the coming season with its "good tidings of great joy," I am

Sincerely yours,
Lewis Carroll

To Lord Salisbury

Christ Church, Oxford
December 12, 1885

Dear Lord Salisbury,

I have been waiting for the Election-storm to blow over, before venturing to trouble you with a matter, which however I think important enough to ask your attention to now. When you have read this letter, you will, I hope, think that I had sufficient grounds for so doing.

The Island of Tristan da Cunha has about 100 inhabitants, and my brother, the Rev. Edwin H. Dodgson, has been for about 4 years "priest in charge," under the Bishop of St. Helena. The people were thriving enough, so long as whalers came that way, who were good customers for fresh meat and vegetables. But the whales have deserted those seas, and no ship comes near them, and, to crown all, the island is now swarming with rats, who eat all the crops. The people are on the verge of starvation, and it is a matter of urgency that some steps should be taken *at once*, to remove them to the Cape, or Australia, or somewhere they can live. My brother is now in England, in hopes of getting something done, and (to come to the point) what I have to ask is that you will be so very kind as to let him come to you and tell you about it. Then you will be able to say what should be done, and would be all-powerful in *getting* it done.

I have myself spoken to many officials on the subject, as for instance Captain Tryon at the Admiralty, and Secretary at the Colonial, Sir Hercules Robinson, also the Cape Premier, also the Government Agent for New Zealand, etc., etc., but I believe one talk with you *yourself* would be of more service than anything *I* have been able to do.

My brother would be able to call on you any day after the 21st.

Always sincerely yours,
C. L. Dodgson

To *Janet Terry Lewis**

Christ Church, Oxford
December 13, 1885

My dear Janet,

It's all very well to declare that your unkindness to Katie is *not* caused by jealousy, but then comes the question, what *else* can cause it? For instance, now, that day that you dragged her through Kensington Gardens, with a dog-collar round her neck, and a rope tied to it, what *could* it have been but jealousy to make you treat her so? And then as to your taking away her jam at tea, of course you *may* be right in saying that "she takes more than is good for her," but still, you know, it *does* look unkind to take it *all*.

But seriously, my dear Janet (for I'm afraid I talk awful nonsense to you, and of course I know quite well that you love Katie very much), would either you, or Lucy, like to have the *Alice in Wonderland Birthday Book*? (Every day has a quotation from *Alice*, and a place where you can get your friends to write their names.) If either of you would like it, I would give the other one the facsimile, that will be out soon, of the book I told you of. But if neither of you would care for it, tell me so. As to Mabel, though you don't

---

* Janet and Mabel were Kate Terry Lewis's second and third daughters, younger sisters of Katie.

mention it, I gave *her Fairies*. But to you and Lucy I fear I've never given *anything* – except those quite useless articles called "kisses."

With much love to *three* (not more) of your sisters, I am

Always affectionately yours,
C. L. Dodgson

To Edith Rix

The Chestnuts, Guildford
January 15, 1886

My dear Edith,

I have been meaning for some time to write to you about agnosticism, and other matters in your letter which I have left unnoticed. And yet I do not know, much as what you say interests me, and much as I should like to be of use to any wandering seeker after truth, that I am at all likely to say anything that will be new to you and of any practical use.

The Moral Science student you describe must be a beautiful character, and if, as you say, she lives a noble life, then, even though she does not, as yet, see any God, for whose sake she can do things, I don't think you need be unhappy about her. "When thou wast under the fig tree, I saw thee," is often supposed to mean that Nathanael had been *praying*, praying no doubt ignorantly and imperfectly, but yet using the light he had: and it seems to have been accepted as faith in the Messiah. More and more it seems to me (I hope you won't be *very* much shocked at me as an ultra "Broad" Churchman) that what a person *is* is of more importance in God's sight than merely what propositions he affirms or denies. *You*, at any rate, can do more good among those new friends of yours by showing them what a Christian *is*, than by telling them what a Christian *believes*....

I have a deep dread of argument on religious topics: it has many risks, and little chance of doing good. You and I will never *argue*, I hope, on any controverted religious question: though I do hope we may see the day when we may freely *speak* of such things, even where we happen to hold different views. But even then I should have no inclination, if we did differ, to conclude that my view was the right one, and to try to convert you to it....

Now I come to your letter dated December 22nd, and must scold you for saying that my solution of the problem was "quite different *to* all common ways of doing it": if *you* think that's good English, well and good; but *I* must beg to differ to you, and to hope you will *never* write me a sentence similar from this again. However, "worse remains behind"; and if you deliberately intend in future, when writing to me about one of England's greatest poets, to call him "Shelly," then all I can say is, that you and I will have to quarrel! Be warned in time.

C. L. Dodgson

To Edith Rix

Christ Church, Oxford
February 14, 1886

My dear Edith,

...I think I've already noticed, in a way, most of the rest of that letter – except what you say about learning more things "after we are dead." *I* certainly like to think that may be so. But I have heard the other view strongly urged, a good deal based on "then shall we know even as we are known." But I can't believe that that means we shall have *all* knowledge given us in a moment – nor can I fancy it would make me any happier: it is the *learning* that is the chief joy, here, at any rate....

I find another remark anent "pupils" – a bold speculation that my 1,000 pupils may really "go on" in the future life, till they *have* really outstripped Euclid. And, please, what is *Euclid* to be doing all that time?...

One of the most dreadful things you have ever told me is your students' theory of going and speaking to any one they are interested in, without any introductions. This, joined with what you say of some of them being interested in *Alice*, suggests the horrid idea of their some day walking into this room and beginning a conversation. It is enough to make one shiver, even to think of it!

Never mind if people do say "Good gracious!" when you help old women: it *is* being, in some degree, both "good" *and* "gracious," one may hope. So the remark wasn't so inappropriate.

I fear I agree with your friend in not liking all sermons. Some of them, one has to confess, are rubbish: but then I release my attention from the preacher, and go ahead in any line of thought he may have started: and his after-eloquence acts as a kind of accompaniment – like music while one is reading poetry, which often, to me, adds to the effect.

C. L. Dodgson

To Charlotte Rix

Christ Church, Oxford
March 21, 1886

My dear Lottie,

The problem you put before me is one that can only be solved by the strictest application of the rules of Logic.

In the first place it is in the highest degree improbable that two *different* people should have sent pens, to Edie and to you, almost exactly at the same time. We may fairly assume that they came from one and the *same* person: and also that that person was a *friend*, as it is a kind of thing *enemies* are never known to do.

The next question is, was it a lady or a gentleman? It seems clear, from your having heard nothing about the unknown person, that it could not have been a *lady*. No lady can keep a secret: and, if a lady had sent you the pens, she would certainly have either written, several years beforehand, to tell you they were coming, or advertised them in the "Agony-column" of *The Times*. I conclude, then, that it was a *gentleman*.

Was he, then, a mere *acquaintance*, or one that knew you fairly well? One who was merely a chance *acquaintance* could not have guessed that such presents would be acceptable, as he would not have known whether you could read or write. I gather that he had known you some time.

"Old, or young?" is the next question. Now the Stylographic Pen Company demand that the money should be sent *with* the order. No *young* gentleman ever *pre*pays a bill: if he pays it a century *afterwards*, he thinks he has done great things. We may make sure that it was an *elderly gentleman, on terms of some intimacy with both of you.*

Lastly, is there any clue by which to judge of his *character*? The only *act* we know of being an act of *giving*, it is only in *that* direction we can expect to test it. Is he, then, of a *generous*, or of a *niggardly*, disposition? The point is a subtle one, but I have traced it out. He is a *niggardly* man: for he has evidently said to himself, "I *must* give these girls *something*. At the same time, I hate expense. How can I do it most cheaply? I will give each of them a *penny* present!"

"But, that being so," you will say, "why should he give us presents *at all*?" *There* I fear, my dear Lottie, that I must abandon the problem. It belongs to an abstruse branch of the subject, called "*Ladies' Logic*," with which I am unacquainted; and can only add that I am

Always affectionately yours,
C. L. Dodgson

To Henry Savile Clarke*

7 Lushington Road, Eastbourne
August 30, 1886

Dear Sir,

There is one, and only one, condition which I should regard as absolutely *essential* before allowing my name to appear as "sanctioning" any dramatic version of *Alice in Wonderland* or *Through the Looking-Glass*. There are one or two *wishes* on the subject, which I will name for your consideration: but the only essential condition is that I should have your written guarantee that, neither in the libretto nor in any of the stage business, shall any coarseness, or anything suggestive of coarseness, be admitted.

Most of the London Pantomimes are entirely spoiled, for children and indeed for any person whose tastes are not debased, by the indecencies introduced into the harlequinade. Setting the question of right and wrong on one side, it is still inexplicable to me how managers can think it to be for their interests to pander to the tastes of dirty-minded youths and men in the Gallery, with the certainty of offending many in the Stalls, etc. It is to the lasting credit of Mr. Gilbert, and I think that the nation ought to feel grateful to him for it, that he has given us so many pure and *absolutely* innocent pieces, like *The Mikado*, to which one can safely take ladies and children.

I have two *wishes* as to what you propose.

One is, that it should not have a harlequinade tacked on to it. It is not that I have any objection to a *decent* harlequinade: but the two things seem to me to be entirely incongruous. This piece ought to be an Operetta (like *The Mikado*), and not a Pantomime.

The other is, that only *one* of the two stories should be dramatised. I do not believe *any* genuine child enjoys mixtures. Their memory of stories (as you will know well if you have ever tried telling a story *twice* to the same child) is accurate down to the smallest detail, and any deviation from what they remember is unwelcome. In the London Pantomimes they constantly make the mistake of mixing *two* Nursery Tales together. I do not believe there is *one* child of their audience who would not be ready to say "Give us the one, or the other, but not *both* in one entertainment."

Of course, if you say "There is not enough material, in either book alone, for an Operetta," I have no more to say: I am not learned in dramatic composition. Still I believe that the *dialogues* alone, in either book, would take at

---

* A minor playwright of the time. He made dramatic adaptations of *Rip Van Winkle* and Thackeray's *The Rose and the Ring*.

least an hour to deliver, and I hope you will not think me very vain if I add that I believe any children, who know the books, would prefer to hear those dialogues reproduced *verbatim* to any *substituted* matter, however much better it might be as dramatic dialogue.

One thing more occurs to me to request. Several of the songs are parodies of old Nursery songs, that have their own tunes, as old as the songs probably. I would much prefer, if you introduce any of these, that the *old* air should be used. The whole of the poetry, in both books, has been already published, with music, many times: people are constantly applying for leave to do this: and they have simply spoiled such pieces as "Will you walk a little faster" by writing new airs. It would take a very good composer to write anything better than the sweet old air of "Will you walk into my parlour, said the Spider to the Fly."

I have already inflicted too long a letter upon you, but as I see you are *en rapport* with the Savoy Theatre, I venture to ask if you would procure for me the address (it is "Southsea," I believe, but I want the street and number) of Mr. Warwick Gray, formerly of the Savoy. He was here lately, with his Children's Opera Company, in which I took some interest, and he was to have left me his address, but I suppose forgot to do so.

My address, as writer of *Alice*, is

> Lewis Carroll, Esq.,
> c/o Messrs. Macmillan & Co.,
> 29 Bedford Street,
> Covent Garden,
> London.

My (permanent) private address is

> Rev. C. L. Dodgson,
> Christ Church,
> Oxford,

but I expect to be at Eastbourne till about October 10.

May I ask you *not* to give any publicity to my real name? *Personal* publicity I dislike greatly, and avoid it as much as possible. Believe me

> Truly yours,
> C. L. Dodgson

P.S. Kindly tell me what plays, etc., you are author of. I am very ignorant of names of dramatic authors.

To Alice (Liddell) Hargreaves

Christ Church, Oxford
November 11, 1886

My dear Mrs. Hargreaves,

Many thanks for your permission to insert "Hospitals" in the Preface to your book – I have had almost as many Adventures, in getting that unfortunate facsimile finished, *Above* Ground, as your namesake had *Under* it!

First, the zincographer in London, recommended to me for photographing the book, page by page, and preparing the zinc-blocks, declined to undertake it unless I would entrust the book to *him* – which I entirely refused to do. I felt that it was only due to you, in return for your great kindness in lending so unique a book, to be scrupulous in not letting it be even *touched* by the workmen's hands. In vain I offered to come and reside in London with the book, and to attend daily in the studio, to place it in position to be photographed, and turn over the pages as required: he said that could not be done because "other authors' works were being photographed there, which must on no account be seen by the public." I undertook not to look at *anything* but my own book: but it was no use: we could not come to terms.

Then Messrs. Macmillan recommended a certain Mr. Noad, an excellent photographer, but in so small a way of business that I should have to *prepay* him, bit by bit, for the zinc-blocks: and *he* was willing to come to Oxford, and do it here. So it was all done in my studio, I remaining in waiting all the time, to turn over the pages.

But I daresay I have told you so much of the story already?

Mr. Noad did a first-rate set of negatives, and took them away with him to get the zinc-blocks made. These he delivered pretty regularly at first, and there seemed to be every prospect of getting the book out by Christmas 1885.

On October 18, 1885, I sent your book to Mrs. Liddell, who had told me your sisters were going to visit you and would take it with them. I trust it reached you safely?

Soon after this – I having prepaid for the whole of the zinc-blocks – the supply suddenly ceased, while 22 pages were still due, and Mr. Noad disappeared!

My belief is that he was in hiding from his creditors. We sought him in vain. So things went on for months. At one time I thought of employing a detective to find him, but was assured that "all detectives are scoundrels." The alternative seemed to be to ask you to lend the book again, and get the missing pages re-photographed. But I was *most* unwilling to rob you of it again, and also afraid of the risk of loss of the book, if sent by post – for even "registered post" does not seem *absolutely* safe.

In April he called at Macmillan's and left *8* blocks, and again vanished into obscurity.

This left us with 14 pages (dotted up and down the book) still missing. I waited awhile longer, and then put the thing into the hands of a Solicitor, who soon found the man, but could get nothing but promises from him. "You will never get the blocks," said the Solicitor, "unless you frighten him by a summons before a Magistrate." To this at last I unwillingly consented; the summons had to be taken out at Stratford-le-Bow (that is where this aggravating man is living), and this entailed 2 journeys from Eastbourne – one to get the summons (my *personal* presence being necessary), and the other to attend in Court with the Solicitor on the day fixed for hearing the case. The defendant didn't appear; so the Magistrate said he would take the case in his absence. Then I had the new and exciting experience of being put into the witness-box, and sworn, and cross-examined by a rather savage Magistrate's clerk, who seemed to think that, if he only bullied me enough, he would soon catch me out in a falsehood! I had to give the Magistrate a little lecture on photo-zincography, and the poor man declared the case was so complicated he must adjourn it for another week. But this time, in order to secure the presence of our slippery defendant, he issued a warrant for his apprehension, and the constable had orders to take him into custody and lodge him in prison, the night before the day when the case was to come on. The news of *this* effectually frightened him, and he delivered up the 14 negatives (he hadn't done the blocks) before the fatal day arrived. I was rejoiced to get them, even though it entailed the paying a 2nd time for getting the 14 blocks done, and withdrew the action.

The 14 blocks were quickly done and put into the printer's hands; and all is going on smoothly at last: and I quite hope to have the book completed, and to be able to send *you* a very special copy (bound in white vellum, unless you would prefer some other style of binding) by the end of the month. Believe me always

Sincerely yours,
C. L. Dodgson

To Henry Savile Clarke

The Chestnuts, Guildford
December 31, 1886

Dear Mr. Savile Clarke,

I got a great deal of amusement and pleasure yesterday afternoon in seeing *Alice in Wonderland*.* I think Phoebe *very good indeed*: and little Dorothy is a genius! I should like to have a long talk with you over the whole thing, and possibly might make a useful suggestion or two: but I hope you would feel *perfectly* free (and it won't wound my vanity a bit) to reject every suggestion I may make.

I could come over any day next week when you have (say) a couple of hours of leisure, morning or afternoon, as suits you best.

I am glad Mrs. Savile Clarke liked the book.

Very truly yours,
C. L. Dodgson

To Mrs. T. Dyer-Edwardes

Christ Church, Oxford
February 12, 1887

Dear Mrs. Dyer-Edwardes,

Will you kindly tell me if there is any one of my books (*Alice's Adventures in Wonderland, Through the Looking-Glass, Rhyme? and Reason?, Alice's Adventures Under Ground*) that Noel does not, and would like to, possess? Or perhaps she might like the first in *French*?

I do *not* (as is popularly supposed of me) take a fancy to *all* children, and instantly: I fear I take *dis*likes to *some*): but I *did* take a fancy to your little daughter – and I hope we may grow to be friends. Believe me always

Yours very truly,
C. L. Dodgson

P.S. My (slightly shy and silent) young friend, Ruth Woodhouse, seemed to enjoy her first visit to a London theatre *intensely*. We had a chatty old gentleman next us, who told us, "The author of *Alice* has written a letter

---

* Savile Clarke's adaptation opened at the Prince of Wales Theatre two days before Christmas and was a critical and popular success. Phoebe Carlo played Alice; Dorothy D'Alcourt, the Dormouse.

to that little girl that plays the part, and has given her a book. And she has written to tell him she will do her very best." "Indeed!" I said, in a tone of pleased surprise. "He is an *Oxford* man," he added confidently: and we were both deeply interested to know it.

To Mrs. H. A. Feilden

Christ Church, Oxford
February 12, 1887

Dear Mrs. Feilden,

I *must* send a line in return, to set at rest your kind anxiety about my health. I have never had *any* serious illness, and when, a couple of years back, I had an attack of ague, the doctor put me through a minute examination, and ended by saying "you are a *thoroughly* healthy man: and, if you want to insure your life, I'll give you a first-class certificate." Nor am I failing in strength: I can stand 10 hours at my desk, or take a 25-mile walk. So it is *quite* possible God may mean me to work for another 20 or 30 years. I *hope* I should be ready to go, if He called me now, but I'm not the *least* anxious to be called yet. I've got *quantities* of work I should like to get finished first. My objection to parties (and most visits) is the *utter* waste of time and brain in talking perfectly useless small-talk – far more at a time than is the least needed for *rest* of brain. I come back, from dinner parties, weary and depressed, feeling that I have *lost* 3 or 4 hours, and have said nothing worth saying, and heard nothing worth hearing. So, now that I have turned 55, I think I may fairly give them up. But I don't mean to forget such friends as you and your lovable daughter. Doesn't *that* show what an old man I am, when I can say to a mother "I love your daughter," and *not* get the reply "what are your intentions, and what is your income?" And I will even be bold enough to add that I *regret* the break (of some years) in my meetings with Helen, which caused us to change from kissing to hand-shaking! Others of my child-friends have kept up the old habit continuously, though married years ago!*

Always sincerely yours,
C. L. Dodgson

---

*Helen Feilden was twenty-eight at this writing and as yet unmarried.

To Charlotte Rix

Christ Church, Oxford
April 1, 1887

So your mother has told you of my offer to take you to call upon Miss Ellen Terry? Well, I think it was very rash to do so, because, you see, the opportunity may never occur, and then you will let disappointment, like a worm i' the bud, prey on your damask cheek – which will become even more damasky than the photographer has made it?

And so you don't agree with my view as to said photographer? Well, *that's* not matter for regret, anyhow: it would be an awfully monotonous world if we all had the same opinions! And you have probably the majority of modern Society on your side: they are all enamoured of the animated milk-jugs that the photographers make of them: and delight in their new faces – cold, hard, shiny, beautifully polished, and not in the least the faces one would care to kiss! But I've a much more real cause than *that*, for not liking your photograph: it does not do you justice at all – nor make you the least like the young lady who beamed so kindly on the shy old bachelor, frightened at finding himself within the walls of a girls' school. Were such a young lady offered to *me*, as companion for a walk, I would say, "thank you, no: she had evidently been just 'put out,' and I'd rather wait till she is put in again." Or, I suppose I ought to say, "till the luxation has been reduced" – isn't that the correct phrase? You do all that kind of thing, don't you?

And now I think, my dear Lottie, I have babbled enough for one while. (But you see that I'm in my second childhood, and will excuse it, I'm sure) so, with love and a kiss for Edith, and a similar consignment for yourself, I am

Your loving friend,
C. L. Dodgson

To his brother Wilfred

Christ Church, Oxford
April 30, 1887

Dear Wilfred,

I want you to notify to me, when the proper times come, which one of your children has reached the age when the possession of a *watch* is desirable.

It is not *my* task to provide so much beef and mutton for little mouths as *you* have to do: hence the giving of watches is more in my line than yours. Surely Willie is old enough now to appreciate, and take care of, a watch? But perhaps some one has forestalled me, and given him one already. Tell me how this is. I would like to earn the character, among your children, of "our *watchful* Uncle!"

Now that I have known scores (almost hundreds) of children, I am perhaps abnormally critical of them: but I must in candour say I *never* met with children of more perfect behaviour, or more sweetly fascinating, than your Nella and Violet. Alice must have some magical way of bringing up her children. Nearly all children *I* have known, with such high animal spirits, are apt to be mischievous and troublesome, teasing one another and making themselves a nuisance generally. Alice has somehow managed to make these children combine the high spirits of children with the good manners of grown-up people. Their presence at the Chestnuts added much to the pleasure of my visit there last week.

Love to Alice, Edith, K.T.Λ.*

Yours affectionately,
C. L. Dodgson

To William Boyd Carpenter

Christ Church, Oxford
May 8, 1887

My dear Lord Bishop,

I feel how great a liberty I am taking, as a total stranger, in addressing your Lordship; but I write, as one of the large University congregation who listened this morning to the Bampton Lecture, to make one single remark – that I feel very sure that the 2 or 3 sentences in it, which were distinctly *amusing* (and of which *one* raised a general laugh) went far to undo, in the minds of many of your hearers, and specially among the *young* men, much of the good effect of the rest of the sermon. Feeling profoundly (as who can fail to do?) what enormous powers have been given to your Lordship for influencing large bodies of men, I feel an equally profound regret that anything should occur likely to lessen their influence for good. I can only *hope*

---

* Καὶ τὰ λειπόμενα ("and the rest, etc."). Dodgson refers, of course, to the other future candidates for watches.

your Lordship will pardon the presumption of such plain speaking, and remain

Your Lordship's most truly,
Charles L. Dodgson

P.S. We have *one* common friend, Mrs. Bickersteth ("Ella" she has always been to me); but I doubt if she would readily forgive me, did she know what a liberty I am taking with her friend.

To Ellen Terry

Christ Church, Oxford
June 9, 1887

Dear Miss Ellen Terry,

I took Ethel out for a walk yesterday, and of course we talked about you: and I write this just to tell you how sorry I was to learn from her that I had given you pain by what I wrote to you about *Faust*. I cannot say more, without needlessly re-opening a painful subject, than that I am very very sorry to have given you pain. You have been much vexed with me, I fear: but do not, dear friend (I would say "dear old friend," only one must not say "old" to a lady) cherish your vexation against me for evermore. Will you not forgive me? And *please* do not say "on what compulsion?" for if *you* play Shylock, who in the world is to play Portia? I am sure it is not for *me* to say "the quality of mercy is not strained," with the sweet words yet ringing in my ears that I heard only last Saturday at the Lyceum. I had with me a grave, silent child-friend of 14, who had never seen anything but a pantomime. She said *very* little about it afterwards, but, as that little was "I never enjoyed anything so much in all my life!" perhaps it is worth repeating.

It has been a great pleasure to me to make friends with a friend of yours, and daughter of an old College friend of mine, Violet Barnes. I went to see her play in *The Butler* the other day. It would be very interesting to know what *you* think of her acting, but perhaps you would rather not criticise a friend.

Believe me always with love, to you, and to Edie when next you see or write to her,

Yours sincerely,
C. L. Dodgson

To Winfrid Burrows

Christ Church, Oxford
January 25, 1888

My dear Burrows,

I want to ask your pardon for any appearance there may have been of harshness or brusqueness in my declining to listen to your anecdote (which probably had little harm in it) about the Ten Commandments. I hate to say such things, and to seem uncourteous: but it is a matter of principle, and I see nothing for it but to bear, when occasion seems to arise, one's testimony for the principle of treating all sacred matters seriously. You may not have noticed the thing so much as I have: but it does seem to me that there is a terrible amount just now, of jesting on sacred things...which *must*, I think, tend to make these things less and less real: so that, in fighting against profane talk, one is practically fighting the battle of faith as against unbelief. If only I were not Curator, I could hold my peace more contentedly, and would gladly do so: but, being thrust into an undesired prominence, I should feel it to be cowardly to be silent, when a word might do good, merely to spare one's own feelings. I don't know if I've put my meaning clearly: but I hope you'll manage to understand it, and to forgive all that seems to need forgiving and that you will believe me to be

Sincerely yours,
C. L. Dodgson

To Mrs. V. Blakemore

Christ Church, Oxford
February 1, 1888

Dear Mrs. Blakemore,

I have at last got my *sisters* to accept the 2 facts (1) that I have *no* unsatisfied wants, (2) that I have *no* room for any extra property; and to send me no more birthday presents. But to get these axioms accepted *elsewhere* seems beyond my power! So I can but say "thank you" for your quaintly devised card-rack.

The awful age (as it looked to me, some 20 or 30 years ago) of 56 seems quite trivial when you get to it. In fact I don't think that, practically, I am a *very* old man as yet: I took a walk of 18 miles the day before yesterday, and came in nearly as fresh as I went out.

My great anxiety is to get my *Book* done, before bodily and mental powers begin to fail. That anxiety gets greater, as life gets shorter: and I am beginning to look forward to another 4 months of hermit-life at Eastbourne, when I may *perhaps* finish it. *Here*, with all manner of petty business constantly interrupting, one can do next to nothing.

I know nothing about the death of the "young man" you mention. Was it a boating-man? I *did* see mentioned the death of a well-known boating-man, but not of anything specially "sad" about it. Death is always sad, I suppose, to us who look forward to it: I expect it will seem very different when we can look *back* upon it.

With love to Edith, I am

Always sincerely yours,
C. L. Dodgson

To the editors of Jabberwock

[c/o Macmillan & Co.]
29 Bedford Street, Covent Garden, London
February 6, 1888

Mr. Lewis Carroll has much pleasure in giving to the editresses of the proposed magazine permission to use the title they wish for. He finds that the Anglo-Saxon word "wocer" or "wocor" signifies "offspring" or "fruit." Taking "jabber" in its ordinary acceptation of "excited and voluble discussion," this would give the meaning of "the result of much excited discussion." Whether this phrase will have any application to the projected periodical, it will be for the future history of American literature to determine. Mr. Carroll wishes all success to the forthcoming magazine.

To Mrs. N. H. Stevens

Christ Church, Oxford
May 30, 1888

Dear Mrs. Stevens,

Thanks for your letter. One reason for your not having seen me is that I do not, as a rule, ever call upon anybody! Another is that I can't walk:

I've been spending my days on the sofa for five or six weeks, with "sub-acute Synovitis" in one knee. Another is that Fate is in opposition to all my attempts to once more enjoy the society of Winnie, whether for a walk, or an expedition to London: even now, I am planning a day in Town, and of course would be only too glad to get her to accompany me, but what's the use proposing it again? I've tried it – it is hard to fix the exact number, something under 40 times – and tried in vain! You know there is no use fighting against – or hoping to change – one's Destiny. Give my love, please, to that most inaccessible, unapproachable, unborrowable, and uneverything-else young lady, and believe me

Sincerely yours,
Charles L. Dodgson

P.S. Quite seriously, if she has the courage to entrust herself to me for one day, and you would allow her to come – I would fix my day to suit her.

To Henry Savile Clarke

7 Lushington Road, Eastbourne
August 5, 1888

Dear Mr. Savile Clarke,

I hope your new "cast" will prove a success.* You say that Dorothy's sister (Clara) is "new": but she was in it when they came to Eastbourne. She played in [the] scene of "all the King's horses and men," and I think was a fairy also.

As to the 2 lyrics you ask for, it is well you mentioned the matter, as *I* have been waiting to hear from *you*. I thought it was understood that you and the composer were to settle what metres were wished for, and I suggested that he had better write the music *first*, and that you should give me a "nonsense-verse" to fit it, from which I could see what metre was wanted. Though I retain my opinion that he had better be content with the existing metres, and merely put new airs to them, I shall be very happy to alter them into any other metres he prefers.

Please bear in mind the two suggestions of mine, which you approved of – one, that *masks* (of heads of animals, etc.) should always partly show the

---

* Savile Clarke's *Alice* would be revived for Christmas of this year, the lead going to Dodgson's newish child friend, Isa Bowman, and lesser parts to her sisters "Maggie" and "Emsie."

human face: the other that *ladies should be warned that bonnets, or hats, are not allowed in the stalls and dress-circle*. This last I consider a *most* important reform to make, for the sake of theatres *generally*: the other managers are almost sure to follow your lead, if once you have the courage to protest against the present senseless practice, by which numbers of the spectators have their pleasure entirely spoiled.

There are a few other matters I want to mention:

(1) In writing your new version of the play, would it not be well to begin by taking the existing one, and ruthlessly erasing all that experience has shown to be flat and ineffective? Then you will see what room you have for new matter.

(2) If you keep the "King's horses and men," *don't* let them carry such absurdly small toy hobby-horses that the wheels are completely off the ground!

(3) I wish to withdraw, *absolutely*, my suggestion of letting boys act any female characters. You were quite right, and I was quite wrong. It would *vulgarise* the whole thing. The rule doesn't work both ways – I don't know why, but so it is. Girls make charming boys (e.g. Little Lord Fauntleroy) but boys should never be dressed as girls.

(4) In giving out the parts to be learned, would it not be well to *underline* the words that ought to be made emphatic? Very likely it wouldn't have saved the Red and White Queens from making nonsense of every sentence by leaning on the wrong word: but they were *exceptionally* idiotic: for people of ordinary common-sense it would be a great help in giving the dialogue its true meaning.

(5) That photographer, who has a studio in the Danish Village (from Tradelle and Young) has done some excellent pictures of your "Tableaux" folk. And he assures me they are from *untouched* negatives – which adds enormously to their value. Could you not arrange with him to do all the *Alice* company ("cabinet" size) and have them on sale in the entrance of the theatre? You might make a very good thing of it, in either of 2 ways: (a) Give him the monopoly of selling in the theatre: let him take them at his own cost, and sell them for a stipulated price, and keep the proceeds himself – he meanwhile paying you a fixed sum, per day, for the privilege. (b) Let him take them for *you*, and supply them to you for a stipulated price: and then *you* sell them at a profit. The profit, per cent, on photographs is enormous. A "cabinet" that sells for 2s., costs (when done in large numbers) about 4d. or 6d. to produce. You might sell at 1s., and yet make a handsome profit. If sold at 1s., they would sell by *hundreds*: every child, that had seen the play, would want to carry off *one*, at least.

(6) One little suggestion which is partly for *my* benefit, though partly for yours as well. Would you mind arranging to have copies of the 2 books on sale in the theatre? It should be the People's Edition, and should include *Alice* (at 2*s*. 6*d*.), *Looking-Glass* (at 2*s*. 6*d*.), and the two bound together (at 4*s*. 6*d*.). We would supply them to you as we do to the booksellers, so that you would make the ordinary "bookseller's profit," while I should make the "author's profit."

Forgive me for boring you with so long a letter!

Yours very truly,
C. L. Dodgson

To J. L. Knight

7 Lushington Road, Eastbourne
September 18, 1888

Dear Sir,

I thank you for your letter, and am very glad to know that I have given pleasure to your children. One of the chief pleasures my books have given me is that of giving them to children: and I like best of all the giving them to *sick* children in hospitals – though perhaps, if I were to express a wish that *your* children were in that condition, in order that I might have more pleasure in giving them books, you would not entirely sympathise with me!

I have received a very loving letter from your little boy, and a very formal letter from Nellie (what does that stand for?) – not that I find the least fault with her for *that*, since nothing could well have been more stiff and formal than my letter, to which it was an answer, and she did quite right to follow suit.

Thank you for your kind offer to show me the beauties of your neighbourhood. I have some recollection of them, as I once spent a day there. But I fear my chance of seeing you, or your children again, is a very slender one: I am a very unwilling and infrequent traveller.

With love to your children, I remain

Truly yours,
C. L. Dodgson

P.S. A letter from Nellie has this moment arrived. Please give her (and Sydney) my love: and tell Nellie I don't think she looks the *least* like a little girl who would say "won't," or "shan't," or "hasn't." And that I feel *sure* that, when next I see her, and when I say "dear Nellie, will you give me a hundred pounds?" she will reply "I *will*!"

To his cousin Mrs. W. E. Wilcox

Christ Church, Oxford
February 6, 1889

My dear Fanny,

It seems to me that I owe you a lot of money. Will you tell me how this is?

Am I right in supposing that Willie was at Selwyn College till the middle of 1888? I find I undertook to contribute (besides my annual gift of £30 to yourself) £30 a year so long as he was at College. Now the last payments made to you, on both these accounts, seem to have been in the middle of 1887.

Consequently, I seem to owe you, on Willie's account, £30 for the year ending in middle of 1888.

And, on your *own* account, I'm not quite clear *what* you are expecting to receive. For I understand that you have (or are *going* to, I'm not clear which) given up keeping school, and thus voluntarily cut off a considerable source of income. Will you kindly tell me if this means that you now find yourself no longer in need of extraneous help. Or does it mean that, though still in need of help, you are physically unable to carry on the school? You will not suppose I am asking with any idea of withdrawing my gifts, so long as they are needed.

With love to Nella, I am

Always affectionately yours,
C. L. Dodgson

To his cousin Mrs. W. E. Wilcox

Christ Church, Oxford
February 8, 1889

My dear Fanny,

I am glad I have rescued this matter from the oblivion it was fading into.

The gifts, for the period that Willie was at College, I would like to continue till June this year, when Theo will have ended his College career. After that, I should like to continue the old half-yearly £15 for *yourself*.

This makes me owe you £90 up to end of 1888: there will be £30 due in June: and £15 more in December.

I am very glad you will be able to say farewell to the fatigue and worry of a life of teaching. And I hope my contribution will make your future years a little more easy and restful than otherwise they might have been.

At any rate it will enable you to supply Nella with the peppermint-drops that she finds so essential to her happiness.

Always yours affectionately,
C. L. Dodgson

I enclose cheque for £90.

To Winifred Holiday *

Christ Church, Oxford
February 28, 1889

My dear Winnie,

If you could see the *heaps* of stupid business I have to get through every day, involving endless letter-writing, over and above the more interesting business of seeing The Nursery "*Alice*" through the Press, you would not wonder that I have left your letter unanswered for a month. Very seldom do I write a letter, unless I have something definite to say: and the definite thing, this time, is to ask you to let me have the pleasure of giving you fresh copies of *Alice* and of the *Looking-Glass*. I don't like writing my name in books not given by me. The copy your father gave you would serve to "lend" (if you *must* indulge in that insane practice), or (if you don't mind giving away a present) to please some less-favoured child who has no copy at all.

Will you have them in red covers, or white? (The white and gold covers look *very* pretty: though of course they need wrapping up more.)

I'm glad you liked the *Alice* play: it was ever so much better than in 1886: and I think my little friend, Isa Bowman, was a more refined and intelligent Alice even than Phoebe Carlo, though *she* was a very good one. Little "Emsie" Bowman (Isa's youngest sister) was delicious as the Dormouse, and as the dancing oyster-ghost. Isa is one of my *chiefest* of child-friends: I had her with me at Eastbourne last summer (I'm a *very* old fogey, now, you know; so I defy "Mrs. Grundy" fearlessly!) for a week's visit, nominally: but we got on so well together, that I kept writing to Mrs. Bowman for

* Daughter of Henry Holiday, the artist who illustrated Dodgson's *The Hunting of the Snark*. Climène Holiday (mentioned later in the letter) was Winifred's first cousin.

leave to keep her longer, till the week had extended to *five*!¹ When we got near the end of *four*, I thought "at any rate I'll keep her over the normal *honey-moon* period." I felt rather curious to see whether there was *any* young person, of the feminine gender, whose company, tête-à-tête, I could endure for a *month*. I hadn't believed it possible: and used to say, when twitted with being a bachelor, "I never yet saw the young lady whose company I could endure for a *week* – far less for *life*!" But alas, I can plead that argument no longer!

Is Climène any better? Less thin and pale than when last I saw her?

I've no end of other letters to write, so will end here.

Your loving friend,
C. L. Dodgson

To his niece Lucy Dodgson

Copy of correspondence between A.B. (Mr. A. Bach) and C.D. (Mr. C. Dodgson) March, 1889.

I.
(A.B. to C.D.)

What colour would you like the face of the watch to be?

2.
(C.D. to A.B.)

It must match the face of the young lady.

3.
(A.B. to C.D.)

Then it had better be a *gold* face – the colour of a child that has Jaundice. All children have Jaundice.

4.
(C.D. to A.B.)

This one hasn't.

5.
(A.B. to C.D.)

I meant that all children *generally* have Jaundice.

6.
(C.D. to A.B.)

This one *doesn't* have it *generally* – not more than two or three times a year.
The watch must match her face when she's *well*.

7.
(A.B. to C.D.)

Then it depends on how many lessons she does every day.

8.
(C.D. to A.B.)

What ever *do* you mean?

9.
(A.B. to C.D.)

Why, if a child does only *one* hour's work a day, her face is bright scarlet:
if she does *two* hours' work, it's a dull crimson: and so on – how many hours'
work does *this* animal do?

10.
(C.D. to A.B.)

She *isn't* an animal.

11.
(A.B. to C.D.)

Well, this *vegetable*, then. Don't be so particular.

12.

(C.D. to A.B.)

About twenty-five, I believe.

———

13.

(A.B. to C.D.)

All right, I know what to do now. The watch shall match her face exactly.
When a child does twenty-five hours' work a day, her face is——

———

14.

(C.D. to A.B.)

Is *what*?

———

15.

(A.B. to C.D.)

———

Never mind, you'll see.

===

I thought there was no good writing any more letters.

===

C.D.

To Mrs. W. Hunter

Christ Church, Oxford
March 10, 1889

Dear Mrs. Hunter,

I have altogether let the time slip by, when I could properly have offered
my congratulations to Dr. Hunter and yourself, on the recovery of your
children. Will you, however, accept them, late as they are, on the plea that
I have, nearly always, more to do than I have time for? There are not *nearly*
hours enough in the day!

One does indeed find it, as you say, hard to understand that there can be
any sufficient reason for pain being permitted in the case of innocent creatures.

It is one of those problems that it will be a *great* satisfaction to know the answer to (as I suppose we shall) in the Other Life. I, as a student of Mathematics, look forward to knowing the answers to several problems that seem hopeless for Human Reason here: some of them seem plainly *outside* the field of our Reason, and yet such as *must* have solutions. But I suppose the unsolved *Moral* Problems will be the most fascinating of all to attack with enlarged powers of reason.

It does not commit me to *much*, to say I shall be happy to call, if ever within reach of Rothesay: for I much doubt if that will ever happen. I was never fond of travelling, and I like it *less* each year, I think. But a much more *practical* promise is to say that if, when next you are in London, you will kindly send me your address, I shall have much pleasure in calling. London and Oxford *are* within reach: a fast train does it under the hour-and-a-half. Believe me

Very truly yours,
C. L. Dodgson

To Mary Brown

Christ Church, Oxford
April 1, 1889

My dear Mary,

The months, and the years, glide away, and now I have 3 reminders of your continued existence to thank you for – (which I do now), a Xmas card 1887, some flowers in June 1888, a Xmas card the same year. I thank you, but must candidly confess I have no use for such presents. I don't like flowers in a room: and can do nothing with Xmas cards except to send them on to some child or other. Far rather would I have a few lines of writing, at any time you feel inclined to write, to tell me something of your life – something that interests you at the moment – that would make you more real to me than presents. For ours is a strange sort of friendship, and we must be getting very unreal to each other by this time. It must be nearly 20 years since we met and it is *very* doubtful if we should even recognise each other now! My memory of you is of a little girl that sat on my knee (a performance that you may have totally forgotten by now) out on the cliffs at Whitby: and yours of me – well, of not quite such an old "lean and slippered pantaloon" as I have now become. That any friendship should have survived at all, through all those years, is something wonderful; and whether it would stand the shock of meeting again, whether our characters have not become by this time hopelessly discordant, is an open question.

Well, I'll tell you about myself now. I'm getting a little book through the Press, which I hope will be out by Easter, to be called, *The Nursery "Alice"* – pictures enlarged, and coloured by Tenniel, and with explanations in easy words just as one would explain the pictures to a child. Would you care to have a copy of it? Can you recall your feelings as a Nursery-child, enough to enjoy a baby book? I go down every summer to Eastbourne and I still make friends with children on the beach, and sometimes even (being now an old man who can venture on things that "Mrs. Grundy" would never permit to a younger man) have some little friend to stay with me as a guest. That will give you some idea what an "aged, aged man" I have become! My last guest was the charming child, who lately acted Alice in Mr. Savile Clarke's play of *Alice in Wonderland*.

There now! I have broken the silence of some 2 years or so, and can contentedly remain for a while at least

Your always affectionate friend,
Charles L. Dodgson

To Charlotte Rix

Christ Church, Oxford
April 10, 1889

My dear Lottie,

I write in a state of very considerable shame and contrition: and can only *hope* for your forgiveness, which is more than I deserve. In going through some old letters today, I came upon one of yours, alluding to an offer of mine (which I had totally forgotten ever having made) to take you to call on Miss Ellen Terry. In some surprise I referred to my letter-register, to see if I had any record of the letter you seemed to allude to: and there, sure enough, is the *précis*: "March 22, 1887. *Mrs. Rix*, offering, if she approves, to take Lottie to call on Ellen Terry." And, immediately afterwards, I came upon your mother's letter, written in answer to it, and stating that she *did* approve.

Now comes the part of the correspondence which covers *me* with disgrace. On January 15, 1889, I got a letter from your mother, thanking me for taking Edith to see Miss Terry, and saying that *you* also would much like to be taken. On this, quite oblivious of *former* correspondence, I considered the question as a *new* one altogether, and at once fancied I saw difficulties in the way, as I had never introduced any but *intimate* friends – which you and I could scarcely claim to be: and accordingly I wrote on January 19, excusing myself from acceding to the proposal (which I supposed *originated* on *your* side, not on *mine*).

Your mother must have been surprised, and (I fear) rather hurt, at my so coolly backing-out of a plan which *I* had originally proposed. I beg *her* pardon, and *yours*, very humbly. Why in the world she, or you, did not at once point out to me that the proposal had come first from *me*, must for ever remain a mystery: such forbearance is *almost* superhuman.

Now, my dear Lottie, will you let me make the only amends I can, by *absolutely* withdrawing all the objections I had conjured up, and returning to my original undertaking? Next time you are in London, I shall be *most happy* to write and get Miss Terry's leave to take you to see her. I do not doubt that she will give leave: she is the very soul of good-nature.

With kindest regards to your mother, I am

Yours always affectionately,
C. L. Dodgson

To his niece Violet Dodgson

Christ Church, Oxford
May 6, 1889

Dear Violet,

I'm glad to hear you children like the Magazine I ordered for you for a year: and if you happen to have seen the book about "Lord Fauntleroy," you'll find an interesting bit about the child that acts the Boy (now they have made a Play of it) in Number Six. She seems to be a child without one bit of pride: a pretty name too, hasn't she? the little "Elsie Leslie Lyde." I grieve to hear your bantam-hen is fond of rolling eggs away. You should remind it, now and then, of "Waste not, want not." You should say "a bantam-hen, that wastes an egg, is sure to get extremely poor, and to be forced at last to beg for hard-boiled eggs, from door to door. How would you like it, Bantam-hen," you should go on, "if all your brood were hard-boiled chickens? You would then be sorry you had been so rude!" Tell it all this, and don't forget! And now I think it's time for me to sign myself, dear Violet,

Your loving Uncle,
C.L.D.*

To Isabella Bowman

Hatfield House, Hatfield, Hertfordshire
June 8, 1889

My darling Isa,

I hope this will find you, but I haven't yet had any letter, written from *Fulham*, so I can't be sure if you have yet got into your new house.

This is Lord Salisbury's house (he is the father, you know, of that Lady Maud Wolmer that we had luncheon with): I came yesterday, and I'm going to stay until Monday. It *is* such a nice house to stay in! They let one do just as one likes – it isn't "Now you must do some geography! now it's time for your sums!" the sort of life *some* little girls have to lead when they are so foolish as to visit friends – but one can just please one's own dear self. There are some sweet little children staying in the house. Dear little "Wang"† is here with her mother. By the way, *I* made a mistake in telling you what to call her. She is "the Honourable Mabel *Palmer*" – "Palmer" is the *family* name: "Wolmer" is the *title*, just as the family name of Lord Salisbury is "Cecil": so that his daughter was Lady Maud *Cecil*, till she married.

Then there is the Duchess of Albany here, with two such sweet little children. She is the widow of Prince Leopold (the Queen's youngest son), so her children are a Prince and Princess: the girl is "Alice," but I don't know the boy's Christian name: they call him "Albany," because he is the Duke of Albany. Now that I have made friends with a real live little Princess, I don't intend ever to *speak* to any more children that haven't titles. In fact, I'm so proud, and I hold my chin so high, that I shouldn't even *see* you if we met! No, darling, you mustn't believe *that*. If I made friends with a *dozen* Princesses,

---

* For another letter in verse disguised as prose, see Dodgson to Margaret Cunnynghame, January 30, 1868, above.

† Lady Mabel Laura Georgiana, daughter of Lord and Lady Wolmer, granddaughter of Lord and Lady Salisbury.

I would love you better than all of them together, even [if] I had them all rolled up into a sort of child-roly-poly.

Love to Nellie and Emsie.

Your ever loving Uncle,
C.L.D.

X X X X X X X

To Mary Brown

Christ Church, Oxford
June 28, 1889

My dear Mary,

I am writing in this way,*in order to keep a copy, without spending the time it would take to copy out my letter. The difficulties you mention are such as I have long felt: and I will try to tell you my thoughts about them, and if anything I say *should* prove, with God's blessing, to be of any use to you, dear Mary, in your spiritual life, it would indeed be happiness to me!

As to the words "today shalt thou be with me in paradise," and the words in the Apostles' Creed "he descended into hell," the usual interpretation is that *both* words refer to the "place of departed spirits," where, as we believe, the disembodied spirits await the time of the resurrection, when they shall be clothed in their "spiritual body" and shall appear before the judgment-seat of Christ, and so shall pass to heaven or to hell.

The parable of the rich man and Lazarus seems to teach that even among the disembodied spirits a *distinction* is made, some being in happiness and others in sorrow. The two separate portions of this world of spirits are called, in the Greek, "paradise" (or "Abraham's bosom") and "hades." This latter word occurs in

Matt. 11. 23

16. 18

Luke 10. 15

16. 23

Acts 2. 27

31

I Cor. 15. 55

Rev. 1. 18

6. 8

* Dodgson is here using the Electric Pen, a device recently invented by Thomas Edison. Dodgson once described the pen as "quite the best thing . . . for taking a number of copies of MSS, drawings, or maps."

20. 13
14

In I Cor. 15. 55 it is translated "grave": in the other 10 places, "hell," which I think a misleading translation, being liable to be confused with the Greek word *gehenna* (which is also translated hell), the name of the place to which the wicked shall be sent *after* the resurrection. The word *gehenna* occurs in 12 places, *viz.* –

Matt.   5. 22, 29, 30

10. 28

18. 9

23. 15, 33

Mark 9. 43, 45, 47

Luke 12. 5

James 3. 6

That it refers to a place not reached till *after* the resurrection is clear from Matt. 10. 28.

I think you would find it a good thing to turn to all these 23 places in your Bible, and write *Hades* in the margin for the 1st set, and *Gehenna* for the 2nd set.

So, in answer to your question "Do you think because a man may drink, he will be sent straight to hell?" I say, in the first place, that it is *not* the teaching of the Bible (though no doubt it *is* taught in many *human* writings, such as sermons and hymns) that *any* one is sent, either to heaven or to hell, *immediately* after death.

But suppose we omit the word "straight" from your question. It then leads to a totally different question, namely, my belief about what is usually called "eternal punishment."

There are many forms of belief, on this subject, which seem to contradict the idea of God's perfect *justice*, or else of His perfect *love*: and people seem sometimes to give up these *latter* beliefs *because* of the contradiction.

In settling one's own belief, when two things are plainly contradictory, all depends on *which* of the two we put *first* and hold *independently* of the truth or untruth of the other.

I can but tell you the order in which *I* believe religious truths. Each person must settle the order for himself.

I believe, *first and before all*, that there is an absolute, self-existent, external, distinction between Right and Wrong. Now put side by side with this the theory that "God is almighty." If any one points out the contradiction, and says "if you grant Him to be *almighty*, you must grant that He can make

Right into Wrong, and Wrong into Right," I reply "if, as it seems, the two are contradictory, I must of course deny *one*. But I do not follow your bidding, and deny the *first*: no, I hold *that independently* of *all* else: I deny the *second*: I say "God is *not* almighty, in this sense."

By "Right" and "Wrong," I mean what *we ought to do*, and *ought not to do*, without any reference to rewards or punishments.

Secondly, I believe I am responsible to a *Personal Being* for what I do.

Thirdly, I believe that Being to be *perfectly good*. And I call that perfectly good Being "God."

Now put side by side with that the theory "God will punish two persons *equally*, who commit the same sin, though the temptation may have been, owing to difference of circumstances, irresistible by one, and easily resisted by the other." I say "this contradicts the *perfect* goodness of God. One of the two must be false. I hold to the *first* theory, namely, that God is perfectly good: and I deny the *second*." That is, I say "God will *not* act thus." If you urge "but such-and-such a text asserts it. Hence, if the Bible is inspired by a God of truth, and if this text be genuine, and rightly translated, then God *will* act so," I reply "then I deny one or other of these conditions: and I say that either the Bible is not inspired, or the text is not genuine, or it is mistranslated."

From the belief that God is perfectly good, I conclude, as *necessary* sequences, that He will take account of *all* circumstances in judging of any action of man – that he will not punish, except for *wilful* sin, where the sinner was free to choose good or evil – that he will not punish *for ever* any one who *desires* to repent, and to turn *from* sin. If any one says "it is certain that the Bible teaches that, when once a man is in *Hell*, no matter how much he repents, there he will stay for ever," I reply "*if* I were certain the Bible taught that, I would give up the Bible." But, as a matter of fact, *that* result is by no means necessary: it is quite enough to say "either that text is not genuine, or you have translated it wrong."

And if any one urges "then, to be consistent, you ought to grant the *possibility* that the Devil himself might repent and be forgiven," I reply "and I *do* grant it!"

You will perhaps think my beliefs strange and wild. But settle *your* belief on that *principle*: i.e. settle, when two things contradict, *which* you will hold to, and I think you will find peace and comfort in such belief.

Enough for one letter.

Always your loving friend,
Charles L. Dodgson

To the Duchess of Albany

Christ Church, Oxford
July 1, 1889

Dear and honoured Madam,

In sending the book, promised for the little Princess Alice, and one also which (as I understand from Miss Maxwell*) I am permitted to give to the little Duke of Albany, I am bold enough to hope that your Royal Highness will honour me by accepting one more book as well, which will follow in a few days.

May I also take the opportunity – perhaps the only one I shall ever have – of adding a few words to what I said on a subject we spoke of, in one of those interesting little talks which I remember with so much pleasure. The subject was the desirability of remembering, or forgetting, a remark made by one of your children, on a scene in the life of Our Lord – a remark which (of course without any consciousness on the part of the child) gave a humorous turn to the passage. I am not going to urge any directly *religious* grounds for reverent treatm[ent of the] sacred narrative – I am persuaded [that] such reasons weigh as fully with your Royal Highness as with myself – and all I wish to say may be put into these few words. Is it not a cruelty (however unintentionally done) to tell any one an amusing story of that sort, which will be for ever linked, in his or her memory, with the Bible words, and which *may* have the effect, just when those words are most needed, for comfort in sorrow, or for strength in temptation, or for light in "the valley of the shadow of death," of robbing them of all their sacredness and spoiling all their beauty?

There are beautiful texts in the Bible, that have been thus spoiled for *me*: and I have never, for years now, repeated any such story, lest I should cause to others the pain I cannot now avoid for myself: for our memories are not under our command, and we often remember best what we most passionately long to forget.

Imagine some poor widow, in the first agony of her grief, opening her Bible to read some of those wonderful words that bring to the mourner peace and the hope of a life beyond the grave, and finding that some wanton hand has scrawled the page with grotesque caricatures – and you will realise what I mean.

---

* Lady-in-attendance on the Duchess of Albany.

I ask pardon for writing so freely, and at such length: but it is a matter about which I feel very deeply.

Permit me to inscribe myself

Your Royal Highness's most sincerely,
Charles L. Dodgson

P.S. I send the Nursery *"Alice"* in brown ink only, because the *coloured* edition has turned out a failure, and will have to be printed again. The new edition will be out by Christmas, I hope: and I will then send a copy for the little Princess – trusting that she will not object to possessing *both* kinds!

To Messrs. Snow & Co.

Christ Church Common Room, Oxford
December 24, 1889

Mr. Dodgson has given directions to return to Messrs. Snow the box of Portugal fruit.

He would have thought it hardly necessary to point out that the Curator, whose duty it is to try to procure the *best* goods he can for Common Room, cannot possibly accept *presents* from any of the tradespeople concerned.

He thinks it only fair to warn Messrs. Snow that any repetition of such attentions may seriously affect their position as Wine-merchants dealt with by Common Room.

To Mary Brown

[The Chestnuts, Guildford]
December 26, 1889

My dear Mary,

I have been putting off, from day to day, writing in answer to your letter of 13th – not from indolence, and not (most certainly) from want of love for you: how can I *help* loving one who has gone on loving me all these years without one single meeting to revive that memory of me since that long-ago when she sat on my knee as a little girl? But I have been almost afraid of writing about subjects so difficult to deal with, in which silence would be safer than to say things in haste, that might prove to be unwise, and harmful rather than helpful. One thing, at any rate, I can safely say to begin with – that I thank you, from my heart, for thus taking me into your confidence, and writing so fully and freely of all your troubles, being sure (as I hope you are) of my sympathy in them all. This is indeed treating me as a real friend and I find it one of the many pleasures of old age (I think at 57 I may call myself an old man?) to be allowed to enter into the inner lives, and secret sorrows, of child-friends now grown to be women, and to give them such comfort and advice as I can. It makes me very humble in view of one's own need of guidance and unfitness to guide, and very thankful to God for thus letting one work for Him. I had better go through your letter, and see what it suggests to me to say. You say "the hardest thing to decide is what is right and what is wrong: the wrong seems to me so often the right somehow." This seems to me confusion of ideas. I will try to put clearly what seems to me to be the position of each human being. God has given him conscience (that is an intuitive sense of "I ought," "I ought not"), and this he ought to obey: God has given him means for learning what is his duty, such as prayer, reading the Bible, etc., and these means he ought to use. If he acts without attending to that inner voice, or if he neglects to use those means of grace, he is, so far, doing wrong, *whatever* the resulting act may be. But if, having duly used all those means, he then does *what seems to him right*, that is right, in the sight of God, whatever the resulting act may be. The principle seems to me to hold both ways. A thing may be quite innocent *in itself*: but suppose a person (suppose from some mistaken information or faulty education, etc., etc.) thinks it wrong, and yet (perhaps for the sake of some advantage to be gained) does it, *he* is doing *wrong* in the sight of God. I will give an instance, as that is a much less common event than the other. In making up my accounts, I make out that my friend owes me £5. I think to myself "he keeps no accounts: he will never find out if I call it £6." But all the while I have made a mistake in adding up, and he really owes me £6, so that my claiming my £6, while quite right in itself, is, so far as I am concerned, and in the sight of God, an act of dishonesty. And so, my dear child (I may call you so, mayn't I?) don't worry yourself with questions of *abstract* right and wrong. When you are puzzled go and tell your puzzle to your Heavenly Father (if it be one that your earthly father cannot solve for you) and pray for guidance, and then do what seems best to *you*, and it will be accepted by Him. Money losses are bitter trials enough sometimes, and I feel for you much in all the anxieties and troubles they have caused you: and your father's illness must be a trouble to you also. But all those are quite endurable sorrows

compared with the miserable history you have given me of your brother.
I feel almost helpless to say anything about so terrible a trial as that sin is the
one unendurable agony of life. One's own sins crush one to the dust more
than all possible sorrows that could come from without. And what must it
have been for the dear Saviour when having made himself one with us, that
he might bear our infirmities, he realised, so far as a sinless soul could, the
intolerable burden of our sin! It is good sometimes to remember that awful
agony in the garden, Jesus *prayed* in that agony. What better advice can I give
you, dear Mary, than to pray His prayer? "Father, if it be possible, let this
cup pass from me: never the less not my will but Thine, be done." Please
whenever you feel inclined to write and tell me about yourself, do so. I shall
never think your letters too long or troublesome. And don't let yourself
think such morbid thoughts as to doubt if there is any use in your life, or
wish to go to your dear Mother before God calls you to join her. Your
being still alive and well and able to attend to your father and little nephew,
and no doubt to other things that are helpful to others, is all good evidence
that God has a meaning and purpose in your life, whether you can see it cr
not. "Thomas, because thou hast seen me," Jesus said, "thou hast believed.
Blessed *are* they that have not seen, and *yet* have believed."

Always your loving friend,
Charles L. Dodgson

To Edith Rix

The Chestnuts, Guildford
December 31, 1889

Dearest Edith,

What a wicked girl you are not to return me Isa's letters! (I would like to
have them in my own possession again: and please, when you send them,
get the letter *registered*.) But then, what a good girl you are to have sent me
What Men Live By. But again, what a wicked girl you were not to put my
name in it! Yet, on the other hand, what a good girl you were to— (I can't
remember any more instances of your goodness, but the clause is needed to
balance the others). And yet again, what a wicked girl you were to send it
without a single line from yourself! Not even "this comes hopping," or
"Edith Rix her mark."

You will see, by the above, what good practice I have had in *analysing
characters*, putting the wicked elements on one side, and the good (when there
are any) on the other.

I have been having quite a new experience in life since we last met. Can you easily believe that I have been standing on a stage, curtain up, foot-lights dazzling me and turning all beyond them into black darkness (I never knew before what it was like, for actors to look over foot-lights into a dark abyss), and telling a fairy-tale, supposed to be addressed to the younger children only, but with an audience of nearly 300? The head-mistress of a large High School at Birmingham had invited me to witness a performance by the girls – scenes from *Julius Caesar* in German, and then Mrs. Freiligrath-Kroeker's dramatic version of *Alice*: and I had rashly offered to tell the little ones a story after it was over. I expected to have an audience of 40 or 50, mostly children, and had no idea there would be such a host of elder girls and parents. However, when I saw what I had to face, I thought I would go through with it, for the sake of the younger children: I tried to ignore the presence of others, after explaining to them that it was a totally different thing from what I had expected, and that I had nothing but a baby-story to tell them. I gave them "Bruno's Picnic," which you may have heard me tell, before now, to children, as it's a kind of "standing-dish" with me. The children, who acted in *Alice*, came on with me, at my suggestion, and sat on the floor, and, with the table of the "Mad Tea Party" to lean against, and the little Alice herself standing by me (her own idea, I think) it wasn't *quite* such a formidable ordeal as it would have been to stand alone on an empty stage. The acting, as a whole, was *very* good: done with great spirit, and they seemed to be absolutely "letter-perfect."

That's a remarkable book of Tolstoi's – fresh and original, and well worth reading. I'm very glad to have it: are any others of his equally good? Love to *all* your sisters (on an occasion like this I wish to make *no* exceptions) and a happy New Year to you all.

Your loving Uncle,
C.L.D.

To Mrs. A. Severn*

The Chestnuts, Guildford
(regular address "Christ Church, Oxford")
January 8, 1890

Dear Mrs. Severn,

It almost feels like taking an unwarrantable liberty, to address you thus: still, we *have* corresponded before now – on the subject of my photograph

* Ruskin's cousin; his companion and attendant during the last years of his life.

of Mr. Ruskin. I share with the British Public the concern with which we heard of his illness. But the last reports I have heard are that he is recovering: so I venture to write a question of my own. About the middle of December I sent him a copy of a new book of mine called *Sylvie and Bruno*. Can you tell me whether it reached him? Very likely he has not been able to read any of it – though it would not fatigue him much to look at the pictures – but, if he ever cares to know anything about the book, I should like him to be reminded that he expressed a hope, years ago, that my next book would not be a mere unconnected *dream*, but would contain a *plot*; and to be told that I have tried to do this in *Sylvie and Bruno* – and that the book contains no *dreams*, this time: what look like dreams are meant for *trances* – after the fashion of Esoteric Buddhists – in which the spirit of the entranced person passes away into an actual Fairyland. Believe me

Very truly yours,
C. L. Dodgson

To Edith Blakemore

[Christ Church, Oxford]
March 31, 1890

...I *do* sympathise so heartily with you in what you say about feeling shy with children when you have to entertain them! Sometimes they are a real *terror* to me – especially boys: little girls I can now and then get on with, when they're few enough. They easily become *de trop*. But with little *boys* I'm out of my element altogether. I sent *Sylvie and Bruno* to an Oxford friend, and, in writing his thanks, he added, "I think I must bring my little boy to see you." So I wrote to say "*don't*," or words to that effect: and he wrote again that he could hardly believe his eyes when he got my note He thought I doted on *all* children. But I'm *not* omnivorous! – like a pig. I pick and choose....

You are a lucky girl, and I am rather inclined to envy you, in having the leisure to read Dante. *I* have never read a page of him: yet I am sure the *Divina Commedia* is one of the grandest books in the world – though I am *not* sure whether the reading of it would *raise* one's life and give it a nobler purpose, or simply be a grand poetical treat. *That* is a question you are beginning to be able to answer: I doubt if *I* shall ever (at least in this life) have the opportunity of reading it: my life seems to be all torn into little bits among the host of things I want to do! It seems hard to settle what to do *first*. *One* piece of work, at any rate, I am clear ought to be done this year, and it will take *months* of hard work: I mean the 2nd Vol. of *Sylvie and Bruno*. I fully *mean*, if I have life and health till Xmas next, to bring it out then. When one is close on 60 years old, it seems presumptuous to count on years and years of work yet to be done.

What's the good of reading the history of King *Arthur*? Isn't it slightly waste of time? (Not that *I* have any business to lecture *you* on waste of time!) But I should have thought more *recent* history would repay study better than such a mythical period as the Arthurian Legend.

It will be a *great* addition to my pleasure, if ever I do come to give an address, to find my old friend *Edith* there (in fact that would be the principal element in deciding to come at one time rather than another): for *she* (perhaps you are acquainted with her?) is rather the exception among the hundred or so of child-friends who have brightened my life. Usually the child becomes so entirely a different being as she grows into a woman, that our friendship has to change too: and *that* it usually does by sliding down, from a loving intimacy, into an acquaintance that merely consists of a smile and a bow when we meet!

That is partly why I have written you all this long letter – that you continue to honour me with an affection that is a *sort* of love, and that we haven't yet got to the "smile and bow" stage! I hope we may continue equally good friends during the years – few or many – that I have still before me.

Your loving friend,
C. L. Dodgson

P.S. I don't think I've ever given you a *Wonderland Stamp-case*.* Shall I send Alice and you one apiece?

To an invalid

April 1890

...Many such sufferers want to know why God has ordered their lives so, and I have been led to think a great deal about the matter, and you may like

---

* Dodgson invented *The Wonderland Postage-Stamp Case* on October 29, 1888, and had it commercially manufactured with an accompanying pamphlet, *Eight or Nine Wise Words about Letter-Writing* (see the Appendix, for the full text).

to know the thought that seems to me to come *nearest*, of any I have found, to a disentanglement of the riddle.

It seems to me that, for everyone of us, life is really a sort of school, or training-time, or trial-time, meant *chiefly* for the building up of a character, and of disciplining the spirit, so that by its own free choice of good rather than evil, and of God's will rather than self-will, it may rise to a higher and higher stage of Christian growth, and get nearer and nearer to God, and more and more like Him, and so more fit for higher forms of existence. Perhaps we are not *at all* fit, at first, for such an existence as we shall enter after death. I fancy that the mere goodness of an innocent child is not the perfection of man's nature, or what is needed by a spirit, to be fit to dwell in His visible Presence. It may need a gradual training of the will – perhaps even the knowledge of what *evil* is, in order to make the choice of *good* more real – well, it has seemed to me that if a person doomed to a life of useless, helpless and hopeless sickness could realise some such thought as this: "Hereafter, in that higher life, looking back on this, I may be able to see clearly that my character needed exactly the training it had: that a healthy, strong, bright life would have been *ruin* to it, and that all these weary hours of suffering were the steps, and the only ones suitable to *me*, for mounting to this better life – it will all be clear, then, and no mystery will remain...."

To Isabella Bowman

Christ Church, Oxford
April 14, 1890

My own Darling,

It's all very well for you and Nellie and Emsie to unite in millions of hugs and kisses, but please consider the *time* it would occupy your poor old very busy Uncle! Try hugging and kissing Emsie for a minute by the watch, and I don't think you'll manage it more than 20 times a minute. "Millions" must mean *2* millions at least.

$$20)\overline{2{,}000{,}000}\text{ hugs and kisses}$$
$$60)\overline{100{,}000}\text{ minutes}$$
$$12)\overline{1{,}666}\text{ hours}$$
$$6)\overline{138}\text{ days (at twelve hours a day)}$$
$$23\text{ weeks.}$$

I couldn't go on hugging and kissing more than 12 hours a day, and I wouldn't like to spend *Sundays* that way. So you see it would take *23 weeks* of hard work. Really, my dear Child, I *cannot spare the time.*

Why haven't I written since my last letter? Why, how *could* I, you silly silly Child? How could I have written *since the last time* I *did* write? Now, you just try it with kissing. Go and kiss Nellie, from me, several times, and take care to manage it so as to have kissed her *since the last time* you *did* kiss her. Now go back to your place, and I'll question you.

"Have you kissed her several times?"

"Yes, darling Uncle."

" What o'clock was it when you gave her the *last* kiss?"

"5 minutes past 10, Uncle."

"Very well. Now, have you kissed her *since?*"

"Well – I – ahem ahem! ahem! (Excuse me, Uncle, I've got a bad cough.) I – think that – I – that is, you, know, I—"

"Yes, I see! 'Isa' begins with 'I,' and it seems to me as if she was going to *end* with 'I,' *this* time!"

Anyhow, my not writing hasn't been because I was *ill*, but because I was a horrid lazy old thing, who kept putting it off from day to day, till at last I said to myself, "Who roar! There's no time to write now, because they *sail* on the 1st of April." In fact, I shouldn't have been a bit surprised if this letter had been from *Fulham*, instead of Louisville. Well, I suppose you *will* be there about the middle of May. But mind you don't write to me from there! Please, *please*, no more horrid letters from you! I *do* hate them so! And as for *kissing* them when I get them, why, I'd just as soon kiss – kiss – kiss *you*, you tiresome thing! So there now!

Thank you very much for those 2 photographs – I liked them – hum – *pretty* well. I can't honestly say that I thought them the very best I had ever seen.

Please give my kindest regards to your mother, and $\frac{1}{2}$ of a kiss to Nellie, and $\frac{1}{200}$ of a kiss to Emsie, and $\frac{1}{2000000}$ of a kiss to yourself.

So, with fondest love, I am, my darling,

Your loving Uncle,
C. L. Dodgson

P.S. I've thought about that little prayer you asked me to write for Nellie and Emsie. But I would like, first, to have the words of the one I wrote for *you*, and the words of what they *now* say, if they say any. And then

I will pray to our Heavenly Father to help me to write a prayer that will be really fit for them to use.

To Gertrude Chataway

7 Lushington Road, Eastbourne
September 7, 1890

"*Seems* like writing to an old friend"? "*Seems*, Madam! Nay it *is*: I know not *seems*!"

Please don't think of me, my dear dear Child, as if I only *seemed* to you like an old friend!

I'm so *very* sorry to hear of your being so out of health. And I've got more to say about *that*: but first, I think, I had better answer about your "governess" protégée. And my answer is "No – I won't vote for her" – very short, and not very courteous, you see. But as you (not *seem* to be, but are) a real old frind, I see no reason for making smooth and showy speeches. Also, as I'm writing to *you*, I'll give my reasons – a thing it is best, usually, *not* to do.

All the help, given by the Institute,* will certainly go to *somebody*: no amount of abstaining from voting would cause it to lie idle, and benefit nobody. I *hope* it will go to whoever is the *best* case for it to go to: but, as I haven't the least idea which *is* the best, and have neither the time, nor the means, to make that out for myself, *I* can do nothing to bring about that desirable result. If, in ignorance of the relative claims of the candidates, I gave a vote, and gave it (as would be highly probable) for some one *not* the best case for it, the effect of my doing so would *not* be that I had in any way caused the money to be spent *charitably* (that will happen in any case), but simply that I had done all in my power to *hinder* the most deserving case from being chosen. I haven't the least doubt that the candidate you plead for is very poor, very unfortunate, and well worthy of help of *some* kind: but I have very great doubt as to hers being a *more* deserving case than every single one of the remaining cases.

There – you won't be "grateful" to me, I fear: but I'm tolerably certain you won't be *angry* with me. *Are* you ever angry? And what do you *look* like, when in that condition? Because *I* can't imagine.

---

* A voting charity, probably the Governesses' Benevolent Institution, which offered governesses annuities, help for those in difficulty, a home for those out of work, and asylum for the aged.

Now for what I wanted to say about you and your health. It is an unusual, and what some people would think a rather uncalled-for and officious suggestion to make. It is this. Do you think a visit to the Seaside (Eastbourne) would benefit you? And, if so, will you come and be my guest here for a while?

I put that question *first*, advisedly: I want you just to get over the shock of so outrageous a proposal a bit: and then you can calmly consider what I have to say in defence of asking a young lady of your age to be the guest of a single gentleman. First, then, if I live to next January, I shall be 59 years old. So it's not like a man of 30, or even a man of 40, proposing such a thing. I should hold it quite out of the question in either case. I never thought of such a thing, myself, until 5 years ago. Then, feeling I really had accumulated a good lot of years, I ventured to invite a little girl of 10, who was lent without the least demur.[1] The next year I had one of 12 staying here for a week. The next year I invited one of 14, quite expecting a refusal, *that* time, on the ground of her being too old. To my surprise, *and* delight, her mother simply wrote "Irene may come to you for a week, or a fortnight. What day would you like to have her?" After taking her back, I boldly invited an elder sister of hers, aged 18. *She* came quite readily. I've had another 18-year-old since, and feel quite reckless now, as to ages: and, so far as I know, "Mrs. Grundy" has made no remarks at all.

But have I had any one who is *grown-up*? (as I presume *you* are, by this time). Well, no, I've not actually *had* one here, yet: but I wrote the other day to invite Irene's *eldest* sister (who must be 23 by this time) and she writes that she can't come this year "but I shall love to come another time, if you'll ask me again!"

I would take moderately good care of you: and you should be middling well fed: and have a doctor, if you needed it; and I shouldn't allow you to *talk*, as that is evidently not good for you. My landlady is a good motherly creature, and she and her maid would look after you *well*.

Another point I may as well touch on, the cost of coming. There has been a difference among my child-guests, in that respect. Some – I fancied, when I began the paragraph, that there had been one, at least, whose railway-fare I had *not* paid. But I find there was none. (You see, I travelled from London *with* most of them, so it was natural to pay: though in some cases perhaps they *could* have afforded it themselves: but there were certainly *some* who couldn't have come at all, unless I had said beforehand "*I* will pay the journey-expenses." Therefore (with no fear that I shall offend you by so doing) I make the same offer to *you*.

Now *do*, my dear Child, get your parents to say "yes" (I mean, supposing sea-air is good for you); and then say "yes" yourself; and then tell me whether you would be competent to travel down here alone, or if I had better come to escort you.

At present there is, lying on the sofa by the open window of my tiny sitting-room, a girl-friend from Oxford, aged 17. She came yesterday, and will perhaps stay a week. After she is gone, if *you* could come for a week or longer, I should love to have you here! It would be like having my Sandown days over again!

Always your loving friend,
C. L. Dodgson

Kindest regards to your parents.

To Ellen Terry

Christ Church, Oxford
November 13, 1890

My *dear* old friend,

(*N.B.* "old" doesn't mean "old in *years*" but "old in *friendship*"!) You are really too nice and kind for anything! What *is* one to do with a friend who does about 100 times more than you ask them to do? The very utmost I hoped for was that, after seeing Isa [Bowman] and ascertaining that she had some "teachableness" in her, you would tell me that, if I applied to the manager of such-and-such a theatre, he would give me the addresses of some good teachers of elocution. It never crossed my thoughts that you would give her any lessons *yourself*! Well, you have earned (if such things can in any way repay you) the deep gratitude of *one* old friend, and the rapturous love of *one* enthusiastic child.

And so you have found out that secret – one of the deep secrets of Life – that all, that is really *worth* the doing, is what we do for *others*? Even as the old adage tells us, "What I spent, that I lost; what I gave, that I had." Casuists have tried to twist "doing good" into another form of "doing evil," and have said "you get pleasure yourself by giving this pleasure to another: so it is merely a refined kind of selfishness, as your own pleasure is a motive for what you do." I say "it is *not* selfishness, that my own pleasure should be *a* motive so long as it is not *the* motive that would outweigh the other, if the two came into collision. The "selfish man" is he who would still do the thing, even if it harmed others, so long as it gave *him* pleasure: the "unselfish man" is he who would still do the thing, even if it gave him no pleasure, so long as it pleased *others*. But, when both motives pull together, the "unselfish man" is *still* the unselfish man, even though his own pleasure *is* one of his motives! I am very sure that God takes real *pleasure* in seeing his children happy! And, when I read such words as "looking unto Jesus, the author and finisher of our faith, who *for the joy that was set before him* endured the cross," I believe them to be *literally true*.

And so in your case, dear friend; I believe that it is real joy to *you* to know that you are filling, full to overflowing, Isa's little cup of happiness; and yet there is no shadow of *selfishness* in what you are doing, but that it is pure, unadulterated, generous *kindness*.

I really believe your great kindness will *not* be wasted on my dear little friend, but that she will take all possible pains to do credit to your teaching.

I wish you could have seen her little sister Nellie play in *Editha's Burglar*! In all my theatrical experience, I have hardly ever seen anything so simple and so sweet.

One thing that made it impossible for me to *bring* Isa to see you, is that I have been ill for the last fortnight, with an aguish attack, and a prisoner to my fireside. But when I *am* able to come to town again, I hope to call, and thank you viva voce for all you are doing for her.

Love to Edy. If she at all desires to have a "stamp-case," she has only to throw out a hint! I'm a capital hand at taking hints!

By the way, I wonder if you ever received a copy of *Sylvie and Bruno*, which I sent to you December 12, 1889? If it failed to reach you, I will send you another copy, as I want you to have the book. Believe me always

Yours affectionately,
C. L. Dodgson

To Mrs. N. H. Stevens

Christ Church, Oxford
February 28, 1891

Dear Mrs. Stevens,

I have lost a considerable fraction (say .25) of my heart to your little daughter: and I *hope* you will allow me further opportunities of trying whether or no we can become real *friends*. She would be about my only child-friend – in Oxford. The former ones have grown up: and I've taken no trouble to find others, it's such a lottery, the finding of any *lovable* ones. *Please* don't think it's only her *beauty* that has attracted me: a face may be very beautiful, and yet very unattractive (for instance if the owner is self-conscious).

I was just going to inscribe a *Nursery "Alice"* for Enid, when, on looking into the list of copies given away, I found I had already given one to *Winnie*: so of course it would be superfluous. I have other children's books on hand, though not of my own writing. I could give her Mrs. Molesworth's *Herr Baby* (plenty of pictures) unless she happens to have it already: or *Fairies* (poetry by W. Allingham, illustrated, mostly in colour, by my friend Miss E. G. Thomson) – the pictures are *lovely* (if you don't mind the fairies being entirely naked!) and I've given many copies to my child-friends. Or I could give her *Evie*, a very naturally written story for children, by a lady-cousin of mine: but it's only got one or two pictures. Please advise: as I suppose I may give her *something*!

Sincerely yours,
C. L. Dodgson

You may have noticed, as one of the Facts of Life, that, if one doesn't blow one's own trumpet, it has a way of not getting blown: so let me humbly mention that I would have *very* much liked a kiss from *another* daughter of yours, besides Enid (as to whom I took it for granted that *any* child under 12 is "kissable"): only, as I had promised I would wait for *her* to indicate if she would like to be on those terms, and as she didn't, I of course forbore, being *more* than content to treat her as she likes best.

I hope I may some day borrow *Enid* for a walk? And perhaps, when she is *quite* at her ease with me, for a day in town. Perhaps, in a year or two, I might even ask for her for a week at Eastbourne: but I daren't ask *that* for Winnie, unless we should ever get again on "kissable" terms. Otherwise it would be a case of the greater (privilege) *not* containing the less: which is contrary to Euclid!

To Mrs. P. A. W. Henderson

Christ Church, Oxford
April 12, 1891

Dear Mrs. Henderson,

Shall you be at home at (say) 4.30 on Wednesday or Thursday? If so, I would like to call, and to bring with me a sweet girl-friend about Frances' age, named Winifred Stevens.

Also please let me know if you are one of the ladies who are "At Home" on a fixed day each week. I ask, that we may *avoid* such a day ! It is an excellent arrangement for your friends who like to meet each other in your house: but *I* should come wishing to see *you* !

Love to Lily.

Always sincerely yours,
C. L. Dodgson

P.S. When the warm days come again, I would much like to fetch Lily (supposing she liked it herself) to try some "studies" in the same dress as last time. I missed the chance of drawing *Annie*, when she was about Lily's present age, though I got plenty of nude "studies" of her as *photos*. However, I merely throw it out as a *suggestion*, and as a thing not to be thought of for a moment unless she *thoroughly* liked it. I've been drawing, in Mrs. Shute's studio, in London, 2 beautiful models, aged 16 and 14: but I'd far rather draw a child of 11 than any number of girls in their teens: the *child*-form has a special loveliness of its own.

To Michael Sadler

Christ Church, Oxford
April 13, 1891

Dear Steward,

I spent Friday in town, and during my absence the window-cleaners came, and cleaned the windows of the large room and octagon towers, instead of beginning (which would have shown more sense) with the bedroom and sitting-room which I am occupying. On Saturday morning, just after I had got out of bed, a ladder was reared against the bedroom window, and a man came up to clean it. As I object to performing my toilet with a man at the window, I sent him down again, telling him "You are not to clean it *now*," meaning, of course, that *that* window was to be left till I was dressed. Instead of moving away the ladder to the next windows (my smaller sitting-room) they went away, and have not returned. So the bedroom-window, the 2 windows of the sitting-room, and the window of the pantry, are not yet cleaned. They are ready to be cleaned at *any* time, whether I am here or not, with the single exception that I object to the bed-room window being cleaned while I am dressing.

Yours ever truly,
C. L. Dodgson

To Mrs. N. H. Stevens

Christ Church, Oxford
April 16, 1891

Dear Mrs. Stevens,

Will you give me the pleasure of *your* company, without Winnie or Enid, some day soon, for a walk and tea? To explain my motive in asking this just now, I must begin further back. Winnie will have told you of our visit at "Torbrex, Headington Hill," and of the very unconventional photographs Mrs. Henderson showed us, of Lily in a most un-society-like costume. I beg to say that *I* didn't ask for them! However, Winnie didn't seem to be *much* scandalised. For my own part, though I have taken many such photographs – and many of them done from the Hendersons, when they were younger, in the even scantier costume of nothing at all (which *I* think much more innocent-looking than *partial* dress) – yet I *never* show them to young friends, until the *mother* has first seen and approved of them.

Now, as I should like to show *some* of these, at any rate, to Winnie, I would be glad if you would kindly look at them first, and tell me which, if any, she may see.

One thing more I want to say. I spoke of taking *Enid* to Mrs. Henderson, to get a photograph done of her. Let me assure you that neither she, nor I, would *dream* of suggesting that Enid should be done in anything short of *full-dress*. So she need not be at all shy of coming. It is quite the exception for children to like being taken in so unusual a style. The little Hendersons enjoyed it thoroughly: but *please* don't think them unmaidenly for having done so. They are as *good*, and innocent, as human children can be!

Yours sincerely,
C. L. Dodgson

To Edith Blakemore

Christ Church, Oxford
April 26, 1891

My dear Edith,

I am writing this (in obedience to my own rule in *Wise Words*) with your letter of March 4 before me. And first, I'm much obliged to Miss Cooper for her kind message, and I have *not* given up the hope of coming to address the elder girls, but (though my *knee* has not troubled me for a long time) I do not feel equal to it just now. More than 2 months ago, I woke up one morning from an uneasy dream, saying to myself "how *very* uncomfortable the pillow is!" and found myself lying on the floor, up in the stalls of the Cathedral. I wouldn't believe it at first, but thought I was *still* dreaming: but in a few moments I was broad awake, and found it really was so. I was lying in a pool of blood, having bled profusely from the nose, which no doubt had received a heavy blow in my fall (in fact the doctor said the bones were loosened, and would take several weeks to get set firm again), and had been lying there exactly an hour. I remembered distinctly the reader of morning-prayers having come to within a few words of the end: and I find I remained kneeling when the others left the building. The 2 tutors, who went last, noticed that I did not get up, but concluded I was only going on in private prayer a little longer than usual, and thought no more of it: and the verger never noticed I had not gone out, but barred the doors, and left by another door. So I had the place all to myself, to sleep off the attack (epileptic, no doubt), and then unbarred the doors and let myself out. Luckily I met no one on my way back to my rooms, for I was a pretty figure! With my face and shirt-front all covered with blood. My doctor found me to be out of health generally – at least the *digestion* was out of order – and this may have caused the attack. Anyhow, the result has been a great deal of headache, and unfitness for brain-work, and the managers of the College Servants' Services decided *not* to ask me to preach this term. I daresay this is wise, as the doctor thought I had been doing too much brain-work, and sitting up too late. You laugh at me for the "fearful agonies" you say I suffer "over a coming sermon," but really I think sermons *may* have had something to do with it. I had preached *3* in the previous month: and I do feel that preparing them takes a good deal *out* of me, in the way of vital force. But I would not have it otherwise: it is work that, if it is to do any good, needs that one should put one's whole self into it.

I have been "taking it easy," now, for a good while, and my headaches are getting fewer, and my brain recovering its usual power: and I should like to know during what periods of this year there would be any use in proposing to come over and give this long-delayed address. In the High School *vacations* I suppose it would be no use, as many of the girls would probably be away.

You can tell Miss Cooper as much of my adventure as you like, and thus save me (who have small time for letter-writing) the time it would take to send her a separate explanation of my not yet coming over.

To Sydney Bowles[*]

Ch. Ch. Oxford.
May 22, 1891.

> My dear Sydney,
> I am so sorry, and so ashamed! Do you
> know, I didn't even know of your existence?
> And it was such a surprise to hear that you
> had sent me your love! It felt just as if
> Nobody had suddenly run into the room, &
> had given me a kiss! (That's a thing that
> happens to me, most days, just now.) If only
> I had known you were existing, I would
> have sent you heaps of love, long ago. And,
> now I come to think about it, I ought to have
> sent you the love, without being so particular
> about whether you existed or not. In some
> ways, you know, people, that don't exist, are
> much nicer than people that do. For instance
> people that don't exist are never cross: and
> they never contradict you: and they never
> tread on your toes! Oh, they're ever so much
> nicer than people that do exist! However,
> never mind: you can't help existing, you
> know; and I daresay you're just as nice
> as if you didn't.
> Which of my books shall I give you, now
> that I know you're a real child? Would you
> like "Alice in Wonderland"? Or "Alice Under Ground"?
> (That's the book just as I first wrote it, with my
> own pictures).
> Please give my love, and a kiss, to Weenie
> and Vera, & yourself (don't forget the kiss to
> yourself, please: on the forehead is the best place)
>   Your affectionate friend
>   Lewis Carroll!

Christ Church, Oxford
May 22, 1891

My *dear* Sydney,

I *am* so sorry, and so ashamed! Do you know, I didn't even know of your *existence*? And it was *such* a surprise to hear that you had sent me your love! It felt just as if Nobody had suddenly run into the room, and had given me a kiss! (That's a thing which happens to me, *most* days, just now.) If only I had known you were existing, I would have sent you *heaps* of love, long

* Elder daughter of Thomas Gibson "Captain Tommy" Bowles, playwright and politician, founder of the society paper *Vanity Fair* and the journal for women *Lady*. Sydney later married the second Baron Redesdale, and their eldest child was the novelist Nancy Mitford. "Weenie" was the younger Bowles daughter, Dorothy; Vera, the daughter of the family with whom the Bowleses were staying at the time.

ago. And, now I come to think about it, I ought to have sent you the love, without being so particular about whether you existed or not. In *some* ways, you know, people that *don't* exist, are much nicer than people that *do*. For instance, people that *don't* exist are never *cross*: and they never *contradict* you: and *they never tread on your toes*! Oh, they're *ever* so much nicer than people that *do* exist! However, never mind: you can't help existing, you know; and I daresay you're *just* as nice as if you didn't.

Which of my books shall I give you, now that I know you're a real child? Would you like *Alice in Wonderland*? Or *Alice Under Ground*? (That's the book just as I first wrote it, with my own pictures.)

Please give my love, and a kiss, to Weenie, and Vera, and yourself (don't forget the *kiss* to yourself, please: on the forehead is the best place).

Your affectionate friend,
Lewis Carroll

To an invalid

August 1891

...I don't feel at all justified in counting on many more years of life – in that last attack it might so very easily have happened that the heart (it *is* weak, I know) might have simply ceased to beat, and my waking up might have been in that strange region we all look forward to seeing, and know so little about!...in that "strange region" there will be one very happy thought to dwell on, "death is over!" and there must be another happy thought for those to whom life here has involved much physical suffering, that all *that* is done with: and that the resurrection-body will be free from all the maladies that the "corruptible" body is liable to....

To Mary Mallalieu

[c/o Macmillan & Co.]
29 Bedford Street, Covent Garden, London
October 11, 1891

My dear Child,

Yesterday I was at Brighton and went to see *The Silver King*, along with some little friends of mine, and we all enjoyed it very much. Now, every time that I have seen it before I've sent little "Cissie" a book, as a sort of reminder of the pleasure she has given me by acting a little girl so nicely. And when one has once made a rule like that it would never do to break it, would it? So I should like to send you – if you don't object – one of the three little books that I have written for children, *Alice's Adventures in Wonderland*, and *Through the Looking-Glass*, and *The Nursery "Alice,"* which has 20 large coloured pictures, and a few bits of the story of *Alice*. If you will say which you would like best I will send you the book, and please say what name I am to write in it, as "Mallalieu" perhaps isn't your real name. I am

Yours affectionately,
Lewis Carroll

To Helen Bowman

[Christ Church, Oxford]

Nov. 1. 1891.

My, Uncle loving
your! Instead grand
-son his to it give to
had you that so, years
80 or 70 for it forgot
you that was it pity
a what and : him of fond
so were you wonder don't
I and, gentleman old
nice very a was he. For
it made you that him
been have must it see
you so: grandfather my
was, then alive was that,

"Dodgson Uncle" only
the. Born was I before
long was that, see you,
then But. "Dodgson
Uncle for pretty thing
some make I'll now",
it began you when,
yourself to said you
that, me telling her
without, know I course
of and : ago years many
great a it made had
you said she. Me told
I's a what from was it?
For meant was it who
out made I how know

you do! Lasted has it
well how and. Grandfather
my for made had you
Antimacassar pretty
that me give to you of
nice so was it, Nelly
dear my.

To Mary Mallalieu

Christ Church, Oxford
November 11, 1891

My dear Polly,

I like the photograph very much, and I thank you for sending it to me: and also for sending me your love, which I like a great deal more than the photograph. Photographs are very pleasant things to have, but *love* is the best thing in all the world. Don't you think so? Of course I don't mean it in the sense meant when people talk about "falling in love"; that's only *one* meaning of the word, and only applies to a few people. I mean in the sense in which we say that everybody in the world ought to "love" everybody else. But we don't always do what we ought. I think you children do it more than we grown-up people do: *we* find so many faults in one another.

I heard a little girl who was asked "*Why* is it that *everybody* loves you, my dear?" And I think her answer was a very pretty one. She said, "I think it must be because *I* love *everybody*."

And I have heard another story – perhaps you have heard it, too – about a very old man called "John," who lived a long time ago. It was when people had only *one* name: so they used to give the name of the father as well; and so *he* was called "John the son of Zebedee." When he was *very* old and feeble they used to carry him into the church to talk to the people; but he was too weak to say much; and at last he used to say nothing but "Little children, love one another." I daresay that people thought "Why doesn't he tell us something *new*? We've learnt *that* lesson over and over again." However, that was 1800 years ago, and I don't think we've learnt it *quite* perfect, even now.

I send you the love of *another* old man: that's *me*.

Yours affectionately,
C. L. Dodgson

To Mrs H. G. Liddell

Christ Church, Oxford
November 12, 1891

Dear Mrs. Liddell,

I have been very busy, and have put off writing to you about your kind invitation, feeling I could not possibly write, in a hurry, and that it is very hard to express, to my own satisfaction, all that is in my mind.

It is *very* hard to find words which seem to express, adequately, how strongly I feel the very *great* loss, to the University, the College, the City, and to myself, involved in the going away of the Dean and yourself. We, as the Governing Body, have had a chief of such exceedingly rare qualities that it would be vain to hope that *any* successor can *quite* fill his place. I am sure that the whole of Oxford, and all the good and charitable work carried on in it, will suffer great and permanent loss by the absence of yourself. And, to *me*, life in Christ Church will be a totally different thing when the faces, familiar to me for 36 years, are seen no more among us. It seems but yesterday when the Dean, and you, first arrived: yet I was hardly more than a boy, then; and many of the pleasantest memories of those early years – that foolish time that seemed as if it would last for ever – are bound up with the names of yourself and your children: and now I am an old man, already beginning to feel a little weary of life – at any rate weary of its *pleasures*, and only caring to go on, on the chance of doing a little more *work*.

It is also *very* hard, at such a time, to say a word that could at all look like a want of readiness to do anything you may happen to wish. But I will trust to your kindness, and tell you candidly what I feel about it.

Years ago, I began declining *all* invitations out, feeling *very* weary of Society, and also thinking I had done my full share of it. But, years before that, I refused all *Sunday* invitations, on principle (though of course allowing to others the same liberty, which I claimed for myself, of judging that question). If you could kindly leave me out of the list of those who have the honour of being asked to meet your Royal guests, I should personally be grateful: and I am sure there are *many* who would be most happy to fill my place: and there is no fear that the Duchess could notice, in the bewildering stream of faces she has to meet, who is, and who is not, present.

Sincerely and gratefully yours,

C. L. Dodgson

To Mrs. H. G. Liddell

Christ Church, Oxford
November 19, 1891

Dear Mrs. Liddell,

I feel that I am largely indebted to *you* (for, if the Royal party had not been staying with *you*, they would assuredly never have come near *me* !) for the unique honour I have enjoyed – enough to make me conceited for the rest of my life. There are, possibly, other commoners who have been honoured by *single* visits from Princesses: but I doubt if any others have ever had *two* visits, in one day from the same Princess !*

The Latin Grammar tells us that the more money we get, the more the love of it grows upon us: and I think it is the same with *honour*. Having had so much, I now thirst for more: and the honour I now covet is that a certain pair of young ladies should come some day and take tea with me. I have a store of ancient memories of visits from your elder daughters but I do not think that Miss Rhoda and Miss Violet Liddell have ever even been inside my rooms: and I should like to add to my store *one* fresh memory at least, of having had a visit from them.

If the idea is not unwelcome to *them* (which is of course essential) I think I could find enough to show them: they would be interested, I think, in my large collection of photos of little friends belonging to that very peculiar class "stage-children."

If they felt any difficulty in coming across here, escorted only by each other, I would gladly come for them.

I do not ever ask more than *2* ladies, at a time, for tea: for that is the outside number who can see the same photographs, in comfort: and to be showing more than one at a time is simply distracting.

If I were 20 years younger, I should not, I think, be bold enough to give such invitations: but, but, I am close on 60 years old now: and all romantic sentiment has quite died out of my life: so I have become quite hardened as to having lady-visitors of *any* age !

If the reply be favourable, will they kindly choose a day, for conferring on me this coveted honour when they have *plenty* of spare time on their hands? I do *not* enjoy brief hurried visits from my young lady friends. A couple of hours would certainly not tire *me* of *them*, however much it might tire *them* of *me* ! Believe me

Sincerely yours,
C. L. Dodgson

---

* "A remarkable day," Dodgson wrote in his diary. "The Duchess of Albany is at the Deanery with her children Princess Alice and Prince Charles: and sent the children . . . to my rooms soon after 10. They had to return very soon, but came for a second visit about 4." Rhoda and Violet Liddell came for tea to Dodgson's rooms on November 25.

V. Last Years

On January 27, 1892, Carroll turned sixty. He had been reasonably healthy all his life, and even in his sixties one detects no obvious decline of physical or mental powers. In fact, a quiet contentment overtook him, and the only anxiety appears in his concern for completing the books he was writing. Even though he speaks of himself as an old man, his interest in his young friends continues unabated—with a difference, however, for Carroll grows interested in more mature women as he himself grows older, and he comes to desire the companionship of some of the mothers of his girl friends even above that of their daughters.

To *Alice* (*Liddell*) *Hargreaves*

Christ Church, Oxford
December 8, 1891

My dear Mrs. Hargreaves,
  I should be so glad if you could, quite conveniently to yourself, look in for tea any day. You would probably prefer to bring a companion; but I must leave the choice to you, only remarking that if your husband is here he would be ~~most~~ very welcome (I crossed out most because it's ambiguous; most words are, I fear). I met him in our Common Room not long ago. It was hard to realise that he was the husband of one I can scarcely picture to myself, even now, as more than 7 years old!*

Always sincerely yours,
C. L. Dodgson

Your adventures have had a marvellous success. I have now sold well over 100,000 copies.

* Mrs. Hargreaves visited Dodgson in his rooms the following afternoon.

213

To Gertrude Chataway

Christ Church, Oxford
January 1, 1892

My dear old Friend,

(The *friend*ship is old, though the *child* is young.) I wish a *very* happy New Year, and many of them, to you and yours: but specially to *you*, because I know you best, and love you most. And I pray God to bless you, dear child, in this bright New Year and many a year to come, and to spare your dear mother to you, for a long time yet, to give you the love that only a mother can give.

At first I couldn't the least understand how my letter *could* have seemed in any way "cross." It seems impossible to feel cross with *you*! I referred to the *précis* of it, in my letter-register, to see what I could possibly have said. And I think I see how it has been. It wasn't *cross*ness, my child: it was, I fancy, only my own *vanity*, and *greed*, that showed itself in the tone of my letter!

Here are the *précis* of the letters concerned.

75151 (to Mrs. Chataway) "If I invite Gertrude, will you let her come?"

75295 (from you) "Would like to come: but cannot leave home 'so soon' (I had named no date; does not say if she would be allowed)."

75304 (to you) "I don't understand 'so soon.' Had named no date."

The fact was (for I want to be quite candid, in return for *your* candour which is delightful to me) that my vanity had desired (what I hadn't the *slightest* right to expect!), first, the assurance that, but for your mother's illness, you would have been *allowed* to come; secondly, that, but for it, you would yourself have *liked* to come; thirdly, a loop-hole left for the *possibility* of your coming, in case I should invite you at a time when you *could* be spared. And I was foolish enough to read, in your declining the invitation before it had been given, and saying "so soon" before I had suggested any *date* for it, a sort of *haste* to put an end to the idea, and the possible existence of *other* objections, besides your mother's illness.

And now let me fully and freely admit that I should have *nothing whatever* to complain of, if there *had* been other objections. If your parents had felt "we cannot let her go and visit a single gentleman in that way," or if *you* had felt "on the whole, I do *not* particularly care to go," what earthly right should I have to feel aggrieved! It was simply a bit of *vanity* on my part, to fancy that *all* parents are willing to trust their daughters with me: and that *all* daughters are willing to come! And now, have I made it clear enough that the fault was *mine*, and mine *alone*? And that *you* had said nothing but what was nice, and kind, and right? If I had you here, I would ask you to give me a kiss, just to show you forgave my folly, and would now forget all about it.

I write all this from my sofa, where I have been a prisoner for about six weeks, with a bad knee (of the nature of "housemaid's knee") which I have to keep up in the horizontal position, and to paint with iodine. It is so nearly well now, that I hope very soon to begin taking walks again. Partly that, but chiefly the *intense* cold at Christmas-time (which made me, with my weak circulation, dread a railway-journey) made my doctor and me agree that I had better not go (as I have always done hitherto) to spend Christmas with my sisters at Guildford. So I had my Christmas-dinner, all alone, in my rooms here: and (pity me, Gertrude!) it *wasn't* a Christmassy dinner *at all*! I suppose— Here came an interruption: a child-friend (not 19 yet: a mere child, you know!) came in to see me, and has been here for half-an-hour or more. She is gone: and I resume the thread of my discourse. I suppose the cook thought I shouldn't care for either roast-beef or plum-pudding: so he sent me (he has general orders to send either fish and meat, or meat and pudding) some fried sole, and some roast mutton! Never, never have I dined, before, on Christmas-Day, without *plum-pudding*. Wasn't it sad?

I am taking advantage of all this abundant leisure and silence, to make a desperate effort to work off my arrears of unanswered letters. I began by making out a list of the people who are waiting (some of them from 5 to 10 years) for letters. There are more than 60 of them.

Now I think you must be content. This is a longer letter than most of them will get. Love to Olive. My clearest (or one of my clearest) memories of *her*, is of a little girl calling out "good night!" from her room, on hearing my step outside, and of your mother taking me in to see her in her bed and wish her good-night. I have a yet clearer memory (like a dream of 50 years ago!) of a little bare-legged girl in a sailor's jersey, who used to run up into my lodgings by the sea. But why should I trouble *you* with foolish reminiscences of *mine*, that *cannot* interest you?

> Yours always lovingly
> (and *not* crossly, *this* time),
> C. L. Dodgson

To Alice (Liddell) Hargreaves

Christ Church, Oxford
January 7, 1892

Dear Mrs. Hargreaves,

I have a favour to ask of you: so please put yourself into a complaisant frame of mind before you read any further. A friend of mine, who is in business involving ivory-carving, has had a lot of umbrella- and parasol-handles carved, representing characters in *Alice* and *Through the Looking-Glass*. I have just inspected a number of them: and, though nearly all are unsuited for use, by reason of having slender projections (hands, etc.) which would be quite sure to get chipped off, thus spoiling the artistic effect, yet I found *one* ("Tweedledum and Tweedledee") which might safely be used as a parasol-handle, without wearing out the life of the owner with constant anxiety.

So I want to be allowed to present, to the original Alice, a parasol with this as its handle – if she will graciously accept it, and will let me know what coloured silk she prefers, and whether she would like it to have a fringe. Wishing you and yours a very happy New Year, I am

Most sincerely yours,
C. L. Dodgson

To Gertrude Chataway

Christ Church, Oxford
February 28, 1892

You dear dear Child!

Though I am distracted with business, and am working nearly all day, I *will* spare a half-hour this morning to answer your sweet letter. You have my truest sympathy in all your troubles. The influenza has been all but universal: nearly all my family have been laid up with it: and my eldest sister (at Guildford) has not yet quite shaken off the attack of pleurisy which it left behind it. But what you tell me about your mother is a very *special* trouble, and is *very* sad to read of. What has happened is (I conclude from what you say) that the paralytic "stroke," which she had had before my last visit, has (perhaps with other "strokes" since) destroyed the working power of the brain. It must be a terrible trial for you all, to see such a change in one so near and dear to you: but, thank God, these "light afflictions" are but "for a moment,"[1] and will seem only like a bad dream of last night, when you meet her again in that brighter world, where there is no more disease to hamper the spirit, nor sorrow, nor sighing.

I suppose Mary* will have left you, by this time, for Vancouver, and you will have many cares, and be very busy: however, letters take only a few minutes to *read*, however long (*I* seem to spend half my working-time on it!) they may take to *write*.

I am once more allowed to walk a few miles every day: and my doctor quite holds out hopes that before long I may venture on my usual walks. There is a favourite round of mine, 18 miles altogether, that I am longing to do again. My College-friends are all too lazy (or too fat, or too old, or something) to come so far with me: but my doctor is young and vigorous: so *he* is going to be my companion, as soon as he thinks I can do it with prudence.

Just now I'm working hard at Common Room business. I have been Curator for 9 years: but the work takes a great deal of time that I *absolutely* need, for finishing some books before my powers fail; and I am hoping to be allowed to resign the office next month. And of course I want to hand over the business, to my successor, in perfect order. Once free of that, I hope to give all the best hours of the day, all this summer, to bringing out *Sylvie and Bruno Concluded*. I *suppose* I gave you the first volume: so I suppose I must (however reluctantly) send you the sequel!

Love to Olive, though no doubt she has forgotten me by this time.

It is sweet to think that you *would* come to me at Eastbourne if you *could*.

Yours very lovingly,
C. L. Dodgson

To William Warner

Christ Church, Oxford
March 12, 1892

Dear Warner,

Let me, at any rate, teach you the Rule I have added to the *Doublets* Puzzle, which is, I think, an improvement, in that it makes many Problems possible which previously were (like your "Iron-Lead" one) impossible. The new Rule is that you may, at any step, re-arrange the letters of the word, instead of introducing a new letter: but you may not do both in the *same* step.

```
IRON
ICON
COIN
CORN
CORD
LORD
LOAD
LEAD
```

Yours ever,
C.L.D.

* Another of Gertrude's sisters.

To Mary E. Manners

Christ Church, Oxford
April 1, 1892

Dear Miss Manners,

The *Alice* tin is indeed a *great* success.* Is it possible to multiply it to any extent in *duplicate*? I've not the least idea how such a thing could be done: they *look* as if all painted by hand. The box you sent was *not* sufficiently packed for a journey: it had received several bruises and indentations, in spite of the paste board: and, if ever I get your brother to take an order for a number of them, and to send them to my little friends, I should wish them to be packed in *wooden* boxes (for which of course I would pay: they might be quite rough, like packing-cases, and with lids *nailed* on, not hinged); but, before making up a list, I would be glad to know

(1) whether there is any *choice* of different sizes or shapes of boxes, or if they would all be duplicates of the one sent to me;

(2) what would be the cost of (say) 50 of them, packing included.

No: I haven't seen, or even heard of, the lines on *Alice* by Sir E. Arnold. I never read anything about myself or my books: but, if these lines are as nice as what *you* wrote about *Alice*, I will read them on your recommendation.

May I reprint your verses in a little book of odds and ends which I am putting together?

Rachel is indeed to be congratulated on having so unique a solo entrusted to her! And who is "Bob," who is to appear on a tin? A bird? Or a human being? Believe me

Very sincerely yours,
C. L. Dodgson

To Eleanora Thorne†

Christ Church, Oxford
April 27, 1892

Oh dear, oh dear, what vague creatures girls are! Here is Norah writing to me (who have undertaken to meet her in London) that she will arrive at

---

* Charles Manners, Mary Manners's brother, had, with Dodgson's permission, designed and manufactured a *Through the Looking-Glass* biscuit tin.

† Nellie Thorne was the daughter of actor Fred Thorne and the niece of actress Sarah Thorne. She was, at the time Dodgson wrote, a budding actress herself. She later married Hollywood film actor Gustav van Seyffertitz, acted on Broadway and in film with Douglas Fairbanks, Sr. Norah O'Neill was Dodgson's cousin, a friend of Nellie Thorne, who was also trying to make a career on the stage.

"Euston" on "Friday": but she names no *hour*: evidently she expects me to stand on that cheerless platform for 24 hours at a stretch. And, while I am still simmering in wrath at *this*, I get a letter from Nellie, telling me she is "going to play" in "a first piece" at the Vaudeville, but naming no *date*, and not giving the *name of the piece*, and adding "I hope if you come to Town while I am acting that you will come and see me": evidently *she* expects me to attend that theatre every night for the next few months, till she appears!

Now I'll give you a heap of good advice. When you ask a friend to come and see you act, state (in round numbers) the *year* in which you expect to appear, and give (within 15 letters) the initials of the *piece*. Also, if his name happens to be "Dodgson," don't omit the "g" in writing to him. Also, if he happens to live at an Oxford College, don't call it "Christ College" ("Christ's College" is at *Cambridge*), but either "Christ Church" or (the usual form) "Ch. Ch." Also, if you *are* reckless enough to send him "love," don't instantly cool down into "yours very sincerely." It's enough to make one shiver, and is nearly as bad as a letter I once got from a little girl (*she* was on the stage, too) ending "now, with best love, I remain, yours truly, Mary White." Also, when you've directed your letter to him, don't suddenly lose your temper, and hurl it to the ground, and trample on it with muddy boots! That has evidently been the fate of your last letter to me: and I've laid the envelope aside, as a memorandum of the sort of child *Nellie* is!

There! I've made you properly angry *this* time, *haven't* I? If ever you recover your temper again, please tell me what's the best way to get from Charing Cross to Ravenscourt Park Station: so that I may call, some fine afternoon when you are sure to be out, and leave my card.

With love,

Yours affectionately,
C. L. Dodgson

To *A. R. H. Wright*

Christ Church, Oxford
May 12, 1892

Dear Sir,

I thank you for your kind and candid letter, with the *principle* of which I am in hearty sympathy, though, as to the practical *application* of that principle, our views differ.

The main *principle*, in which I hope all Christians agree, is that we ought to abstain from *evil*, and therefore from all things which are *essentially* evil. This is one thing: it is quite a different thing to abstain from anything, merely because it is *capable* of being put to evil uses. Yet there are classes of Christians (whose *motives* I entirely respect), who advocate, on this ground only, total abstinence from

(1) the use of wine;
(2) the reading of novels or other works of fiction;
(3) the attendance at theatres;
(4) the attendance at social entertainments;
(5) the mixing with human society in any form.

All these things are *capable* of evil use, and are frequently so used, and, even at their best, contain, as do *all* human things, *some* evil. Yet I cannot feel it to be my duty, on that account, to abstain from any one of them.

I am glad to find that *you* do not advocate total abstinence from No. (2), which would have obliged you to return the book I sent to your little daughter. Yet *that* form of recreation has sunk to far more hideous depths of sin than has ever been possible for No. (3). Novels have been written, whose awful depravity would not be tolerated, on the stage, by any audience in the world. Yet, in spite of that fact, many a Christian parent would say "I do let my daughters read novels; that is, *good* novels; and I carefully keep out of their reach the *bad* ones." And so *I* say as to the theatres, to which I often take my young friends, "I take them to *good* theatres, and *good* plays; and I carefully avoid the *bad* ones." In this, as in all things, I seek to live in the spirit of our dear Saviour's prayer for his disciples: "I pray not that thou shouldest take them out of the world, but that thou shouldest keep them from the evil."

Yours, in all Christian sympathy,
C. L. Dodgson

To Mrs. N. H. Stevens

Christ Church, Oxford
June 1, 1892

Dear Mrs. Stevens,

I had better write all I want to say. If I called to say it, very likely I should find you surrounded by callers, and should have to leave much of it unsaid.

First, *many* thanks for again lending me Enid. She is one of the dearest of children. It is *good* for one (I mean, for one's spiritual life, and in the same sense in which reading the Bible is good) to come into contact with such sweetness and innocence.

Next, there are 5 things I want to write about.

(1) Five years ago, I asked Mrs. Earle to propitiate you, so that I might try to make friends with Winnie (an attempt that was, more or less, successful). *Now* I am asking you, in your turn, to perform the same kind office, and to propitiate Mrs. Gamlen and Mrs. Sidgwick, in order that I may try if I can add, to my *very* small list of child-friends here (which contained, till Saturday, *one* name only!), Ruth (I don't know if she has any sisters) and *Margie and sisters.* For a little bird has whispered to me that she has 2 elder sisters, and that *Rose* is *specially* lovable.

(2) I have at least *five* bags, and small portmanteaus, any one of which I could easily carry a mile. I think Winnie had better have a rather larger one than I named, and bring a second dress, which she might find convenient (e.g., if caught in a shower). I want her to take the dimensions of a folded dress, and then let me fetch her here to choose which bag, etc., to take. My minimum portmanteau will, I fancy, do much better than a bag.

(3) I want to know what pictures, etc., in London Winnie has seen. That I may plan our *morning* in town on the 8th.

(4) I am planning to bring Isa Bowman with us on Friday. Miss Lloyd (96 Holywell) will kindly give her a bed, but thinks 9 p.m. will be an inconvenient hour, in her small establishment, to provide *supper* on Friday night. We mean to leave town at 6.40 and reach Oxford 8.28. I'll take a cab (I can't carry *both* sets of luggage!) and we ought to reach you about 8¾. Could you give Supper to Isa and me? (All *I* take, at such an hour, is cold meat, bread and butter, and *tea*: not beer or wine).

(5) Will keep. Haste.

> Yours very sincerely,
> C.L.D.

To Mrs. N. H. Stevens

> Christ Church, Oxford
> June 4, 1892

My dear Mrs. Stevens,

One question I have forgotten to ask, that needs asking before I take Winnie to Guildford.

When there, I always use my bedroom as a sitting room also, and spend my morning there. I can't do my own reading and writing in the drawing-room, where visitors might at any moment come in. And when any young friend of mine is on a visit there, I like her to come and keep me company instead of sitting alone in the drawing-room (for my sisters are never there in the morning). My eldest sister allows this arrangement, *when she knows that the mother approves*: otherwise, if the young lady is to be regarded as under *her* chaperonage, she would consider it too unconventional to let her be alone with a single gentleman, and would limit her to the *drawing-room*.

So I always have to get distinct leave from the mother. Will you give it?

When would darling Enid like me to come and play Castle Croquet? I could come Monday, or Tuesday, or (with Isa) Saturday or following days. It wants *four* players, but *could* be reduced to *three*. I don't care whether I play myself or not. I could superintend just as well without playing. There had better not be more children than can join in *playing*: a child would find it dull to look on.

> Very sincerely yours,
> C. L. Dodgson

To Mrs. H. Beerbohm Tree

> The Chestnuts, Guildford
> June 9, 1892

Dear Mrs. Beerbohm Tree,

I am going to make the most shameless use of the friendliness with which you received us yesterday, by inflicting on you what may prove to be a long letter. (Still I have proved by actual trial that a letter, that takes an hour to *write*, takes only about 3 minutes to *read*!)

My hope is, to interest you in a certain cousin of mine, who is now in London, hoping, against hope, to get a theatrical engagement – something, however small: something to begin with, just to "get her head above water," and to make a beginning.

Please, then, kindly bear with me for a few minutes, while I tell you her history.

Her mother was a contemporary of mine, and I used to meet her, some 30 years ago, before she married. She married an Irish gentleman, a Mr. Quin: and they lived in Ireland for many years. Both he and she have been dead for some years, leaving 5 daughters, of whom one is married, and the other four live together near Liverpool. They have but little to live upon;

* On the previous April 30, Dodgson had seen the Beerbohm Trees play *Hamlet* at the Haymarket. "It was a real treat," he wrote in his diary. "Mrs. Tree was good as Ophelia."

and, last summer, Minna, the eldest, wrote to me asking advice. She said she had done a great deal of acting in private – that she believed she had some talent in that direction – and that, if she *could* turn her talent to account, she thought it would be her duty to try, in order to earn some money for herself and her sisters. I thought that, anyhow, she ought to do some work on the *real* stage, to begin with, and not rest only on the untrustworthy evidence of acting in drawing-rooms among admiring friends.

So I wrote to Miss S. Thorne about her, and it was arranged that she should join her Company for 6 months, as a pupil. That period ended about a month ago: and she had then played in a fairly varied series of parts, though of course all were very small parts.

When the Company came to Banbury, with a Pantomime, I went over from Oxford to see it. The only chance Minna got, in it, was in a dumb-show piece (*à la L'Enfant Prodigue*), made out of *Robert Macaire,* in which she was the wife. It seemed to me, though of course an amateur's opinion is worth *very* little, that she had some power of pathos, that she was *in* her part, and that she showed no consciousness of there being an audience. Also she seems to me to be a girl of courage and resolution, ready to face hard work and hard living. (She is about 24.) Also, what is surely an advantage over a very large number of would-be actresses, she is a *lady*: can look like a lady, *walk* like a lady, and, above all, *talk* like a lady. One sometimes sees a play, otherwise well acted, almost spoiled by the "lady" of the piece, who seems to be the kitchen-maid dressed-up in her mistress's clothes. Also (I think I've kept the best for the last, almost!) she is most distinctly *pretty*. I'm afraid that weighs, with a large number of play-goers, quite as much as good *acting*.

Of course she has her name down at several agents, and I have utilised (in the same reckless way as I am now doing *your* kind reception of me) my limited acquaintance among actors, managers, and dramatic critics.

Now for the favours I am (almost) counting on, from yourself.

First, will you let me bring Minna (by the way, her *stage*-name is "Norah O'Neill") to call on you? I should so much like you to see for yourself what she is like. Or, even if I were unable to come with her, I don't *quite* despair of your allowing me to send her to call by herself.

Secondly, will you put this letter by, for reference, and kindly bear the matter in mind, on the chance of something favourable occurring – some vacancy for an "understudy" in your own company, or some opportunity of naming her to some other manager having a vacancy, for which he might require a real lady.

Mr. Beerbohm Tree can not, of course, be expected, in the midst of the *host* of aspirants he must so constantly meet, to remember a single individual, however urgently recommended. But *you*, I imagine, are *not* obliged to interview all these people, and have *not* got your memory burdened with a dictionary of names: so that I have real hope that *you* (specially if I am permitted to bring her within the circle of your personal acquaintances) may remember, if ever a suitable time should come for so doing, the name of "Miss Norah O'Neill."

(Her present address is "160 Warwick Street, Pimlico": but a London address is of course liable to change. Anything for her, addressed to me at "Christ Church, Oxford" would be sure to find her.)

I *did* so enjoy our call, and the sight of your lovely little daughter. I almost think she and I might, under favourable circumstances, at last become friends ! I'll send her book from Oxford, whither I return tomorrow.

Sincerely yours,
C. L. Dodgson

To Charles Manners

Christ Church, Oxford
June 22, 1892

Dear Sir,

I am very much obliged to you for your generous offer dated April 11 of 50 *Looking-Glass* boxes, filled with biscuits, but would much rather not accept so large a present, which would be too like selling, for a valuable "consideration," the use of my name. But I would be happy to accept 5 more, in addition to the one you have sent me: and I would rather have them *empty*. They might be packed in *one* box, as I should convey them, by hand, to friends in Oxford.

If you will kindly let me know what the selling price will be, for *empty* boxes, and what the charge for packing each in a wooden case and sending by parcel post, I will then decide how many I would like to give away, and will send you a list of the addresses to which they should be sent.

The box, which you kindly wished me to send back for repair, is so slightly bruised that it really is not worth while to trouble about it. Believe me

Very truly yours,
C. L. Dodgson

To Mrs. W. Mallalieu

Christ Church, Oxford
July 1, 1892

Dear Mrs. Mallalieu,

Thanks for your letter. I shall be very glad to have Polly's company to church: and hope we may be allowed to read a little of the Bible together, as I love to do with my young friends.

"Straps" do not sound a good way of packing frocks without crushing. She will like to have one or two extra ones. Besides the one she comes in, which will do for walking, she might like one for such a thing as an evening concert, and perhaps a second morning one, in case of being caught in a shower. My little friend Isa Bowman is rather apt to dress in *gaudy* colours, which I don't much like, as it makes us too conspicuous: but I think I need not fear *that*, in *Polly's* case, after seeing how quietly and tastefully she was dressed, the day I had the pleasure of her society. It will be *very* little trouble to bring my small portmanteau (it is *very* small) and then she can bring frocks without any risk of creasing. Please send, with her, enough things for a *week*, at least. I don't like to *name* more than 3 days, to begin with. After that, one can judge whether she would like to go home or stay a little longer.

Mrs. Dyer, or her maid, will be able to give her *all* the help she can need, whether for dressing or undressing.

Of course any theatre-engagement would prevent, or would bring to an end, her visit. That is why I want to have her as *soon* as I can, while she is still un-engaged.

I don't see a chance of getting to Eastbourne till next Wednesday or Thursday: but, as soon as I am settled there, I will propose a day for fetching my newest little friend.

Very sincerely yours,
C. L. Dodgson

It is a great pity that theatre-companies use so much, of what God means to be our "day of *rest*," in travelling about: and I am glad to think that you and Polly are having, just now, plenty of Sundays that are *not* "spent in the train."

To his sister Mary

7 Lushington Road, Eastbourne
July 10, 1892

Dearest Mary,

Thanks for your tract. You were right in thinking I do *not* read tracts, usually. (Most of them are not worth it: they put commonplace thoughts into commonplace language.) And you were *also* right in thinking I *should* read yours. I like your treatment of the text, though it is only *expansion*, by filling in details: for that is just what uneducated readers (for whom I presume it is intended) need. But – if you won't mind a critical remark (perhaps the having done so much correcting for the Press has made me extra-sensitive) – you ought not to be content, in writing for *print*, with grammar and punctuation which would be a *little* slipshod, even in a letter. Good *English*, and graceful arrangement, are higher qualities, not attainable by *rule*, but only by having read much good English, and so having got a musical "ear," so to speak. But grammar and punctuation are matters of ordinary *rule*; and your tract, to put it mildly, is capable of improvement in both these particulars. If you like to send me a copy that I may mark, I will treat it as if I were correcting it for the Press; and then you will see what I mean.

I think *newspapers* are largely responsible for the bad English now used in books. How few novels of the day are written in correct English! To find any such, you must go back 50 years or more. That is one reason why I like reading the *older* novels – Scott's, Miss Austen's, Miss Edgeworth's, etc. – that the *English* is so perfect. We have one living novelist, whose English is *lovely* – Miss Thackeray. I have brought a volume of hers with me, to read a bit, now and then, and get my ear into *tune*, before going on with *Sylvie and Bruno Concluded*, which will be, I hope, my principal occupation for 3 months to come.

I haven't yet heard whether Polly Mallalieu can come with me on Wednesday. If not, I shall perhaps come *direct* to Guildford, and not round by London.

I'm sorry Mr. E. Allen has got into Parliament, as I fear he will do mischief there.

Ever yours affectionately,
C. L. Dodgson

Very glad you report so well of your '49.

To William Mallalieu

7 Lushington Road, Eastbourne
July 17, 1892

Dear Mr. Mallalieu,

Every day that I have your dear little daughter with me I am learning to love her more. I am sure I ought to be all the better for having the example before me of so sweet and tractable and loving and pure a character as I am sure hers is.

Partly on her account, and partly on yours, I wish to write on another matter – not one I *like* to write about: indeed I think it very likely that what I have to say will offend you: but I must run the risk of *that*, as I feel that it would be wrong in me to keep silence.

When I measured Polly yesterday, and told her she was 4ft. 10½ins. *without* her shoes, and that she was quite mistaken in thinking she was only 4 ft. 10 in. *with* them, she said, in the most innocent way, as if it was a perfectly unobjectionable thing, that perhaps you had said she was an inch shorter than she really was, in order to secure some engagement she was trying for. Now you must not be angry with her for having, in her innocence, told me this. I don't suppose she saw any harm in it: but to *me* it is *very* sad to think that any such teaching should be possible in her young life, when children learn good (and also evil) so readily. Perhaps you think I am making a fuss about a mere trifle: but *no* sin is a trifle in the sight of God: and a lie *is* a sin. (I know "lie" is an ugly name for it, and one very likely to give offence: but it is the *true* name.) Also, if you had got her that engagement, by means of that lie, you would most likely have also incurred the guilt of *theft*. If some other child had thereby *lost* the engagement (some child who would have got it, had Polly's height been truthfully stated), you would have been guilty of *robbing* that child of valuable property, just as truly as if you had taken her purse.

Please do not suppose I am saying all this as if I were looking down from a height, on one whom I regard as a sinner, while regarding myself as a good man. Most truly, I feel my own sinfulness more strongly than I could easily say in words: but I think, the more one feels one's own sin, and the *wonderful* goodness of God who will forgive so much, the more one longs to help others to escape the shame and misery one has brought on one's-self.

Besides the fact, that to try to get engagements dishonestly is, for *yourself*, a sin in God's sight, you have the far stronger motive, for avoiding it, that it is to teach your innocent child to think lightly of sin. And, just as the little brook, that looks so trifling if you see it at its source, becomes a great river further on, so the beginning of evil – the regarding falsehood and cheating as mere trifles – which your example may be introducing into your child's life, may become, in future years, the cause of sin and misery for her, which you would (I hope) be ready to give your life to save her from.

I beg you, most earnestly, to forgive my boldness in saying all this, and to resolve, if only for Polly's sake, that any engagement you ever get for her shall be got *truthfully* and honestly, so that you may hope for God's blessing on it.

Very sincerely yours,
C. L. Dodgson

To William Mallalieu

7 Lushington Road, Eastbourne
July 19, 1892

Dear Mr. Mallalieu,

It was to *you*, not to Mrs. Mallalieu, that I addressed my letter, written in consequence of Polly's remark "I think" (or "I believe": I forget which she said) "that Papa took an inch off my height, because he wanted to get me an engagement." Had I been writing to your *wife*, I should probably have tried to express myself more gently: but, writing as man to man, it seemed to me that plain speaking was best.

Most likely Polly has *heard* of such tricks being played (I fear they are *very* common, in all lines of business), and so fancied *that* was the explanation of what was really (as I am *most* happy to know) a mistake.

Now let me express, as strongly as I can, *two* things I feel about it.

The first is, that I most deeply *regret* all the pain my letter has given, both to your wife and to yourself.

The second is, that I most sincerely *rejoice* that (after several times almost deciding to say nothing about it) I at last said to myself that I *ought* to write that letter. Just consider what the result would have been if I had *not* written. I should have gone on in the full belief that Polly's father was one of those who think nothing of the difference between truth and falsehood, and that Polly herself was in danger of learning the same indifference. It would have been, for years to come, a dark cloud over all my thoughts about that dear child. I cannot tell you what a relief it is to know that I may lay aside all such fears about her, and to know that her parents do feel the value of *truth*, and will bring her up as a *truthful* child.

I pass over, as it seems best to do, all that Mrs. Mallalieu has said about my letter being "unjust," "uncharitable," etc. She no doubt wrote in a moment of displeasure, not knowing how completely I was *obliged*, by the evidence then before me, to write as I did: and she may be sure I shall think no more about those words.

There is *one* sentence that I think, for the sake of the theatrical profession, I had better reply to. Mrs. Mallalieu says "had I not been a member of the theatrical profession, I venture to think I should have been spared such humiliation." Please let me assure her she could hardly make a greater mistake than to think that I regard the theatrical profession as less truthful than other professional people, or less truthful than non-professional people. I have a *very high* opinion of theatrical people. Possibly my acquaintance with them is too limited to judge by, but those I know are so honourable and estimable in character, that it inclines me to rank the whole profession very high indeed. The only memory I have, of detecting any friend of mine in telling *me* a direct falsehood, was in the case of a lady who did not belong to the theatrical, or any other, profession. It is one of the saddest memories of my life: and my feeling was "now I can never again be *sure* that you are telling me the truth: we cannot be friends any longer!"

With kindest regards to Mrs. Mallalieu, I am

Very sincerely yours,
C. L. Dodgson

Polly sends "best love, and I'm sorry Auntie's going away before I can see her." I expect to bring her to you by about 4 on Thursday afternoon.

To Isabella Bowman

7 Lushington Road, Eastbourne
[?July 31, 1892]

My own darling Isa,

The full value of a copy of the French *Alice* is £45: but, as you want the "cheapest" kind, and as you are a great friend of mine, and as I am of a very noble, generous disposition, I have made up my mind to a *great* sacrifice, and have taken £3 10s. 0d. off the price. So that you do not owe me more than £41 10s. od., and this you can pay me, in gold or bank-notes, *as soon as you ever like*. Oh dear! I wonder why I write such nonsense! Can you explain to me, my pet, how it happens that when I take up my pen to write a letter to *you* it won't write sense? Do you think the rule is that when the pen finds it has to write to a nonsensical good-for-nothing child, it sets to work to write a nonsensical good-for-nothing letter? Well, now I'll tell you the real truth. As Miss Kitty Wilson is a dear friend of yours, of course she's a *sort* of a friend of mine. So I thought (in my vanity) "perhaps she would like to have a copy" from the author, "with her name written in it." So I've sent her one – but I hope she'll understand that I do it because she's *your* friend, for, you see, I had never *heard* of her before: so I wouldn't have any other reason.

I'm still exactly "on the balance" (like those scales of mine, when Nellie says "it won't weigh!") as to whether it would be wise to have my pet Isa down here! how *am* I to make it weigh, I wonder? Can you advise any way to do it? I'm getting on grandly with *Sylvie and Bruno Concluded*. I'm afraid you'll expect me to give you a copy of it? Well, I'll see if I have one to spare. It won't be out before Easter-tide, I'm afraid.

I wonder what sort of condition the book is in that I lent you to take to America? (*Laneton Parsonage*, I mean). Very shabby, I expect. I find lent books *never* come back in good condition. However, I've got a second copy of this book, so you may keep it as your own. Love and kisses to any one you know who is lovely and kissable.

Always your loving Uncle,
C.L.D.

To Princess Alice

7 Lushington Road, Eastbourne
August 15, 1892

My dear Alice,

There's just a chance that this note will get to you before you've quite forgotten me. Somebody asked me if they might copy some of the *Alice* pictures on what they call "Children's Tins." Did you ever hear of such things? I never did, till now. They say children use them to keep biscuits in or sweets, or anything. But I think you can find a much better use for the one I'm sending you. Whenever Charlie is very naughty, you can just pop him in, and shut the lid! Then he'll soon be good. I'm sending one for him, as well: so now you know what will happen when you're naughty! I've written your names on your boxes, that you may know which is which. Please excuse the writing: it's not very easy to write on tin, you know.

I send my best love, for you to divide with your brother: and I would advise you to give two-thirds to him, and take three-quarters for yourself.

Yours affectionately,
C. L. Dodgson

To Mrs. A. S. Walford

7 Lushington Road, Eastbourne
August 17, 1892

Dear Mrs. Walford,

I hope I am man enough to "own up," as the Americans say, when I have made a mistake, and to beg pardon for it, which I sincerely do.

It looks, no doubt, an inordinate piece of vanity, to have supposed that it was because of books of mine that you had wished to know me: but I may plead, as an excuse, the actual fact that people are *constantly* doing it: for years I have suffered from applications, from perfect strangers, who persist in ignoring my "anonymous" position – some seeking autographs, some interviews, some personal acquaintance. I have had to keep a printed form ready, and constantly use it, in answer to such people, stating that I acknowledge *no* connection with books not bearing my name.

I will give myself the pleasure of calling again, before long, and of making sure that we are still on friendly terms: but I must ask you to excuse me, on quite other grounds, from accepting any *definite* invitiation, even to tea. For years I have retired from "Society," of which I am weary, and find neither a pleasure nor a profit: and I decline *all* invitations without exception. I have passed the age when the years ahead seem infinite: I feel that the number of working hours, now left, is very finite indeed: and I would like to give all that is left, of time and brain-power, to *work*. I may not even be able to say "Lord, thy pound hath made five pounds": but trust not to have kept it simply wrapped up in a napkin.

Very truly yours,
C. L. Dodgson

To Enid Stevens

Christ Church, Oxford
December 12, 1892

I wonder *what* it is, my darling, that you think you have "found out"? You have sent me 7 beautifully-written sums; and they all come to £12.18.11. But you don't say *what* you have "found out" from them! Do you think you have found out that *every* sum of money, that you could possibly think of, *must* come to that? If *that's* what you think, suppose we try it some other way. Suppose you walked out one day, and met 7 men, one after another; and suppose every one of them had a stick in his hand – would you go home and say to your mother "I've *found out* something about men in Oxford – every man always has a stick in his hand!" And *then* suppose that, next time you walked out, you met a man with an umbrella! What *would* you think about the rule that you thought you had found out? Now go back to the money-puzzle. Suppose that, the very next example you tried, it came to £10.15.9. Would you *still* say "I have found out your puzzle"?

Now here's another puzzle for you. Will your mother lend me a daughter next Friday? In the usual funny way, of course. What? Don't you know what "the usual funny way" is? Well, *this* is the way your mother lends a daughter. She says "you may come to my house, and you may sit there as long as you like, and you may have her on your knee, and you may kiss her once in every half-hour (mind you don't do it oftener than that); but *you mustn't take her out of the house.*"

Now, suppose you went to Janet (by the way, I'm *so* sorry to hear that you've quarrelled again!) and said "Janet, dear, will you lend me an umbrella?" And suppose she said "yes, Enid, darling. Here's my umbrella for you; and you may sit here as long as you like, and you may hug it in your arms, and you may kiss it once in every twenty minutes (mind you don't do it oftener than that): but *you mustn't take it out of the house.*" If she was to say *that*, I wonder what you would think? I'm afraid you would quarrel with her worse than ever!

Your loving friend,
C. L. Dodgson

To Charlotte Rix

Christ Church, Oxford
December 14, 1892

My dear Lottie,

In May, 1891 (how time *does* run away!), I wrote to Miss Ellen Terry about you, touching as lightly as possible on the many glaring defects in your character, bringing forward, as plausibly as I could, the few commendable qualities I have been able to discover, and petitioning for leave for you to call.

This produced no result whatever – unless you reckon "silence" as something. And this, being merely the absence of sound, is about as near to being a *thing* as vacuum is to being a *substance*.

However, having to write, the other day, on another matter, I mentioned *en passant*, my ancient letter about you, and that no reply had ever reached me. Now I'll copy for you what she says in her letter received this morning –

"Perhaps little 'Lottie' would like to come and see *King Lear*? If so (in about 2 weeks time) I would send my Box, and she might bring some young friends, and then I would see them all in my room after the play was over."

I'm so glad she has said all this, as I feel sure you will be pleased. She has a real kind heart.

Now, if I might venture to advise, I would *not*, if I were you, take so full an advantage of her offer as to take a *lot* of young friends. I fancy if you were to read "one" for "some," and to go with *Edith* only, you would find it quite enough. If it would make it any easier for you, I *might* be able to go with you: but I'm not very hopeful of this.

If you wish to go, you had better name as large a period as you can, within which you could go, any day that she could spare the Box: and then I would write – unless you would like to write yourself. Do so, by all means, if you like. I'm sure she would take it kindly. Her address is "22 Barkston Gardens, Earl's Court." With very kind remembrances to your parents, I am

Always yours affectionately,
C. L. Dodgson

P.S. When does Edith come to you?

To Charlotte Rix

Christ Church, Oxford
December 22, 1892

My dear Lottie,

I'm *so* glad Miss Terry has written to you, and that I have been of some service to you in this matter: and I shall be most happy to be of *further* service, by procuring you a ticket of admission to Hanwell,* as soon as you are ready to go.

On second thoughts, I had better *not* come to the Lyceum with you. Of course I should *not* be admissible to Miss Terry's dressing-room: and she evidently contemplates your coming with *girl*-friends only. I shall be much interested to hear all about it. My address will be "The Chestnuts, Guildford," till January 10th.

You will very likely meet *another* "Edie" when you go: *viz.*, Edith Wardell. You may if you like (as of course you will find it *very* difficult to think of anything to say!) give her my love – and ditto to Miss Ellen Terry.

Best love to my silent old friend.

Yours affectionately,
C.L.D.

To E. Gertrude Thomson

Christ Church, Oxford
February 27, 1893

My dear Miss Thomson,

Your letter was most welcome. While you are doing so much for *my* pleasure, it were churlish not to try to do something for *yours*: so, though I am writing "Logic" about 6 hours a day, I have spared the time to copy out these two little Acrostic poems for you. I won't bar you from showing them to members of your own family; but please let them be seen by no one else, for the present. I'm going to apply to the Duchess for leave to print them, along with many other such things written for other children: till I get that leave, I can only show them to special friends. The allusion to "pistols" refers to my having taught the children, when they came to my rooms, how to fold paper into (so called) "pistols," which will make a *real* bang, to the great delight of children.

As to your letter:

In the "bower" picture, surely the elder child has the form of a *girl*?

* A lunatic asylum.

It is not an easy subject to discuss with a lady, but perhaps to a lady-*artist* I may mention, without offence, that the breasts are those of a girl, not a boy. To the best of my recollection, you have given them just the curvature which I noticed in the last child-model (Maud Howard, aged 14) whom I had the privilege of trying to copy in Mrs. Shute's studio. If you would add to the hair, and slightly refine the wrist and ankles, it would make a beautiful girl. I had much rather have *all* the fairies *girls*, if you wouldn't mind. For I confess I do *not* admire naked *boys* in pictures. They always seem to me to need *clothes*: whereas one hardly sees why the lovely forms of girls should *ever* be covered up!

If ever you fancy any of the pictures look too like real *children*, then by all means give them wings.

I shall be very grateful to be allowed to see future drawings in the "pencil" stage, when any alterations can easily be made.

One whole hour has gone since I began copying those verses! Now I must really return to my Logic.

Very sincerely yours,
C. L. Dodgson

The "bower" picture from *Three Sunsets*

To Edith Miller

Christ Church, Oxford
April 9, 1893

My dear Edith,

It was a *great* pleasure to get your letter, just a month ago: and I thank you heartily for writing it. And please don't measure my feelings by my promptness in answering it. I fear I keep all my friends waiting a long time for letters they may be expecting: and I have had it in my mind for some time to write to you again – if only to tell you that I have not forgotten my promise to pray for you. I have done so ever since, morning and evening. There are a good many names that I specially mention: and yours has been one. Absence of temptation is no doubt sometimes a blessing: and it is one I often thank God for. But one has to remember that it is only a short breathing-space. The temptation is sure to come again: and the very freedom from it brings its own special danger – of laying down the weapons of defence, and ceasing to "watch and pray": and then comes the sudden surprise, finding us all unprepared, and ready to yield again. I speak my own experience, the result of many many failures in my own life: and I *am* truly thankful when God grants me the happiness of helping others (as I think he has granted in *your* case) in the battle we all have to fight. I can see no harm in your being happy in your present surroundings, and in having found some genuine work to do for God and for others. And I *don't* call your letter a selfish one; because you know I *asked* you to write it all about yourself.

A week ago I had a very happy day in town, taking a child-friend from here, aged nearly eleven – the first time I have been trusted with her. Her mother brought her to meet me at the station, about 5 minutes to 9 *a*.m.: and I delivered her up to her mother again at 5 minutes to 9 *p*.m. So I had her society for exactly 12 hours. She *seemed* to enjoy her day thoroughly: I know *I* did! There seems a fair chance now of her being allowed to come with me to Eastbourne, in which case I hope to be able to introduce her to you. She is one of my child-friends with whom I can feel at my ease – not one whose shyness makes *me* shy also, and makes both of us wretched! We went to Edwin Long's pictures, to the Cyclorama of "Egypt" at the Niagara Hall, to luncheon with Lord and Lady Maud Wolmer and their children, and then to the Matinée of that delightful play *Liberty Hall* – which I think Ruth enjoyed most of all.

Kindest regards to your mother: love and a kiss to May; and ditto ditto to yourself, from

Your loving friend,
C. L. Dodgson

To Mrs. G. J. Burch *

Christ Church, Oxford
May 20, 1893

Dear Mrs. Burch,

In discussing any scientific questions, it is always best to begin with a few *axioms*, i.e. propositions that cannot be disputed. Here are my axioms.

(1) When I travel, with only so much luggage as I can carry for short distances, I save a good many odd shillings that would otherwise go on cabs and porters (e.g. I can cross London by Metropolitan R.W. instead of cab).

(2) "Though on pleasure I am bent, I have a frugal mind."

(3) When, lately, I took Winifred Stevens to town, one Saturday, and on to my sisters' house at Guildford for the Sunday, I lent her a small portmanteau, each half of which is (measured inside) $16 \times 11 \times 3$. In this she managed to pack an evening dress, and all else needed for her visit. And this I easily carried, on our return, from the Station to Canterbury Road, and similar distances at Guildford, etc.

(4) Had it been too small, I could have lent her one (*she* having nothing convenient on hand) each half being $19 \times 11 \times 4$: and this also I carry easily.

That is enough of axioms, I think.

Now, I *may* be able, on June 3rd, or else the 10th (I do not yet know which) to make a similar expedition with *you*, if you can come. Do you think one or both of those days will be free? And could Irene & Co. spare you from Saturday morning till Monday evening?

If you can come (as I *much* hope you will be able) could you manage with that amount of luggage? (If not, never mind.)

* Two months before he wrote this letter, Dodgson met a new child acquaintance, Irene Burch, at the home of some friends he had called on. Through Irene, he then met her sister, Dorothy, and their mother. This is one instance where Dodgson's friendship with the mother surpassed that with the daughters. Mrs. Burch became a true friend of his, went on outings to London with him, and chaperoned some of his visits with younger friends.

You would, I hope, allow me to take my usual course of paying *all* expenses, including your cab down to the Station: for I should want you to meet me there at 9 a.m., and could not conveniently come for you so early.

I had almost forgotten to say what my Saturday plans would be. They would include pictures (either R.A. or New) and a Matinée of *The Merchant of Venice*. Believe me

Sincerely yours,
C. L. Dodgson

To his nephew Bertram Collingwood

[Paddington Station] Great Western Railway [London]
June 17, 1893

My dear Bertram,

Many thanks for sending me so truly welcome a piece of news. I sincerely rejoice to think that your undergraduate life at Cambridge has so entirely matched Stuart's at Oxford, not only in the negative quality of being *sans peur et sans reproche*, but also in having won real honour in the Schools. My chief ground of satisfaction, however, is (as I doubt not it is *yours* also) the thought of the *deep* joy you will have thus given to your father and mother by your success, and by the proof it gives that your career has been one of hard and steady *work*.

It is pleasant to think that I have helped a little, in the matter of £.s.d., to enable you to have this career: but all would have been in vain if there had not been supplied by *you*, the far more important item of *work*.

May it prove a happy omen of much success in the future !

Always your affectionate Uncle,
C. L. Dodgson

To his cousin Dorothea Wilcox

Christ Church, Oxford
June 27, 1893

My dear Dora,

I don't know who that lady was, whom I met at the Club but I observed that, when we talked of Miss Ellen Terry ("Mrs. Wardell"), she put on a *sour* expression; and I think it very likely that, after I had gone, she would tell you the story, as if on good authority, that I am constantly hearing, of the (alleged) immoral life of Miss E. T. and Mr. Irving. It is to me simply *astounding*, the wicked recklessness with which people repeat scandalous reports about actresses, without taking the *slightest* trouble to verify them. I have more than once investigated such stories, and have found them to be (as I *know*, on perfectly good evidence, *this* one to be) simply *false*.

If the lady *did* tell you this story, will you kindly accept *me* as decidedly a more competent witness on the subject than she is: and, if you hear the story told again, will you kindly say that you have reliable authority for declaring it to be *absolutely* false?

I know all Miss Ellen Terry's history, and, knowing it, am proud to still regard her as my *friend*. I have introduced to her several girl-friends – always first telling the *mother* of the girl the whole history, and asking leave to introduce the daughter; and, in every case, leave was given.

Always yours affectionately,
C. L. Dodgson

To Gertrude Chataway

7 Lushington Road, Eastbourne
August 30, 1893

My dear old friend,

I think there is no higher privilege given us in this life than the opportunity of doing something for *others*, and of bearing one another's burdens, and praying, one for another. And I believe, and *realise* it more as life goes on, that God hears, and answers, our prayers for *others*, with a special love and approval that does not belong to prayers offered for *ourselves*. In that hope I pray for you, and your father and sister, to give you in your sorrow the peace and strength that only He can give. And you have my true deep sympathy, dear child, in your present trial.*

Your loving old friend,
Charles L. Dodgson

P.S. Of course I pray *also* for your dear mother, that God will be with her in these her last hours, and then take her to that rest that remaineth for his children.

---

* Gertrude's mother died on the day that Dodgson wrote this letter.

To Enid Stevens

7 Lushington Road, Eastbourne
September 13, 1893

Dearest Enid,

I've had it in my mind, for ever so long, "Enid would like to hear about your adventures at Eastbourne," and I've been *meaning* to write you a letter. But I *am* so busy, dear child! *Sylvie and Bruno Concluded* takes up (when I'm in the humour for it, which I generally *am*, just now) 6 or 8 hours a day. And there are letters that *must* be written. And a new thing has come to take up my time: last Sunday I preached the first sermon I ever preached in Eastbourne, though I have come here for 17 summers (so my landlady says): and next Sunday I am to preach another: and these take up a lot of time, thinking them over.

But the *great* difficulty is, that *adventures don't happen*! Oh, how *am* I to make some happen, so as to have something to tell to my darling Enid? Shall I go out, and knock down some man in the road? (I should choose a little weak one, you know.) *That* would indeed be an adventure, both for him and for me. And *my* share of it would be the being walked off by the policeman, and locked up in a cell at the police-station. Then my adventures *could* be written to you. Only *I* couldn't do it, you know. It would have to be done by the policeman. "Honord Mis, You will be pleazd to no that Mr. Dodgson is now kiking at the dore of his sell. I tuk him sum bred and water jus now: but he sed he woodnt have eny. He sed as how heed just had his diner." How would you like *that* sort of thing, my Enid?

Well, here is a little adventure. I was taking a walk the other day, and I came on a boy and girl about 12 and 10 years old; and they seemed to be in some trouble; and they were carefully examining her finger. So I said "Is anything the matter?" And they told me she had just been stung by a wasp. So I told them to put some hartshorn to it, as soon as they got home, and that would take away all the pain. And I gave them a tiny lesson in chemistry, and explained that, if you mix an acid and an alkali, they fizz up, and the acid loses its acidity: and that wasp's poison is an *acid*, and hartshorn is an *alkali*, When I got home, I thought "Now I won't be so badly provided, next time I come across a stung little girl" (or "a little stung girl" – which is the best way to say it?) so I bought myself a little bottle of strong ammonia (which is better than hartshorn): and I put it in my pocket when I go a walk. And now, if it happens again, I can make the little girl happy in a minute.

But *no* little girl has ever got stung since, that *I* have met with. Isn't it a sad sad pity?

Now here's *another* adventure for you. I have a very dear girl-friend here (about twenty-five, so she's a *little* older than you): and the other day I took her in the steamer to Brighton. It's about 2½ hours' voyage: and it was deliciously rough: and we pitched up and down all the way. And every now and then a wave struck the bow, and a lot of it splashed over the deck. At first there was in the bow a young man (a passenger) and my friend (May Miller) and me. Soon the young man got so wet, that *he* fled. May bore 2 or 3 more shower-baths, and then she said *she* was getting drenched. So we went back to the middle of the steamer: and all the passengers, up on the "bridge" and the upper deck, clapped their hands, in honour of the brave young lady. However, *I* was so wet by this time that I had got reckless: so I went back to the bow, and climbed up to the very point, and sat there, riding up and down *grandly* over the waves, and every now and then getting a wave all over me. I turned my back to the side from which they came: and it felt very much as if some one gave me a heavy blow with a soft hearthrug! And then the warm water would come *pouring* round my ears, and over my shoulders, and, as it flew away in the wind, I saw the most *lovely* little rainbows in the spray: for the sun was shining bright all the time. When we got to Brighton, I was wet to the skin, and May nearly as bad. We *had* meant to go and have tea with my sister, who lives in Brighton: but we decided it wouldn't be wise to risk a chill, by going into a house *at all*. It wanted about an hour to the time of the train back to Eastbourne: and we spent it walking up and down in the sun and wind, and trying to get dry. It didn't take long enough, in the train, to get chilled: so neither of us took cold. When we got to my lodgings, May thought at first she had better go straight home (about a mile further) in order to get dry things. But I told her she had far better dine with me, and I was sure Mrs. Dyer could lend her enough clothes to dine in, and would dry her own things while we dined. So she agreed, and came to dinner dressed up in clothes lent her by the maid! (Mrs. Dyer's things would have been too large.) And she *did* look so pretty in the maid's Sunday-gown! It might have been made for her, it fitted her so beautifully.

"What stupid little adventures!" I hear Enid muttering to herself. Well, I can't help it, my pet. These are *true*. If I were to *invent* some, why, they wouldn't be *ad*-ventures, you know. They would be *in*-ventures: and that's *quite* a different thing.

Well, my darling, I've been writing to you for 3 quarters of an hour, and I think I must go a walk now, to Beachy Head, my favorite walk. I hope you'll like getting it (just a *little* bit, you know: of *course* I don't expect you to like it *much*).

Heaps of love, and 3 kisses (isn't that our regular number?). And ditto ditto to Winifred. And kindest remembrances to your Mother. And respectful compliments to Scamp.

Your very loving old friend,
Charles L. Dodgson

To Margaret Bowman

7 Lushington Road, Eastbourne
September 17, 1893

Oh, you naughty, naughty little culprit! If only I could fly to Fulham with a handy little stick (ten feet long and four inches thick is my favourite size) how I would rap your wicked little knuckles. However, there isn't much harm done, so I will sentence you to a very mild punishment – only one year's imprisonment. If you'll just tell the Fulham policeman about it, he'll manage all the rest for you, and he'll fit you with a nice comfortable pair of handcuffs, and lock you up in a nice cosy dark cell, and feed you on nice dry bread and delicious cold water.

But how badly you *do* spell your words! I *was* so puzzled about the "sacks full of love and baskets full of kisses!" But at last I made out why, of course, you meant "a sack full of *gloves*, and a basket full of *kittens*!" Then I understood what you were sending me. And just then Mrs. Dyer came to tell me a large sack and a basket had come. There was such a miawing in the house, as if all the cats in Eastbourne had come to see me! "Oh, just open them please, Mrs. Dyer, and count the things in them!"

So in a few minutes Mrs. Dyer came and said, "500 pairs of gloves in the sack and 250 kittens in the basket."

"Dear me! That makes 1000 gloves! four times as many gloves as kittens! It's very kind of Maggie, but why did she send so many gloves? for I haven't got 1000 *hands*, you know, Mrs. Dyer."

And Mrs. Dyer said, "No, indeed, you're 998 hands short of that!"

However the next day I made out what to do, and I took the basket with me and walked off to the parish school – the *girls'* school, you know – and I said to the mistress, "How many little girls are there at school today?"

"Exactly 250, sir."

"And have they all been *very* good all day?"

"As good as gold, sir."

So I waited outside the door with my basket, and as each little girl came out, I just popped a soft little kitten into her hands! Oh what joy there was! The little girls went all dancing home, nursing their kittens, and the whole air was full of purring! Then, the next morning, I went to the school, before it opened, to ask the little girls how the kittens had behaved in the night. And they all arrived sobbing and crying, and their faces and hands were all covered with scratches, and they had the kittens wrapped up in their pinafores to keep them from scratching any more. And they sobbed out, "The kittens have been scratching us all night, all the night."

So then I said to myself, "What a nice little girl Maggie is. *Now* I see why she sent all those gloves, and why there are four times as many gloves as kittens!" and I said loud to the little girls, "Never mind, my dear children, do your lessons *very* nicely, and don't cry any more, and when school is over, you'll find me at the door, and you shall see what you shall see!"

So, in the evening, when the little girls came running out, with the kittens still wrapped up in their pinafores, there was I, at the door, with a big sack! And, as each little girl came out, I just popped into her hand two pairs of gloves! And each little girl unrolled her pinafore and took out an angry little kitten, spitting and snarling, with its claws sticking out like a hedgehog. But it hadn't time to scratch, for, in one moment, it found all its four claws popped into nice soft warm gloves! And then the kittens got quite sweet-tempered and gentle, and began purring again!

So the little girls went dancing home again, and the next morning they came dancing back to school. The scratches were all healed, and they told me "The kittens *have* been good!" And, when any kitten wants to catch a mouse, it just takes off *one* of its gloves; and if it wants to catch *two* mice, it takes off two gloves; and if wants to catch *three* mice, it takes off *three* gloves; and if it wants to catch *four* mice, it takes off all its gloves. But the moment they've caught the mice, they pop their gloves on again, because they know we can't love them without their gloves. For, you see, "gloves" have got "love" *inside* them – there's none *outside*!

So all the little girls said, "Please thank Maggie and we send her 250 *loves*, and 1000 *kisses* in return for her 250 kittens and her 1000 gloves!!" And I told them [they had the numbers of loves and kisses] in the wrong order! and they said they hadn't.

Your loving old Uncle,
C.L.D.

Love and kisses to Nellie and Emsie.

To his sister Mary

7 Lushington Road, Eastbourne
September 21, 1893

My dearest Mary,

It is indeed a welcome hearing – the excellent report you give of your husband's health. And I *hope* you are having better weather than we are having *here* (it has been raining hard for hours), in order that he may get plenty of open air.

I *do* like getting such letters as yours. I think all you say about my girl-guests is most kind and sisterly, and most entirely proper for you to write to your brother. But I don't think it at all advisable to enter into any controversy about it. There is no reasonable probability that it would modify the views either of you or of me. I will say a few words to explain my views: but I have no wish whatever to have "the last word": so please say anything you like afterwards.

You and your husband have, I think, been very fortunate to know so little, by experience, in your own case or in that of your friends, of the wicked recklessness with which people repeat things to the disadvantage of others, without a thought as to whether they have grounds for asserting what they say. I have met with a good deal of utter misrepresentation of that kind. And another result of my experience is the conviction that the opinion of "people" in general is absolutely worthless as a test of right and wrong. The only two tests I now apply to such a question as the having some particular girl-friend as a guest are, first, my own *conscience*, to settle whether I feel it to be entirely innocent and right, in the sight of God; secondly, the *parents* of my friend, to settle whether I have their *full* approval for what I do. You need not be shocked at my being spoken against. *Anybody*, who is spoken about at all, is *sure* to be spoken against by *somebody*: and any action, however innocent in itself, is liable, and not at all unlikely, to be blamed by *somebody*. If you limit your actions in life to things that *nobody* can possibly find fault with, you will not do much!

Sylvie and Bruno Concluded goes on fairly well. I *think* it will be out by Christmas. But it won't do to "whistle" *much*, while still as deep in "the wood" as I am at present.

September 22, Weather has quite changed today, and Gertrude has gone off for the morning, having Edith Miller as her companion, to finish a little picture she is making of a bit of the coast.

Ever your affectionate brother,
C. L. Dodgson

To E. Gertrude Thomson

7 Lushington Road, Eastbourne
September 21, 1893

My dear Miss Thomson,

I must be very brief, to catch the post. My girl-friend's sister, Mrs. Bell, 98 Portland Place, has a little girl Cynthia, aged 6, who it seems would be a lovely model for you: and there is every hope that you would be allowed to draw her nude. Please call soon, and see Mrs. Bell, and settle about it. Whether she would have to be drawn at home, or could be fetched to you, can be settled hereafter. The great thing is for you and Mrs. Bell to get to know each other.

Best take this note with you, and send it up for Mrs. Bell to read. It will do as an introduction. Best call between 2 and 3.

Very sincerely yours,
C. L. Dodgson

To Mrs. C. F. Moberly Bell

7 Lushington Road, Eastbourne
September 22, 1893

Dear Mrs. Bell,

I feel that I really *must* write to thank you for the great friendliness you have so kindly expressed towards me, who am (except for Gertrude:* I grant that that makes a *great* difference!) an entire stranger to you. I will certainly take an early opportunity of calling to make the personal acquaintance of you and yours: and I will give you due notice of the proposed call.

Generally speaking, to have people much praised, to one, before one sees them, prejudices me a little *against* them: and I doubt if I am very peculiar in this: it's more or less a human weakness, I think. But what *Gertrude* tells me I believe, pretty much as if I had seen it myself: so I shall come with a decidedly *favourable* bias in my mind: and when once the mind gets warped in that way, it takes some trouble to bend in the other way. I wonder if you and your children could invent a little bias in my favour? It would add to the chances of our meeting being a pleasant one.

There is another thing I really must send you my *special* thanks for: it is a thing that I consider quite an extraordinary favour, under the circum-

* Gertrude Chataway, Mrs. Bell's sister.

stances – that you should have expressed a willingness to let your little Cynthia be drawn by my friend Miss Gertrude Thomson in the *very* unusual character of a nude model. Of *course* I understand that such an expression is only provisional, and that it entirely depends on what you think of Miss Thomson, after you have seen her. In order that no time might be lost, I sent her a hasty note last night, urging her to call on you as soon as she could. If, when you have seen her, you do really give her the permission (*and* if Cynthia herself is perfectly willing to be so drawn – a condition that I regard as *absolutely* essential in any such matter) I am sure Miss Thomson will regard herself as a highly-privileged artist. And I am also sure that *I* shall regard myself as a highly-privileged person, in being permitted to include in the book, which Miss Thomson is illustrating for me, so very exceptional a picture (or possibly pictures) as that (or those) which she might thus obtain. Believe me

Sincerely and gratefully yours,
C. L. Dodgson

Gertrude sends her love, and she is going home again tomorrow (Saturday).

To Mrs. C. F. Moberly Bell

7 Lushington Road, Eastbourne
September 27, 1893

Dear Mrs. Bell,

The reason I chose yesterday for coming to see you was that I have long regarded *Tuesdays* as my "lucky days." Not that I exactly believe in any superstition about luck: but certainly, as a matter of fact, a great many of the happiest days in my life have been *Tuesdays* – more, I think, than any other day of the week.

Forgive me for making the remark; but, before you had been in the room a minute, I felt you were a person with whom I couldn't possibly be *shy* (*some* people make me *awfully* shy!) but óne with whom I *had* to be confidential!

I must go back to the first paragraph. I had meant to say, at the end of it, that I didn't find yesterday at all an exception to the rule. My $2\frac{1}{2}$ hours in your house were *most* enjoyable. Your children and I will, I think, learn to love each other when we are a little better acquainted. It takes some time to *understand* a child's nature – particularly when one only sees them all together, and in the presence of their elders. I don't think anybody, who has only seen children so, has any idea of the loveliness of a child's *mind*. I have been largely privileged in tête-à-tête intercourse with children. It is very healthy and helpful to one's own spiritual life: and humbling too, to come into contact with souls so much purer, and nearer to God, than one feels oneself to be.

Some day I shall be asking you to let me borrow one of your dear girls – not only for "a day out" in London (*that*, I imagine, there would be no difficulty about. I always get *two* tickets, when I go to a Matinée, and then cast about for a companion), but I shall perhaps ask you (*next* year, I'm too busy now to have *any* more guests) to let me have one down here, for a week, all to myself, and see if we can make friends!

I'm writing to tell Miss Thomson that I don't want her to make *complete* studies of any child of yours, but only hasty sketches (which would not be tiring) that I may have the pleasure of feeling, as to some of the fairies, "*this* is Cynthia," and (possibly) "*this* is Iris."   Believe me

Very sincerely yours,

C. L. Dodgson

Will you kindly tell me who's got which of my books?

To Hilda Moberly Bell

7 Lushington Road, Eastbourne

October 5, 1893

My dear Hilda,

It *is* sweet, of you children, to sign your letters to me, after only *once* seeing me, as you do! When I get letters signed "your loving," I always *kiss* the signature. You see I'm a sentimental old fogey! But *what* a pity that *Iris* won't forgive me! She doesn't write: she sends no message: and I've looked, in vain in the "Agony-Column" of the *Standard* (the only paper I see) for her advertisement! And that reminds me – a little bird (could it have been a "German-Bulfinch"? It was something beginning with "Ger"*) told me that you always had *two* copies of *The Times*. I wonder if you could cut out, and send me, *The Times* critique on *Sowing the Wind*? I would advise *you* to read it, also, so as to have some idea what the play is about.

* "Auntie Ger"; that is, Gertrude Chataway.

It's *very* nice to think that we are engaged for the 14th. And now I hope that, the next time that wealthy architect, that admires you so much (you know the one I mean? The one that lives across the street, and who always takes off his hat, if he meets your party out walking when you are not with them), the next time he comes under your window, to serenade you with his hurdy-gurdy, and begins to sing

> Hilda! Hilda!
> Give me your answer true;
> I'm a crazy builder,
> All for the love of you!

I hope you'll just open the window about three inches, and shout softly, through the opening, "my 'answer true' is that I'm engaged to Mr. Dodgson!" And then, if you listen carefully, you'll hear him begin again in a minute (as soon as he's recovered his presence of mind),

> Enid! Enid!
> Give me your answer true;
> It wasn't Hilda I meanëd,
> It was only you!

And that reminds me – please tell Enid I'll write to her *some* year. She mustn't be in such a hurry. And she mustn't get so cross about it. And I'm not exactly *crushed*, as yet, by her cleverness in "burying" my pseudonym of "Carroll." In fact, a more dismal failure, than she has achieved in turning it into "Carrel," I *never* yet met with! And I doubt *very* much if the girl's surname is *really* "Car." There *is* such a name: but "Carr" is much more common. And I think, if she were *really* a noble wise child, who can hear the sound of the tram-car rolling in the street, she'd have made a better job of burying my name!

Now I've got letters from *three* of you four (excuse the liberty) darlings. Of course I can't expect one from *Cynthia*. She would only say, if you asked her to send one, "I never *do* write, you know: I always do *wrong*!"

> Your ever loving,
> C.L.D.

P.S. I've sent a card to ask whether you'd like the books in white-and-gold, or red-and-gold. I shall treat your Mother's suggestion with all the contempt that such a suggestion deserves!

To Enid Moberly Bell

7 Lushington Road, Eastbourne
October 10, 1893

My dear Enid,

I'll tell you what I'll do for *you*, my dear child (to make amends for taking Hilda to a play, you know); I'll take you to a Matinée of *Utopia*. It doesn't seem as if they were going to have any more Matinées of *A Woman's Revenge*: and I fancy *Utopia* is a far nicer play: and I certainly want to see it, myself: and if it turns out good (the *Standard* praises it tremendously) I shall be going a second time: and then, you know, I *might* take Iris: who knows? No, I *don't* want to take both of you at once! So it's no use your hinting at it. I *hate* parties of *three*: duetts are *ever* so much nicer! I remember once telling a friend I had been to a good many theatres that winter, and had taken a good many children with me (10 or 12, I think). And *he* said "Why didn't you take them all at once, and get it over?" Oh, the idiot! As if *that* were the way to enjoy children's society! He talked of them as if they were doses of medicine!

By the way, I feel *sure*, now, that Iris was *not* angry with me about that hoax, as she has written, and signed herself "your *very* loving." Oh, the amount of tears and groans I've spent on that affair! Really it's *too* provoking to find they've all been wasted!

To give you some idea of what it has cost me, I'll just describe breakfast-time, the day before that letter came. ("D" means "Mr. Dodgson, "L" "landlady," "M" "maid.")

Time, 8.30 a.m.

Enter D, who rings bell, and then lies down, with face on hearthrug, and groans.

D. Oh, Iris!

Enter M. What ever *is* the matter, Sir?

D. Oh, Iris!

M. (calls landlady) Oh, Mum, Mum! The poor gent is took ill!

D. Oh, Iris!

Enter L. Won't you eat some breakfast, Sir?

D. Oh, Iris!

M. It's something about *diaries*, I fancy.

L. Ah, he's been writing 'em all night, maybe. Shall us burn 'em, Sir? Then they'll be off your mind.

D. Oh, Iris!

M. He says the *fire is* – summat or other.

L. Oh, the *fire is* burning all right, Sir! Do eat some breakfast!

D. Oh, Iris!

M. He says a *liar is* – summat or other.

L. A *liar is* a bad bad man, Sir! But cheer up: *you're* not a liar!

D. goes on groaning till luncheon-time: then, instead of luncheon, he has his breakfast: then he groans till dinner-time: then, instead of dinner, he has his luncheon: then he goes to bed without any dinner.

It isn't a comfortable plan. *Aren't* you glad it's all over now?

Your very loving old new friend,
C.L.D.

To Harry Furniss

7 Lushington Road, Eastbourne
October 21, 1893

Dear Mr. Furniss,

On further examination, with a magnifying-glass, of this drawing, I find that Bruno *has* a waist. *Without* the glass, the effect is, distinctly, that his right side is bounded by the line of light that runs down the front of Sylvie's skirt, and thus that he is in a loose sort of shirt. Yet there is a piece of window-sill between the 2 figures, which (if it were as much illuminated as the portion to the left-hand of Bruno) would clearly show where Bruno's figure ended. But this bit, for some inexplicable reason, you have shaded. *What* is supposed to cast a shadow on it?

I must really *beg* you to make *both* dresses more opaque. If you look through a magnifying-glass, you will see that the "hind-quarters" still show very plainly through: in fact, this is quite visible, even *without* a glass. The only dress, that Sylvie has, behind her, from the waist downwards, seems to consist of a few torn shreds of wet muslin!

All the upper part of the picture is so *lovely*, that I should greatly regret not being able to use it.

Do you mean that small "thing," close to Bruno's left elbow, to be cut, as you have drawn it, quite separate from the surroundings? Is it a falling leaf, or what?

Very sincerely yours,
C. L. Dodgson

brown eyes, and that not Sylvie's but an angel's
voice was whispering

" 𝕴𝕿 𝖎𝖘 𝕷𝖔𝖇𝖊."

The final illustration in *Sylvie and Bruno Concluded*

To Edith Ball

[Christ Church, Oxford]
November 6, 1893

My dear Edith,

I was very much pleased to get your nice little letter: and I hope you won't
mind letting Maud have the *Nursery "Alice,"* now that you have got the real
one. Some day I will send you the *other* book about Alice, called *Through
the Looking-Glass* but you had better not have it just yet, for fear you should

get them mixed in your mind. Which would you like best, do you think, a horse that draws you in a cab, or a lady that draws your picture, or a dentist, that draws your teeth, or a Mother, that draws you into her arms, to give you a kiss? And what order would you put the others in? Do you find Looking Glass writing easy to read? I remain

Your loving,
Lewis Carroll

Nov 6, 1893.

My dear Edith,
I was very much pleased to get your nice little letter: and I hope you won't mind my little Mabel have the Memory... that you have got the real one. Some day I will send you the other book about, called "Through the Looking-Glass," but you had better have it just yet, for then you...

Looking-glass letter to Edith Ball, November 6, 1893

To Edith Lucy

Christ Church, Oxford
November 26, 1893

My dearest Edith,

Why *will* you insist on my beginning so, when you know what a lot of Ediths I know (one of them my own niece), and how awfully hard it is to decide which of them is the dearest! Many thanks for your trouble in copying my advertisement; they are going off tonight. Katie will have to wait some time for her looking-glass, I'm afraid. However, there'll be all the less temptation to *vanity*, which is *some* comfort. Seriously, it's *very* lucky I had run short of copies, and had to send for more: or I might never have found out this "fiasco" in printing, till the whole 1000 were sold. As it is, only *60* are gone, and there are 940 available to give away. I expect the 60 will come in with a *rush*!

As I really believe you *like* helping me by writing, I will propose another job for you – *viz.*, to come here at 4, any day this week that best suits you, to write out, from my address-book, from 150 to 200 labels, to be pasted on the parcels of the presentation-copies of *Sylvie and Bruno Concluded*. I want to take them with me, ready-written, when I go to town to inscribe the books.

First, we would have tea – then labels – then dinner – then I would either take you home *directly* after dinner, or, if you preferred it, you might stay a few minutes longer.

Your loving friend,
C. L. Dodgson

To Mary Mallalieu

Christ Church, Oxford
February 16, 1894

My dear Polly,

What a nice photograph of you! Thank you *very* much, dear, for sending it to me. I'm very glad to have it, to remind me of you. If only I lived a little bit nearer to Leicester I would come and see you play.... I've seen (a pantomime) lately that was *quite* charming – *Cinderella*, at the Lyceum. I took two nieces and a nephew, and a dear little girl-friend, 7 years old, with me. She and the little boy had never been inside a theatre before. They let me bring her without a ticket, to sit on my *knee*: and about once in every half-hour she turned round to give me a kiss. I *think* she meant it as a sort of way of saying "thank you *so* much for bringing me!"

If ever you are to play in London, or are going on a tour again, let me know, as it will give me *some* chance of seeing – I won't say "my *little* Polly," but my tall Maypole of a Polly, so tall that I shall have to get up on a chair next time I want to give her a kiss!

Kindest regards to your father and mother, love to your (little?) brother, and love and a kiss for yourself, from

Your affectionate old friend,
C. L. Dodgson

To Mrs. J. C. Egerton

Christ Church, Oxford
March 8, 1894

Dear Mrs. Egerton,

It was a very pleasant experience for me – the hour or so that I spent, the other day, with you and your family. And I should like to try, if you do not object, to make real friends of your girls: of course we are only just *acquaintances* as yet. Much of the brightness of my life, and it has been a wonderfully happy one, has come from the friendship of girl-friends. Twenty or thirty years ago, "ten" was about my ideal age for such friends: now "twenty" or "twenty-five" is nearer the mark. Some of my dearest child-friends are 30 and more: and I think an old man of 62 has the right to regard them as being "child-friends" still.

But I have very little time, now, for society. (In fact, years ago, I began to decline *all* invitations.) The remaining years may be very few: and there is *much* work I still want to do.

The time I can best spare is from 7 to 9 or 10: as it only means my dining in my rooms instead of hall, and *not* returning to work (which indeed is never wise to do) directly after dinner. So I have for some years had dinner-parties of a novel kind – *one* young lady as guest! And I would like, if you do not object, to try the experiment with Gussie. I would come for her at about 6, and escort her home as late as you would allow her to stay. I *write* this request rather than call to *ask* it, as, if you do mean to refuse it, it is much pleasanter, for both, to do so in *writing*. *Any* day would suit me. Believe me

Very truly yours,
C. L. Dodgson

To Mabel Scott

Christ Church, Oxford
March 29, 1894

Oh dear, oh dear. What ever is Society coming to! Here's a young person of *over 17* (that I surmise) sending her "love" to a young gentleman of *under 70* (that I guarantee)!

Evidently your head has been turned with *anagrams*. *Your* idea of a good anagram is, no doubt,

AMIABLEST?
'TIS MABEL!

(i.e. "Who is the most lovable young lady at present extant?"
"It is so-and-so.")

That's all very well: but *I* can make you a much better anagram.

WHERE MABEL?
WE BLAME HER.

(i.e. "In what condition is so-and-so, at present?"
"She's in that state of mind, that all *judicious* friends shake their heads at her!")

Give my love to Edith, please, and believe me (it's all *your* fault, you know, not mine)

Yours affectionately,
C. L. Dodgson

To Mrs. J. F. Baird

Christ Church, Oxford
April 12, 1894

Dear Mrs. Baird,

There are two questions that I want to put before you for consideration.

The first is as to that friend of mine to whom Dolly wishes to be introduced. I have now introduced to her four of the daughters of my friends of ages between 18 and 25; but in every case, *before* doing so, I told the mother the history of my friend and asked her whether, now she knew all the circumstances, she still wished her daughter to be introduced. In each case the answer was "Yes." So now, before giving any more promises to introduce Dolly, I would like to know what *you* think about it.

If you already know what is popularly said against my friend (which is usually a good deal more than the truth) and if, knowing it, you still wish Dolly to be introduced, I am quite satisfied and no more need be said.

If you do not know of any such tales, current in society, then I think I had better come and tell you the true history (you yourself, I mean; I had rather not talk about the matter to your daughters) and then you can settle what you wish to be done.

The other question is, may Dolly come and dine with me? I ask this, not knowing your views as to "Mrs Grundy." And you may be sure I shall not feel in the least hurt if you think it best to say "No." It is only in these last two or three years that I have ventured on such unique and unconventional parties. Winifred Stevens was my first guest.

If you say "Yes" and will name a day (I've no engagements) I would come for her about 5½ and would escort her back at any hour you named (but I hope you would fix it as late as you can). Believe me

Sincerely yours,
C. L. Dodgson

When she was scarcely more than a child (17, I think), a man nearly three times her age professed to be in love with her. The match was pushed on by well meaning friends who thought it a grand thing for her. From the first, I don't think she had a fair chance of learning her new duties. Instead of giving her a home of her own he went on living as a guest with an elderly couple and the old lady was constantly exasperating the poor child by treating her as if she were still in the schoolroom and she, just like a child, used to go into fits of furious passion.

Quarrels began at once and very soon a separation was agreed on. He cynically told his friends that he found he had never *loved* her; it had only been a passing fancy. He agreed to make her an annual allowance so long as she lived respectably.

This she did for a while, then she rebelled and accepted the offered love (of course without ceremonial of marriage) of another man.

I honestly believe her position was, from her point of view, this:

"I am tied by *human* law to a man who disowns his share of what ought to be a *mutual* contract. He never loved me and I do not believe, in God's sight, we are man and wife. Society expects me to live, till this man's death, as if I were single and to give up all hope of that form of love for which I pine and shall never get from *him*. This other man loves me as truly and faithfully as any lawful husband. If the marriage ceremony were *possible* I would insist on it before living with him. It is *not* possible and I will do without it."

I allow freely that she was headstrong and wild in doing so; and her real *duty* was to accept the wreck of her happiness and live (or if necessary die) *without* the love of a man. But I do not allow that her case resembled *at all* that of those poor women who, without any pretence of *love*, sell themselves to the first comer. It much more resembles the case of those many women who are living as faithfully and devotedly as lawful wives without having gone through any ceremony and who *are*, I believe, married in *God's* sight though not in Man's.

A lady (wife of a clergyman) to whom (before I would introduce her daughter to my friend) I told this story said, "She has broken the law of man; she has *not* broken the law of God."

She lived with this man for some years and he *is* the father of her son and daughter. Then came the result she must have known was possible if not probable and which perhaps her mad conduct deserved; the man deserted her and went abroad.

When her lawful husband found out what she had done, of course he sued for and got a divorce. Then of course she was, in the eye of the law, free to be legally married and if only the other man had been as true as she, I have no doubt, meant to be to him, they would have married and it would have gradually been forgotten that the children were born before the ceremony.

All this time I held no communication with her. I felt that she had [so] entirely sacrificed her social position that I had no desire but to drop the acquaintance. Then an actor offered her marriage and they were married. It was a most generous act, I think, to marry a woman with such a history and a *great* addition to this generosity was his allowing the children to assume *his* surname.

The actor's father, a clergyman, so entirely approved his son's conduct that he came from the North of England to perform the ceremony. This second marriage put her, in the eyes of Society, once more in the position of a respectable woman. And then I asked her mother to ask her if she would like our friendship to begin again and she said "yes." And I went and called on her and her husband.

It really looked as if the misery of her life was *over*. But another misery came on of quite another kind. The man drank. She knew he was addicted to it before she married him but she fancied (very foolishly, I fear) she could cure him. This got worse and worse till they had to live apart and I believe he drank himself to death.

So she is now a widow.

To Ellen Terry

Christ Church, Oxford
April 24, 1894

My dear Miss Ellen Terry,

Many thanks for your kind message, through Minna, about my wanting to bring "nice girls" (as if *I* knew any such!) to the Lyceum, and your idea of giving us a box. May I make a candid confession? I don't like boxes at all: and I always go to the stalls: and really I don't want to have them *given* me (except that presents from *friends* are always nice), but am very happy to buy them, and so add a trifle to the receipts of the best of our theatres. I *would*, however, gratefully accept it as a gift to myself, if you would give a box to Minna's sisters, for some Matinée when *you* play. It would be a *great* treat for them, and one they cannot afford to buy themselves.

Now I have a favour, to ask you. (What a lot I've asked of you, and what a lot you've granted!) I have a very nice girl-friend here, aged about 20. She has set her heart on going on the stage. She has a good many things in her favour. She is a very fine handsome girl, with plenty of spirit and energy. I have seen her in amateur-theatricals, and thought her performance *very* promising.

She has also set her heart on being introduced to *you*: and this I have promised to manage, if I can. *Would* you mind naming a day and hour, when you would see her for a few minutes? I would most likely come with her: but my life is *very* busy, and she might have to go alone.

She is taking lessons in acting, from a Mrs. Dowson, who has been on the stage. And is also taking lessons in *fencing*! (I didn't know that was necessary.)

She had a wild idea that, if she could see you *soon*, there might be a chance of her being taken on as a "super" for your next provincial tour. I have *not* encouraged that hope.

Love to Minna, and Edith too if she will accept it.

Affectionately yours,
C. L. Dodgson

To Ellen Terry

Christ Church, Oxford
June 7, 1894

My dear Miss Ellen Terry,

I want to thank you, as heartily as words can do it, for your true kindness in letting me bring Dolly behind the scenes to you. You will know, without my telling you, what an *intense* pleasure you thereby gave to a warm-hearted girl, and what love (which I fancy you value more than mere *admiration*: I know *I* do!) you have won from her. Her wild longing to try the Stage will not, I think, bear the cold light of day, when once she has tried it, and has realised what a lot of hard work, and weary waiting, and "hope deferred" it involves. She doesn't, so far as I know, absolutely *need* (as Norah does) to earn money for her own support. But I fancy she will find life rather a *pinch*, unless she can manage to do *something* in the way of earning money. So I don't like to advise her strongly *against* it, as I would with any one who had no such need.

Also, thank you, thank you, with all my heart, for all your great and constant kindness to Norah. She *does* write so brightly and gratefully about all you do for her and say to her! I was very nearly writing a line to Mr. Irving, to thank him for his most welcome proposal that Norah should stay on: but on second thoughts, never having had the pleasure of meeting him, I will not trouble him with a letter. Perhaps you will *tell* him some time, will you?, how grateful I am.

Once I wrote to you about *Faust*, and was so unfortunate, I fear, as to vex you a little, by a remonstrance (probably very unskilfully worded) about the "business" in the chamber scene. I only allude to it again because I noticed the other day, that you have quite altered the "business," and now wholly omit what I had feared might make some of the audience uneasy. Would you mind telling me, some time, whether the alteration is a permanent one, or merely an accidental difference that day; and, if permanent, whether the change is connected at all with my letter?

Our interview the other day was *awfully* short! That isn't *at all* the sort of interview I like best with old friends. Tête-à-tête's are what I like best. Now that I have entered on the stage of being a "lean and slippered panta-loon," and no longer dread the frown of Mrs. Grundy, I have taken to giving tête-à-tête dinner-parties – the guest being, in most cases, a lady, of age varying from 12 to 67 (the maximum I have yet had): and they are *very* pleasant! If *you* were staying in Oxford, I really think (however incredible it may sound) that I should have the "cheek" to ask *you* to come and dine so!

Would you give my love to Norah, when next you see her, and accept the same yourself from

Your affectionate old friend,
Charles L. Dodgson

Oh, and heaps of thanks for treating Norah's sisters to a sight of *Faust*. You have brightened *their* lives also.

To E. Gertrude Thomson

Christ Church, Oxford
June 19, 1894

My dear Miss Thomson,

I find it so hard to explain, to a lady, why I cannot use this picture, that I *hope* you will excuse anything that seems offensively plain-spoken, as being quite contrary to my *intention*. When this business began, I told you I could have no *clothed* fairies at all. My feeling is this. First, I object to all *partly* clothed figures, altogether, as being unpleasantly suggestive of impropriety. So I will have none but *wholly* clothed, or *wholly* nude (which, to my mind, are not improper *at all*).

This figure is partly clothed; i.e. her hair is utilised, in a way artists often do utilise it and other things, as a partial concession to propriety, and to the principle, maintained by some, that a *wholly* nude figure is improper.

The presence of this picture in my book would make all the others look improper.

I have two other objections to the picture: but, without them, what I have said is enough by itself to prevent my using it.

The other two are, first, that the head is too large for the feet: she looks *top-heavy*. Secondly, I don't like the smiling and beckoning to supposed spectators. Even in a *draped* figure, such an expression would look a *little* too "bold": in an *undraped* one, it is, to me, unpleasantly so.

I'm afraid all this is unpleasant reading: but I don't see how I can avoid that result.

Very sincerely yours,
C. L. Dodgson

To Mary Brown

7 Lushington Road, Eastbourne
August 21, 1894

My dear Mary,

I wonder if you have an idea what sort of thing it is to have with you, every day (for I bring it with me here from Oxford), a bundle of unanswered letters, the oldest more than $5\frac{1}{2}$ years old! The very sight of it suggests, "You've many an hour of steady work before you, before I shall be got rid of!" and then one is apt to think "work that has waited so many *years* can easily wait another day!" The temptation to procrastinate, with such formidable arrears on hand, is almost irresistible! Four of these letters are from *you*! The oldest – I was going to say when it was *dated*, but on looking at it I find it has no date at all (it's a way ladies have in letter-writing): nor is No. 2 dated at all. No. 3 is merely dated with the highly satisfactory and intelligible date "Thursday." No. 4 *is* dated. However, all are recorded in my letter-register, with a *précis* of each: so I know when they came. No. 1 came September 4, 1891. I will see what there is to answer in it....No. 2 (received September 24 – 1892) is to thank (with some doubt) for the biscuit box with *Alice* pictures. Yes – it was from me. I gave away 200 or 300 of them, no great *gift*, as they wouldn't let me *pay* for any! My friends find strange uses for theirs, one little girl writes that *her* box "just holds her unanswered letters"! One of my brothers is prosaic enough to use his as a tobacco-box!

This letter No. 2 has some remarks with which I heartily agree, on the folly of people learning nothing about housekeeping before they marry – I think *cooking* should be part of every girl's education!

No. 3 (received December 30, 1893) begins "what ages it seems since I heard from you!" Well, it's quite true – I *have* treated you very badly, my dear old friend. But it's *also* quite true, as you kindly add that you "suppose," that my life is a busy one: in spite of that, I get about 2000 letters off, every year: but it isn't enough!...

No. 4 has *two* dates, I see "December 29" at the beginning, and "January 16" at the end. So it took 18 days to write! Always write *deliberately*, my dear child! never be in a hurry! This contains thanks for *Sylvie and Bruno Concluded*. I'm very glad you like having it.

Also it asks for a sketch of "Nine Men's Morris" and the rules. I'll write them down, and enclose them with this.

In No. 3 you ask what books I have done, naming the Child's Bible and Girl's Shakespeare. I fear neither of these will ever be done – at least by me. Life is very short! I'm 62, and though I'm in good working order now (I can easily work 10 hours a day) I can't in reason expect many more years of it. At present I'm hard at work (and have been for months) on my Logic-book. (It has really been on hand for a dozen years: the "months" refer to preparing for the Press.) It is *Symbolic Logic*, in 3 Parts – and Part 1 is to be easy enough for boys and girls of (say) 12 or 14. I greatly hope it will get into High Schools, etc. I've been teaching it at Oxford to a class of girls at the High School, another class of the mistresses (!), and another class of girls at one of the Ladies' Colleges. I believe it's one of the *best* mental exercises that the young could have: and it doesn't need *special* powers like mathematics. I may *perhaps* get Part 1 out early next year. The next will take another year at least.

I think I once gave you my *Game of Logic*? This is a more serious attempt: but with much shorter (and, I hope, better) explanations.

And now what am I to tell you about myself? To say I am quite well "goes without saying" with me. In fact my life is so strangely free from all trials and troubles, that I cannot doubt my own happiness is one of the "talents" entrusted to me to "occupy" with, till the Master shall return, by doing something to make other lives happy. I only wish I could lighten your burdens a little, dear friend! Perhaps you will be interested (though scandalised) to know how terribly "unconventional" I have become in my old age. And if you would like to send some severe remarks on my great imprudence in defying "Mrs. Grundy," please do so! Having given up society for the last 6 or 8 years, by refusing all invitations (I want all my time and brainpower now for the work still to be done: and "Society" is a weary work!) I console myself by giving dinner-parties of a new type: *viz.*, *one* lady guest only. I've done that now for years in Oxford, and here. I find tête-à-tête parties very pleasant, and refreshing. Oxford society is surprised no doubt: but it bears my eccentricities patiently: and something like 20 lady friends, of ages varying from 12 to 30 or 35 (but nearly all between 20 and 30) come and dine with me. But "worse remained behind"! I've tried the same plan with *guests* here. I began with a child of 10, whom I had here for a week. Next year I had one of 12: the next year one of 14. Then I got reckless as to ages: and many of my girl friends of 20 and 30 have come in that way. On Monday I'm expecting an Oxford friend (who is, I think, about 25, and whom I've known about 20 years) to come for a few days. Now aren't you terribly shocked at me? Last year an Oxford friend proposed herself for a week's visit.... She has quite broken the record as to age and I can now say to any mother whose daughter I invite, "I've had an older guest, in fact she is older than I am." And I've known her about 40 years. But she's a wonderful old lady, as lively as a kitten. She did enjoy her visit to me. Believe me always

Your loving old friend,
Charles L. Dodgson

To Winifred Schuster

7 Lushington Road, Eastbourne
September 25, 1894

My dear Winifred,

Suppose you were to ask the Mistress at your school whether she, and a few of the elder girls, would like to try to learn Symbolic Logic, and, if so, whether she could find a spare half-hour, every other day, when I might come and teach them, what do you think she would say? If she says "yes," I would advise *you* to attend, even though you've heard it all before: it will make you understand it all the better.

Yours affectionately,
C. L. Dodgson

Looking-glass letter to Winifred Schuster, September 25, 1894

To Winifred (Stevens) Hawke

The Chestnuts, Guildford.
January 1, 1895

My dear Winifred,

(No – I am *not* going to address you as "Mrs. Hawke"! You may expect it as much as you like, but *I shan't do it*! If *that's* what you want, you must go to another shop, if you please 'm. We don't keep the article *here*.)

"Who shall my *first* letter in the New Year be written to?" is a question that I daresay many a one is asking today. My answer to the question is "at any rate it must be to somebody whom I *love*." And, though the avowal is of course a highly improper one to make to a married lady, yet that *is* my reason for writing this my first letter with the new date. I suppose (and *hope*, for the sake of your mother, and your disagreeable little sister) that this will find you still at Oxford: and that there is no use in my presenting myself *yet* at your London mansion, with or without any small friend of mine, for luncheon or any other selfish purpose. But you may be sure that I shall do so, the first chance I get: and, though I hardly eat anything *myself* at luncheon, I think it highly probable that I shall have somebody or other with me who will want *dinner*: and who will have an *appetite*!

I'm down here with a small selection of sisters – three only out of the seven I possess – and working as hard as ever at the Logic Book that seems so hopeless to get finished. I'm sitting up in my bed-room, with an asbestos fire, that I can light for myself at any moment, which is a great luxury; and where I can get on with my work without interruption, and in *silence*. I've long lost the power of doing any *work*, worthy of the name, in a room with others, and with conversation going on.

As yet, I've not made *any* plans for Matinées in London. The large majority of the plays, now being acted, are such as *I* at any rate, don't want to see, however popular they may be. But I think I shall be going, *some* day soon, and with *some* child-friend, to see *Santa Claus* at the Lyceum: and then, if you are back in town, I'll come down on you for a meal. When do you mean to go back to town? And couldn't you manage to take *Enid* with you? To take her and you to *Santa Claus* would *indeed* be a treat!

If ever you want a *light* mental recreation, try the "30 letter" puzzle. I tried it for the first time, the other day, with one of my sisters: and I think it very interesting. I have taught it to Enid, I think: but we have improved it. Here is our rule.

"Take 4 or 5 complete alphabets. Put the vowels into one bag, the consonants into another. Shake up. Draw 9 vowels and 21 consonants. With these you must make 6 real words (excluding proper names) so as to use up *all* the letters. If *two* people want to do it, then after drawing a set of 30, pick out a set of duplicates for the other player. Sit where you cannot see one another's work, and make it a *race*. It seems to take from 5 to 10 minutes. It makes a shorter, but very good, puzzle, to draw 6 vowels and 14 consonants, and make 4 words; and a yet shorter one to draw 3 vowels and 7 consonants and make 2 words."

Kindest regards to your mother. Much love to you and Enid, and a kiss apiece, if you'll have it!

Your loving friend,
C. L. Dodgson

To Edith Blakemore

The Chestnuts, Guildford
January 1, 1895

Yes, my dear Edith, you are quite correct in saying it is a long time since you heard from me: in fact, I find that I have not written to you since the 13th of last November. But what of that? You have access to the daily papers. Surely you can find out, negatively, that I am all right? Go carefully through the List of Bankruptcies: then run your eye down the Police Cases: and, if you fail to find my name anywhere, you can say to your mother, in a tone of calm satisfaction, "Mr. Dodgson is going on *well*."

I've brought with me here, as a sort of holiday-task, a bundle of 50 or more letters requiring answers. It needs *great* energy to begin on them. You might think that the more there are, the more easy it would be to begin: but it isn't so. If you have *one* mutton-chop before you, you can eat it: but, suppose I were to put 50 on your plate at once, would you have the heart to begin? All the time, that I can spare from writing to little girls like you, I spend on writing my "Logic" for the young. I hope to publish about Easter. I think I'll send you a copy, on the chance of your being still young. I wish you all a very happy New Year, and am

Always yours affectionately,
C.L.D.

To Margery Worthington

[Christ Church, Oxford]
January 24, 1895

My dear Margery,

Please excuse this horrid thing. It *would* walk about on the letter. It said it wanted to see who I was writing to.

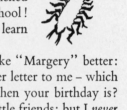

I'm very glad you like *Alice*: but what wicked wicked sisters you have not to let you read it till they go to school! But perhaps the mistress had told them they had to learn a page of it by heart as a lesson?

I'm sorry I spelt your name "Marjorie," if you like "Margery" better: but you see Miss Evans had spelt it "Marjorie," in her letter to me – which was very naughty of her. Please will you tell me when your birthday is? I have a book in which I write the birthdays of my little friends: but I *never* give birthday presents: I think that *un*-birthday presents are much nicer: don't *you* think so? When I come to Bushey, to see Miss Evans, may I come and see *you*?

Your loving friend,
Lewis Carroll
★ ★ ★

To A. H. J. Greenidge

Christ Church, Oxford
May 24, 1895

Dear Mr. Greenidge,

I would like you to know, from myself, how *entirely* I approve of Edith's wise suggestion that she and I had better now drop the "kissing" which used to mark our greetings. It is a real pleasure to me to feel that, in carrying out her suggestion, I am doing what will I hope be satisfactory to one she loves so well.

Will you give tangible proof that you regard me (through her) as a *friend* (and *not* as an unwelcome interloper!) by coming to dine with me, in Hall, any day that suits you? We dine at 7 (evening-dress *quite* optional: I don't use it myself in this summer-term).

Sincerely yours,
C. L. Dodgson

To Mrs. G. J. Rowell

Christ Church, Oxford
June 25, 1895

Dear Mrs. Rowell,

The being entrusted with the care of Ethel for a day is such a great advance on mere acquaintanceship, that I venture to ask if I may regard myself as on "kissing" terms with her, as I am with many a girl-friend a great deal older than *she* is. Considering that – she being 17 and I 63 – I am quite old enough to be her *grandfather*, I hope you won't think it a very out-of-the-way suggestion. Nevertheless, if I find you think it wiser that we should only shake hands, I shall not be *in the least* hurt. Of course I shall, unless I hear to the contrary, continue to shake hands only.

Very truly yours,
C. L. Dodgson

To Lord Salisbury

7 Lushington Road, Eastbourne
August 30, 1895

Dear Lord Salisbury,

It has occurred to me that it may be worth while to put before you an idea (though probably it will not be a novelty to you) as to a very useful work which the Government might do in London. It is to have look-out stations, at the highest accessible points, where men should be on watch, day and night, for the first symptoms of a fire, and then, by being in electric communication with all the fire-engine stations, rouse all those who are nearest to the scene of the fire – which they might often be able to do some time before the alarm could be given by those on the spot, and thereby great saving of property, and sometimes of life, might result.

The plan is in operation in some foreign cities, but I never heard of its being attempted in London: and I believe any Government that set it going in London would earn the thanks of the population of London, and indeed of the nation, when once they had realised how great an additional security for life and property was thus initiated.

The details I need not discuss: they will suggest themselves. The top of the Victoria Tower, and the top of St. Paul's, would probably be the best two places to command large areas of London: and of course each station would be provided with a minute map of the district commanded by it, and with a good telescope.

One great use of such a commanding view would be to secure proper *division* of resources, in case of *two* great fires occurring at once. At present, in such a case, fire-engines would receive summons from *both* places as neither of them would know of the other fire: whereas the officer, who saw both, could instantly decide to *which* fire each engine ought to go.

I will not trespass further on your valuable time, but sign myself

Sincerely yours,
C. L. Dodgson

To Lord Salisbury

7 Lushington Road, Eastbourne
September 3, 1895

Dear Lord Salisbury,

I am much obliged to you for your letter, and for your *not* treating my suggestion as a mere "fad," unworthy of notice. I can desire nothing better for it than that it should be considered by the authorities in the Fire Brigade Department.

Two other ideas of mine I have often thought of submitting to you, and have again and again given up the thought of doing so, from a consciousness of my great ignorance of politics. However, I will venture on it, now that you are probably less overwhelmed with business than you will be when the next Session begins. Both ideas refer to the possibility of strengthening, and popularising, the position of the House of Lords, and bringing it more thoroughly into "touch" with the other House – objects which seem to me *most* desirable.

Both ideas, if carried out, would perhaps involve real *constitutional* changes, and, as such, ought surely to commend themselves to the Radicals!

One is, that Members of the Government, to whichever House they belong, should be free to appear in the other, to answer questions, and join in discussion (of course not to *vote*), in all matters connected with their own Department. Surely it would be more satisfactory to the Commons, when some important question was raised as to our Foreign relations, to find that you yourself appeared to answer their questions, instead of speaking through a subordinate: and the idea that, when Liberals are next in power, Lord Rosebery would be free to speak in the House of Commons, and Sir William Harcourt in the House of Lords, would, I fancy, commend itself to most of the Opposition.

The other idea is that the House of Lords might do more of the work that now falls on, and almost crushes, the House of Commons, by having first class Government Bills introduced in their House, debated, amended, and sent to the other House in the same finished condition in which Bills are now sent up to them from the Commons.

I must content myself with merely putting these two ideas before you "in the rough." To discuss their consequences, necessary conditions, etc., is, I feel, entirely beyond my capacity. Believe me

Sincerely yours,
C. L. Dodgson

To Mrs. B. Dyer

The Chestnuts, Guildford
December 28, 1895

Dear Mrs. Dyer,

I am glad, for your sakes, that you have found quarters that suit you. But, for myself, I am considerably frightened about the *distance from the sea*. How far is it? It is important, specially for any child-friend I might have to stay with me, that the sea-front should be within easy reach; and, if it is not so, I greatly fear I should have to find some lodgings nearer to the sea – even though yours, being further off, would no doubt be much cheaper.

However there is plenty of time to consider all details, before I shall be wanting to come to Eastbourne again. Will you please let me know

(1) How far are you from the sea?

(2) Shall you be able to let me have a first-floor sitting-room?

(3) And two bed-rooms?

(4) What rent do you think of charging?

I should consider it as a *real* misfortune to have to look out for other quarters! Wishing you, and your husband and sons, a very happy New Year, I am

Very truly yours,
C. L. Dodgson

To Mrs. B. Dyer

The Chestnuts, Guildford
January 15, 1896

Dear Mrs. Dyer,

Perhaps you are wishing to know whether I am likely to come to you in the summer. The distance from the sea, and the ground-floor sitting-room, are certainly *drawbacks*. But at any rate I would like to come and *try* the rooms for a week, in June or July. It would take a good many drawbacks to drive me to look out for another lodging !

Yours very truly,
C. L. Dodgson

To Mrs. A. L. Mayhew

Christ Church, Oxford
February 29, 1896

Dear Mrs. Mayhew,

When, several years ago, it seemed desirable that your children should forget all about me and my photography which was not to your liking, I imagined that our acquaintanceship had come to an end – not, I hope, with any angry feeling on either side, but simply extinguished as no longer desirable to keep up.

Now, however, that chance has made me acquainted with your little Margaret, I see no reason, unless you desire it, to repel the friendship she is ready to offer. That you allowed her to keep the book I sent her is a sort of sign that you do not object. However, in *writing* to her, I think it best to send the letter to *you* – leaving you free either to hand it on, or to destroy it and tell her nothing about it, whichever you think best   Believe me

Very truly yours,
C. L. Dodgson

To Mrs. N. H. Stevens

Christ Church, Oxford
March 3, 1896

Dear Mrs. Stevens,

Instead of having dear *Enid* to dine, it occurs to me that her *mother* ought to be the next to come. I have several times *nearly* had that pleasure, but have always been prevented. Won't you name a day, when I may have the pleasure of coming for you at 6.15? I think you know that *my* guests are never expected to come in evening-dress. Any day but Thursday and Saturday would suit me.

Very sincerely yours,
C. L. Dodgson

To Mrs. A. L. Moore

Christ Church, Oxford
July 24, 1896

Dear Mrs. Aubrey Moore,

You and your children seem so well disposed to regard me as a friend (though a *little* too much inclined to treat me as a "lion" – a position I cordially detest) that I should like to try, if I may, to know them better. Child-friends *will* grow up so quick! And most of mine are now grown up, though by no means ceasing to be "child-friends." But my life is *very* busy, and is nearing its end, and I have *very* little time to give to the sweet relief of girl-society. So I have to limit myself to those whose society can be had in the only way in which such society is worth having, *viz.*, one by one.

Would you kindly tell me if I may reckon *your* girls as invitable (*not* "inevitable"!), to tea, or dinner, *singly*. I know of cases where they are invitable in *sets* only (like the circulating-library novels), and such friendships I don't think worth going on with. I don't think anyone knows what girl-nature *is*, who has only seen them in the presence of their mothers or sisters.

Also, are they kissable? I hope you won't be shocked at the question, but nearly all my girl-friends (of all ages, and even married ones!) are now on those terms with me (who am now sixty-four). With girls under fourteen, I don't think it necessary to ask the question: but I guess Margery to be *over* fourteen, and, in such cases, with new friends, I usually ask the mother's leave. When my girl-friends get *engaged* (as they are always doing) I always decline to go on with the practice, unless the *fiancé* gives his permission: and sometimes he gives it – which is rather a wonder to me, as I feel sure that, if I were in his case, I should *not* give it! Believe me

Sincerely yours,
C. L. Dodgson

To Mrs. R. L. Poole

Christ Church, Oxford
November 7, 1896

Dear Mrs. Poole,

I have a request to make of you; and I do it in writing, rather than viva voce, because I think it possible you may not be willing to grant it, and it is not a pleasant task to have to think, on the spur of the moment, how to word a *refusal*. My request is that I may be allowed to try the experiment of making friends with Joy (or whatever is the name she answers to, as to which I am rather puzzled). The friendship of children has always been a great element in my enjoyment of life, and is very *restful* as a contrast to the society of books, or of men. But I don't go *out* into Society now; and my only spare time, for such pleasures, is in the *evenings*; and tête-à-tête parties are the only kind I care for! If you give your sanction, I will ask to be allowed to fetch her, some evening, to dine with me. And I think she already regards me with sufficient friendliness to give *her* consent. But, as I have made a similar request, in vain, as to her friends the Aubrey Moores, I don't feel *quite* confident of success on *this* occasion. Believe me

Very truly yours,
C. L. Dodgson

To Dorothy Joy Poole

Christ Church, Oxford
November 11, 1896

———

What shall I call thee?
"I happy am –
Joy is my name."
Sweet Joy befall thee!*

———

There, my dear Dorothy; if you happen *not* to have seen these lines before, and if you can guess, *from the style*, who wrote them, I will admit that you are a fairly good judge of modern poetry!

Having now allowed a year or two (more or less) to elapse, in order to give you time to recover your courage, I write to ask whether you are disengaged for next Saturday evening, and, if so, whether I may fetch you, at 6½, to one of my grand dinner-parties.

* William Blake, "Infant Joy," *Songs of Innocence*.

Do not be alarmed at the *number* of the guests: it will be .99999, etc. It *looks* alarming, I grant: but circulating decimals lose *much* of their grandeur when reduced to vulgar fractions!

Two things need to be mentioned.

One is, evening-dress is *not* expected. I wear morning-dress *myself*: so why should my guests be more ceremonious? (I do so *hate* ceremony!)

Another is, what do you usually drink at dinner? My lady-guests *mostly* prefer draught-lemonade. But you can have any of the following beverages:

(1) bottled lemonade;
(2) ginger-beer;
(3) beer;
(4) water;
(5) milk;
(6) vinegar;
(7) ink.

Nobody has yet chosen either No. 6 or No. 7.

By the way, "morning dress" includes morning-*shoes* (or boots). So don't bother yourself to bring *evening*-shoes, unless it is a positive discomfort to you to wear the others. In that case, perhaps the *best* thing to bring would be a pair of those lovely morocco *slippers*, with fur-edges. (*N.B.* I once tried to buy such a pair, for myself: but only got the crushing reply that "slippers of *that* kind are *only* worn by *ladies*"!)

> Affectionately yours,
> C. L. Dodgson

To Mrs. R. L. Poole

> Christ Church, Oxford
> November 16, 1896

Dear Mrs. Poole,

I fancy I did thank you, in anticipation, for the loan of Dorothy for an evening: but I now wish, in retrospect, to send a *double* measure of thanks, for the treat you have given me, and for the hope that I have secured a new *real* child-friend. She has good *sense*: she is a pleasant and interesting companion: and I like her. (I do not fear that this last avowal will suggest any such question as "What are your *intentions*?") Now I wonder whether *you*, encouraged by the circumstance that your daughter has returned alive, will brave the ogre's den, and come and dine with me? Child-society is very delightful to me: but I confess that grown-up society is much more interesting! In fact, *most* of my "child"-friends (specially those who come to stay with me at Eastbourne) are now about 25.

I wonder if you and Mrs. Aubrey Moore will ever allude to your acceptance of an invitation which *she* declined? If so, it would be an amusing discussion to overhear! I rather *think* she will be simply *horrified* at the laxity of your views about the chaperonage of young ladies! I enclose a book for Dorothy, with my love, and am

Sincerely yours,
C. L. Dodgson

My only engagements are Tuesday and Thursday.

To H. L. Thompson

Christ Church, Oxford
December 2, 1896

My dear Thompson,

Your letter causes me to write, *now*, a letter I had meant to keep waiting till your installation as Vicar of St. Mary's.

That you may not misunderstand it, I begin by saying that to preach the sermon to undergraduates, which you propose I should do, would be, to me, a privilege to be most deeply thankful for. But it is not a matter in which one's own feelings should be regarded, till the question has been settled what is *best* to be done, in the spiritual interests of others.

Please regard what I now tell you as confidential.

When the Services for College Servants began here, I was asked to help; and I generally preached a sermon every Term, at the request of Warner, who has throughout been the principal actor in the affair, and has done, I am sure, *great* good, in organising and maintaining the services.

Whether my sermons were at all worth preaching, or worth listening to, is a question *I* am of course wholly unfit to discuss – and which I had much rather *not* discuss. So I will simply state the fact that my help ceased to be asked for, nearly 3 years ago. I held my peace, for there are *two* things I dread doing – and I don't know which I dread most. One is, the declining to preach when invited to do so: this feels to me like a wanton throwing away of an opportunity, that perhaps God meant me to take, of doing something, however trivial, in His service. The other is, the offering when *not* invited. This feels like a deliberate courting of failure (for I generally feel, on the eve of such an attempt, as if a failure were nearly *certain*).

However, I did venture, after all that long interval, to name the matter to my dear friend the Dean. It is obvious how difficult he would have felt it to say "your sermons were not thought to be worth hearing," and how gladly he would name any other sufficient reason. The reason he gave was that it was wished to make the services more *parochial*, so that preachers had been invited who were used to *parish* work (in which *I* have had next to no experience).

But the possibility of the *other* reason existing *also* makes me write this, to suggest that, before asking any help from me, you should talk to Warner (without telling him you have received this letter). You can easily learn from him (and need not repeat to me) *all* his reasons. And you will then be able to judge for yourself whether or no to renew your application to me. I hope and pray that you may do what is *best* for your congregation.

Sincerely yours,
C. L. Dodgson

To Dora Abdy

[Christ Church, Oxford]
[December 8, 1896]

My dear Dora,

In correcting the proofs of *Through the Looking-Glass* (which is to have *An Easter Greeting* inserted at the end), I am reminded that in that letter (I enclose a copy), I had tried to express my thoughts on the very subject we talked about last night – the relation of *laughter* to religious thought. One of the hardest things in the world is to convey a meaning accurately from one mind to another, but the *sort* of meaning I want to convey to other minds is that while the laughter of *joy* is in full harmony with our deeper life, the laughter of amusement should be kept apart from it. The danger is too great of thus learning to look at solemn things in a spirit of *mockery*, and to seek in them opportunities for exercising *wit*. That is the spirit which has spoiled, for me, the beauty of some of the Bible. Surely there is a deep meaning in our prayer, "Give us an heart to love and *dread* Thee." We do not mean *terror*: but a dread that will harmonise with love; "respect" we should call it as towards a human being, "reverence" as towards God and all religious things.

Yours affectionately,
C. L. Dodgson

To Mary Barber

The Chestnuts, Guildford
January 12, 1897

My dear May,

In answer to your question, "What did you mean the Snark was?" will you tell your friend that I meant that the Snark was a *Boojum*. I trust that she and you will now feel quite satisfied and happy.

To the best of my recollection, I had no other meaning in my mind, when I wrote it: but people have since tried to find the meanings in it. The one I like best (which I think is partly my own) is that it may be taken as an Allegory for the Pursuit of Happiness. The characteristic "ambition" works well into this theory – and also its fondness for bathing-machines, as indicating that the pursuer of happiness, when he has exhausted all other devices, betakes himself, as a last and desperate resource, to some such wretched watering-place as Eastbourne, and hopes to find, in the tedious and depressing society of the daughters of mistresses of boarding-schools, the happiness he has failed to find elsewhere.

With every good wish for your happiness, and for the priceless boon of health also, I am

Always affectionately yours,
C. L. Dodgson

To Lord Salisbury

Christ Church, Oxford
June 7, 1897

Dear Lord Salisbury,

Before entering on the matter which is the main cause of my writing this letter, let me assure you that it has been with much concern, and much sympathy with you and your family, that I have heard, from time to time, such grave reports as to the health of Lady Salisbury. Even apart from the *friendship* that has existed between us for a quarter of a century, mere *gratitude*, for all the kindness I have received from her and from all your family, would make me feel deeply with you in the anxiety that must be caused by so serious an illness.

Although I was boorish enough to decline (on the ground of having now settled down into the hermit-life of old age) Lady Salisbury's last kind invitation to Hatfield, yet I do not consider communications with your family to have *ceased*. I still occasionally venture to appear in Arlington Street and I *frequently* take advantage of the always-ready hospitality which Maud provides, for me and any friend I happen to bring, in Mount Street. Once, not long ago, she gave luncheon, on *four* consecutive Saturdays, to me, her *old* friend, and to a new *young* friend each time!

The matter I now venture to write to you about is connected with *Ireland*; and I earnestly hope, considering the *extreme* importance of the point I wish to put before you, that you will not think I am taking an unwarrantable liberty, as an outsider, and one very ignorant of political matters, in thus writing to so experienced a statesman, whose time is necessarily so fully occupied. No doubt I am transgressing that most salutary rule "Do not speak to the man at the helm": still I think there *are* occasions – when the ship is in real danger – that may be held to justify even *that* extreme measure.

The thing has been on my mind for years. Summer after summer I have felt a profound regret (which I fancy *you* also may have felt) to see that our beloved Queen, amidst all her frequent excursions to Scotland, and to foreign countries, seemed to be *never* able to find an opportunity to gladden the hearts of her *Irish* subjects, by appearing among them. And I have felt a profound conviction that, if she had done otherwise – if, once in every few years, during the past 60 years, she had paid a visit to Ireland, it would have made an *incalculable* difference in the history of Great Britain. Those two miserable Home-Rule Bills would never, I feel quite sure, have been even heard of – much less would they have come so near, as they did, to running the old ship upon the rocks, in spite of all the helmsman could do!

More than this, she would have converted the Irish, from a discontented and almost hostile race, into loyalists of a quite passionate enthusiasm. Take the case of Mr. Arthur Balfour (for whose talents and statesmanship I feel the most profound respect) as an illustration of what marked effects may be produced by a little display of sympathy and of an unselfish readiness to take trouble. His tour in Ireland, with Miss Balfour, seems to have won all hearts, and I have heard him spoken of as "the most popular man in Ireland."

Her Majesty's long reign has been remarkable for the great benevolence, and the deep wisdom, which she has shown during all these years. But we are all liable to make mistakes: and her long neglect of Ireland has been, I feel convinced, an enormous and most disastrous mistake.

Perhaps there may yet be time to undo *some* of the mischief. But *who* is the right person to bring this most vital matter before her, and to persuade her to glorify the concluding years of her reign by winning the hearts of her Irish subjects? Is there any one living, whose opportunities, and whose fitness for the task, can for a moment be compared with *yours*? Oh, pardon the boldness with which I say all this: it is not for myself, it is for thousands and thousands of my fellow-subjects that I am urging it: but do, do, if by any possibility you can, bring this vital question to the notice of the Queen, and induce her – as probably only you can do – to see how vast an opportunity, for doing good, she is throwing away! It would be by no means the *least* of the boons, to the people of Great Britain and Ireland, by which you will have signalised your present Premiership.

Do, also, if I have not already taken up too much of your valuable time, read the enclosed cutting, on the same topic, from the *St. James's Gazette*. Believe me always, dear Lord Salisbury,

Sincerely yours,
C. L. Dodgson

To E. Gertrude Thomson

2 Bedford Well Road, Eastbourne
August 10, 1897

My dear Miss Thomson,

It was careless of Messrs. Macmillan and their binder to forget that a specimen of the linen had been already approved by you. I have asked them, in case they kept a bit themselves, to send a part of it to me, in order to make sure it is right: in case they have *not*, I have told them you will send them the original piece in September. The thing can very well wait till then. We haven't got the book* anything *like* ready yet.

Your description of the sands, and the naked children playing there, is very tempting, and I might *possibly* make an expedition there, some day (would your landlady take me in?), on the chance of getting some picturesque victims to sketch. But, alas, it is impossible *this* year. Dolly comes to me on Friday, and may perhaps stay till the end of the month; and by that time the summer-*heat* will have gone, and your live fairies will have ceased to dress in "nothing."

Yet it is doubtful if I should not, after all, find I had come in vain – and that it was a hopeless quest to try to make friends with any of the little nudities. A *lady* might do it: but what would they think of a *gentleman* daring to address them! And then what an embarrassing thing it would be to *begin* an acquaintance with a naked little girl! What *could* one say to start the

---

* Dodgson's last book, *Three Sunsets and Other Poems*, illustrated by Gertrude Thomson. It would appear posthumously.

conversation? Perhaps a poetical quotation would be best. "And ye shall walk in silk attire." How would *that* do? I'm afraid she would reply "Do I *look* like it?" Or one *might* begin with Keats' charming lines "Oh where are you going, with your love-locks flowing, And what have you got in your basket?" She would *have* "love-locks flowing," most likely: they wouldn't be the kind you have to hang up till you've done bathing. And, even without clothes, she might still find some use for a basket – if only a *clothes*-basket! Or a quotation from Cowper (slightly altered) might do. *His* lines are "The tear, that is wiped with a little address, May be followed perhaps by a smile." But *I* should have to quote it as "The tear, that is wiped with so little a dress"!

You will think that Eastbourne air makes me talk nonsense. Perhaps it does. To return to sense. Haven't you got your little camera with you? And could you not make friends with some of these girl-fairies, and do me a photo of one, or of a group, with a background of rocks? And, if you chance to make friends with any exceptionally *nice* little nudity (no matter whether she is *beautiful* or not: only *nice* ones will do) who is willing to be victimised for my benefit, I will send you a book to give her.

Very sincerely yours,

C. L. Dodgson

P.S. The quotation to put, as a motto, *under* a photo of your little "sea-fairy," would no doubt be from Sir Noël Paton's poems:

> And there, upon the gleaming sands,
> Between the ripples and the rocks,
> Stood, mother-naked in the sun,
> A little maid with golden locks.

To Robert Allen

2 Bedford Well Road, Eastbourne
September 2, 1897

Dear Mr. Allen,

I shall be most happy to come over to you on the 19th to talk to your children. After that, if the weather is fine enough for me to take a walk, and return to you for the evening-service, I should like to do so: if not, I had better return here by the 4.47.

How long an address do you usually give? *Catechising* I fear I could not manage: I can only tell them a story.

Also, could the children be *let alone* while I talk to them, and *not* have (as was the case during my first address here) people going about among them, stirring up the inattentive ones, and effectually taking *off* the attention of at least *half-a-dozen attentive* children for every *one* they thus stirred up, and doing much more harm than good. I told this to Mr. Hewett, and that so much interruption worried *me* greatly: and he kindly stopped it on the second occasion (all but *one* female teacher, who *wouldn't* let her little victims alone !).

> Sincerely yours,
> C. L. Dodgson

To George Davis

> Christ Church, Oxford
> October 16, 1897

Dear Sir,

On Thursday last, in the train from Red Hill to Guildford, I had a very pleasant 5 minutes' interview with your bright and intelligent-looking daughter. Being an old clergyman, fond of children, and also fond of mathematics (a subject on which I gave lectures at Oxford for 25 years), I spent the very short time we had together in teaching her what I believe is an entirely new rule in Arithmetic that I have lately discovered, and had just been teaching to a girls' school at Brighton. After she got out, my remaining fellow-passenger told me she was the daughter of the Station-Master at Betchworth. I am glad to know it, as it enables me to send the enclosed paper, which I have written out for her, and which I hope you will kindly give her.

> Truly yours,
> C. L. Dodgson

To his cousin Mrs. W. E. Wilcox

> The Chestnuts, Guildford
> January 4, 1898

My dear Fanny,

I'm glad you reminded me of the half-yearly gift. I had meant to send it in December, but somehow overlooked it. You will probably find me here, when you come next week; but you had better have the money at once. Love to Nella.

> Always affectionately yours,
> C. L. Dodgson

To H. L. M. Walters

The Chestnuts, Guildford
January 5, 1898

Dear Mr. Walters,

My note to your wife was written too briefly and hastily to explain my position with regard to giving help in church. The hesitation, from which I have suffered all my life, is always worse in *reading* (when I can *see* difficult words before they come) than in speaking. It is now many years since I ventured on reading in public – except now and then reading a lesson in College Chapel. Even that I find such a strain on the nerves that I seldom attempt it. As to reading the *prayers*, there is a much stronger objection than merely my own feelings: every difficulty is an interruption to the devotions of the congregation, by taking off their thoughts from what ought to be the *only* subject in their minds. I am sorry that I cannot undertake what you ask.

Sincerely yours,
C. L. Dodgson

To his sister Mary

The Chestnuts, Guildford
January 5, 1898

Dearest Mary,

You know, better than I can say it, all that my heart feels for you in your irreparable loss.* And you know, better than I can tell you, where to go for strength, and guidance, and, in God's good time, comfort and peace. I would certainly have come to you, if I could have done so with reasonable prudence: but, with a feverish cold, of the bronchial type, and the risk of ague (a form my colds usually take), Dr. Gabb forbids me to risk it.

I am so glad to think you have two sons to help and comfort. Please give them my love and *deep* sympathy.

You will very likely be in need of some ready money: so I enclose £50 "on account."

Your loving brother,
C. L. Dodgson

---

* Her husband had died earlier that day. Dodgson received the news by telegram.

To his nephew Stuart Collingwood

[The Chestnuts, Guildford]
January 5, 1898

My dear Stuart,

I have sent you a message, of love and sympathy, through your mother. This note is on a business-matter that will not wait.

When my dear Father died in 1868, we gave almost *carte blanche* to the undertakers, without any stipulations as to *limit* of expense. The consequence was a *gigantic* bill – so large, that we had great difficulty in getting the authorities at Doctors' Commons to sanction such extravagance.

If I had the thing to do again, I should say to the undertaker "Now that you know *all* that is required, I wish you to give me a signed promise that your charges *shall not exceed a stipulated sum.*" I should then take the advice of experienced friends as to whether the limit named was a reasonable one; and, if they said "no," I should apply to another undertaker.

You and your mother will have to live with the strictest economy: you have no money to throw away.

Your affectionate uncle,
Charles L. Dodgson

VI. Death

On December 23, 1897, Carroll travelled down to Guildford to join his family for the Christmas holidays. But this was not to be a festive season. On January 5, he learned that his brother-in-law had suddenly died, and by then he had himself come down with a fever and chest cold. Today we would deal with the symptoms routinely, with antibiotics, but over eighty years ago, bronchial infections were serious, and sometimes fatal. Carroll's condition worsened, and on January 14, thirteen days before his sixty-sixth birthday, he died of pneumonia.

Carroll had requested that his funeral be "simple and inexpensive, avoiding all things which are merely done for show, and retaining only what is, in the judgement of those who arrange my Funeral, requisite for its decent and reverent performance." He also requested that "there be no expensive monument. I should prefer a small plain head-stone." His wishes were carried out. According to his friend Gertrude Thomson, who was present, "On a grey January day . . . a few mourners slowly climbed the hill in silence, while borne before them on a simple hand-bier was the coffin, half hid in flowers." He was buried where he died, in Guildford, the only home he had known away from Oxford.

Appendix

Dodgson published the essay below in a miniature pamphlet, $4'' \times 3''$, so that it would fit into the envelope of *The Wonderland Postage-Stamp Case*.

Eight or Nine Wise Words about Letter-Writing

1. On Stamp-Cases

SOME American writer has said "the snakes in this district may be divided into one species – the venomous." The same principle applies here. Postage-Stamp-Cases may be divided into one species, the "Wonderland." The title is entered at Stationers' Hall: the two Pictorial Surprises, and the "Wise Words," are copyright.

You don't see why I call them "Surprises"? Well, take the Case in your left-hand, and regard it attentively. You see Alice nursing the Duchess's Baby? (An entirely new combination, by the way: it doesn't occur in the book.) Now, with your right thumb and forefinger, lay hold of the little book, and suddenly pull it out. *The Baby has turned into a Pig!* If *that* doesn't surprise you, why, I suppose you wouldn't be surprised if your own Mother-in-law suddenly turned into a Gyroscope!

This Case is *not* intended to carry about in your pocket. Far from it. People seldom want any other Stamps, on an emergency, than Penny-Stamps for Letters, Sixpenny-Stamps for Telegrams, and a bit of Stamp-edging for cut fingers (it makes capital sticking-plaster, and will stand three or four washings, cautiously conducted): and all these are easily carried in a purse or pocket-book. No, *this* is meant to haunt your envelope-case, or wherever you keep your writing-materials. What made me invent it was the constantly wanting Stamps of other values, for foreign Letters, Parcel Post, &c., and finding it very bothersome to get at the kind I wanted in a hurry. Since I have possessed a "Wonderland Stamp-Case," Life has been bright and peaceful, and I have used no other. I believe the Queen's Laundress uses no other.

Each of the pockets will hold 6 stamps, comfortably. I would recommend you to put them in, one by one, in the form of a *bouquet*, making them lean to the right and to the left alternately: thus there will always be a free *corner* to get hold of, so as to take them out, quickly and easily, one by one: otherwise you will find them apt to come out two or three at a time.

According to *my* experience, the 5*d*., 9*d*., and 1*s*. Stamps are hardly ever wanted, though I have constantly to replenish all the other pockets. If your experience agrees with mine, you may find it convenient to keep only a couple (say) of each of these 3 kinds, in the 1*s*. pocket, and to fill the other 2 pockets with extra 1*d*. Stamps.

2. *How to Begin a Letter*

If the Letter is to be in answer to another, begin by getting out that other letter and reading it through, in order to refresh your memory, as to what it is you have to answer, and as to your correspondent's *present address* (otherwise you will be sending your letter to his regular address in *London*, though he has been careful in writing to give you his *Torquay* address in full).

Next, *address and stamp the Envelope*. "What! Before writing the *Letter*?" Most certainly. And I'll tell you what will happen if you don't. You will go on writing till the last moment, and, just in the middle of the last sentence, you will become aware that "time's up!" Then comes the hurried wind-up – the wildly-scrawled signature – the hastily-fastened envelope, which comes open in the post – the address, a mere hieroglyphic – the horrible discovery that you've forgotten to replenish your Stamp-Case – the frantic appeal, to every one in the house, to lend you a Stamp – the headlong rush to the Post Office, arriving, hot and gasping, just after the box has closed – and finally, a week afterwards, the return of the Letter, from the Dead-Letter-Office, marked "address illegible"!

Do not, however, in your anxiety to observe this rule, commit the error of *addressing two Envelopes at once*! The inevitable result of *that* would be that the Letters would get into wrong Envelopes, and if (as is most probable) one was a Letter of congratulation, and the other of condolence, the outcome of your morning's work would be to turn two of your best and oldest friends into *bitter enemies for life*! *Verb. sap. sat.*

Next, put your own address, *in full*, at the top of the note-sheet. It is an aggravating thing – I speak from sad experience – when a friend, staying at some new address, heads his letter "Dover," simply, assuming that you can get the rest of the address from his previous letter, which of course you have destroyed.

Next, put the date *in full*. It is another aggravating thing, when you wish, years afterwards, to arrange a series of letters, to find them dated "Feb. 17,"

"Aug. 2," without any *year* to guide you as to which comes first. And never, never, dear Madam (N.B. this remark is addressed to ladies *only*: no *man* would ever do such a thing), put "Wednesday," simply, as the date ! " *That way madness lies.*"

3.   *How to Go On with a Letter*

Here is a golden Rule to begin with. *Write legibly.* The average temper of the human race would be perceptibly sweetened, if every body obeyed this Rule ! A great deal of the bad writing in the world comes simply from writing *too quickly*. Of course you reply "I do it to save *time*." A very good object, no doubt: but what right have you to do it at your friend's expense? Isn't *his* time as valuable as yours? Years ago, I used to receive letters from a friend – and very interesting letters too – written in one of the most atrocious hands ever invented. It generally took me about a *week* to read one of his letters ! I used to carry it about in my pocket, and take it out at leisure times, to puzzle over the riddles which composed it – holding it in different positions, and at different distances, till at last the meaning of some hopeless scrawl would flash upon me, when I at once wrote down the English under it: and, when several had been thus guessed, the context would help one with the others, till at last the whole series of hieroglyphics was deciphered. If *all* one's friends wrote like that, Life would be entirely spent in reading their letters !

This Rule applies, specially, to names of people or places – and *most* specially to *foreign names*. I got a letter once, containing some Russian names, written in the same hasty scramble in which people often write "yours sincerely." The *context*, of course, didn't help in the least: and one spelling was just as likely as another, so far as *I* knew: it was necessary to write and tell my friend that I couldn't read any of them !

My second Rule is, don't fill *more* than a page and a half with apologies for not having written sooner !

The best subject, to *begin* with, is your friend's last letter. Write with the letter open before you. Answer his questions, and make any remarks his letter suggests. *Then* go on to what you want to say yourself. This arrangement is more courteous, and pleasanter for the Reader, than to fill the letter with your own invaluable remarks, and then hastily answer your friend's questions in a postscript. Your friend is much more likely to enjoy your wit, *after* his own anxiety for information has been satisfied.

In referring to anything your friend has said in his letter, it is best to *quote the exact words*, and not to give a summary of them in *your* words. You know, yourself, how aggravating it is to have "words put into your mouth" – so to speak – which you have neither said nor meant to say. This caution is specially necessary when some point has arisen as to which the two correspondents do not quite agree. There ought to be no opening for such writing as "You have quite misunderstood my letter. I never said so-and-so, &c. &c.," which tends to make a correspondence last for a life-time.

A few more Rules may fitly be given here, for correspondence that has unfortunately become *controversial*.

One is, *don't repeat yourself*. When once you have said your say, fully and clearly, on a certain point, and have failed to convince your friend, *drop that subject*: to repeat your arguments, all over again, will simply lead to his doing the same; and so you will go on, like a Circulating Decimal. *Did you ever know a Circulating Decimal come to an end?*

Another Rule is, when you have written a letter that you feel may possibly irritate your friend, however necessary you may have felt it to so express yourself, *put it aside till the next day*. Then read it over again, and fancy it addressed to yourself. This will often lead to your writing it all over again, taking out a lot of the vinegar and pepper, and putting in honey instead, and thus making a *much* more palatable dish of it! If, when you have done your best to write inoffensively, you still feel that it will probably lead to further controversy, *keep a copy of it*. There is very little use, months afterwards, in pleading "I am *almost sure* I never expressed myself as you say: *to the best of my recollection* I said so-and-so." *Far* better to be able to write "I did *not* express myself so: these are the words I used."

My fifth Rule is, if your friend makes a severe remark, either leave it unnoticed, or make your reply distinctly *less* severe: and, if he makes a friendly remark, tending towards "making up" the little difference that has arisen between you, let your reply be distinctly *more* friendly. If, in picking a quarrel, each party declined to go more than *three-eighths* of the way, and if, in making friends, each was ready to go *five-eighths* of the way – why, there would be more reconciliations than quarrels! Which is like the Irishman's remonstrance to his gad-about daughter – "Shure, you're *always* goin' out! You go out *three* times, for *wanst* that you come in!"

My sixth Rule (and my last remark about controversial correspondence) is, *don't try to have the last word*! How many a controversy would be nipped in the bud, if each was anxious to let the *other* have the last word! Never mind how telling a rejoinder you leave unuttered: never mind your friend's supposing that you are silent from lack of anything to say: let the thing drop, as soon as it is possible without discourtesy: remember "speech is silvern, but silence is golden"! (N.B. If you are a gentleman, and your friend a lady, this Rule is superfluous: *you won't get the last word*!)

My seventh Rule is, if it should ever occur to you to write, jestingly, in *dispraise* of your friend, be sure you exaggerate enough to make the jesting *obvious*: a word, spoken in *jest*, but taken as *earnest*, may lead to very serious consequences. I have known it to lead to the breaking-off of a friendship. Suppose, for instance, you wish to remind your friend of a sovereign you have lent him, which he has forgotten to repay – you might quite *mean* the words "I mention it, as you seem to have a conveniently bad memory for debts" in jest: yet there would be nothing to wonder at if he took offence at that way of putting it. But, suppose you wrote "Long observation of your career as a pickpocket has convinced me that my only hope, for recovering that sovereign I lent you, is to say 'Pay up, or I'll summons yer!'", he would indeed be a matter-of-fact friend if he took *that* as seriously meant!

My eighth Rule. When you say, in your letter, "I enclose £5 bank-note", or "I enclose John's letter for you to see", get the document referred to – and *put it into the envelope*. Otherwise, you are pretty certain to find it lying about, *after the Post has gone*!

My ninth Rule. When you get to the end of a note-sheet, and find you have more to say, take another piece of paper – a whole sheet, or a scrap, as the case may demand: but, whatever you do, *don't cross*! Remember the old proverb "*Cross-writing makes cross reading*." "The *old* proverb?" you say, enquiringly. "*How* old?" Well, not so *very* ancient, I must confess. In fact, I'm afraid I invented it while writing this paragraph. Still, you know, "old" is a *comparative* term. I think you would be *quite* justified in addressing a chicken, just out of the shell, as "Old boy!", *when compared* with another chicken, that was only half-out!

If doubtful whether to end with "yours faithfully," or "yours truly," or "yours most truly," &c. (there are at least a dozen varieties, before you reach "yours affectionately"), refer to your correspondent's last letter, and make your winding-up *at least as friendly as his*: in fact, even if a shade *more* friendly, it will do no harm!

A Postscript is a very useful invention: but it is *not* meant (as so many ladies suppose) to contain the real *gist* of the letter: it serves rather to throw into the shade any little matter we do *not* wish to make a fuss about. For example, your friend had promised to execute a commission for you in town, but forgot it, thereby putting you to great inconvenience: and he now writes to apologize for his negligence. It would be cruel, and needlessly crushing, to make it the main subject of your reply. How much more gracefully it comes in thus! "P.S. Don't distress yourself any more about having omitted that little matter in town. I won't deny that it *did* put my plans out a little, at the time: but it's all right now. I often forget things, myself: and 'those, who live in glass-houses, mustn't throw stones,' you know!"

My tenth Rule. When your letter is finished, read it carefully through, and put in any "not" that you may chance to have omitted. (This precaution will sometimes save you from saying what you had not quite intended: *e.g.*, suppose you had *meant* to write "Dear Sir, I am not prepared to accept the offer you make me of your hand and heart.") Then fold up the letter with all the enclosures *in* it, so that all must come out *together*. Otherwise your friend will simply draw out the letter, and put the envelope into the fire, and it will only be when he reaches the words "I enclose £5 bank-note" that he will turn to watch, with tearful gaze, a fragment of white paper-ash, as it flickers up the chimney!

My eleventh Rule. Do not fasten up the envelope till Post-time is close at hand. Otherwise, you will have to tear it open again, to insert something you had forgotten to say.

My last Rule. When you take your letters to the Post, *carry them in your hand*. If you put them into your pocket, you will take a long country-walk – I speak from experience – passing the Post-Office *twice*, going and returning, and, when you get home again, will find them *still* in your pocket!

4. *On Registering Correspondence*

Let me recommend you to keep a record of Letters Received and Sent. I have kept one for many years, and have found it of the greatest possible service, in many ways: it secures my *answering* Letters, however long they have to wait; it enables me to refer, for my own guidance, to the details of previous correspondence, though the actual Letters may have been destroyed long ago; and, most valuable feature of all, if any difficulty arises, years afterwards, in connection with a half-forgotten correspondence, it enables me to say, with confidence, "I did *not* tell you that he was 'an *invaluable* servant in *every* way,' and that you *couldn't* 'trust him too much.' I have a *précis* of my letter. What I said was 'he is a *valuable* servant in *many* ways, but *don't* trust him too much.' So, if he's cheated you, you really must not hold *me* responsible for it!"

I will now give you a few simple Rules for making, and keeping, a Letter-Register.

Get a blank book, containing (say) 200 leaves, about 4 in. wide and 7 high. It should be *well* fastened into its cover, as it will have to be opened and shut hundreds of times. Have a line ruled, in red ink, down each margin of every page, an inch off the edge (the margin should be wide enough to contain a number of 5 digits, easily: *I* manage with a ¾ inch margin: but, unless you write very small, you will find an inch margin more comfortable).

Write a *précis* of each Letter, received or sent, in chronological order. Let the entry of a "received" Letter reach from the left-hand edge to the right-hand marginal line; and the entry of a "sent" Letter from the left-hand marginal line to the right-hand edge. Thus the two kinds will be quite distinct, and you can easily hunt through the "received" Letters by themselves, without being bothered with the "sent" Letters; and *vice versa*.

Use the *right-hand* pages only: and, when you come to the end of the book, turn it upside-down, and begin at the other end, still using right-hand pages.

Write, at the top of every sheet of a "received" Letter, and of every copy you keep of a "sent" Letter, its Register-Number in full.

I will now give a few (ideal) specimen pages of my Letter-Register, and make a few remarks on them: after which I think you will find it easy enough to manage one for yourself.

29217	/90.	
(217) sendg, J., a	Ap. 1 (Tu.) *Jones, Mrs.* am as present from self and Mr. white elephant.	27518 225
(218) grand	do. *Wilkins & Co.* bill, for piano, £175 10s. 6d. [pd	28743 221,2
(219) 'Grand to borr	do. *Scareham, H.* [writes from Hotel, Monte Carlo'] asking ow £50 for a few weeks' (!)	⊙
⊙	(220) do. *Scareham, H.* would know *object*, for wh loan is and what *security* is offered.	like to asked,
218 246	(221) Ap. 3. *Wilkins & Co.* vious letter, now before me, undertook to supply one for decling to pay more.	in pre- you £120:
23514 218 228	(222) do. *Cheetham & Sharp.* written 221 — enclosing previou ter — is law on my side?	have s let- [
(223) G. N. dressed 'very	Ap. 4. *Manager, Goods Statn, R.* White Elephant arrived, ad- to you — send for it at once — savage'.	226

29225	/90.	
217 230	(225) Ap. 4. (F) *Jones, Mrs.* th|anks, but no room for it at present: am|send-ing it to Zoological Gardens.	anks, send-
223	(226) do. *Manager, Goods Sta*|tn, G. *N. R.* please deliver, to bearer|of this note, case containing White Ele|phant addressed to me.	tn, G. of this phant
223 229	(227) do. *Director Zool. Gardens.* closing above note to R. W. Ma|call for valuable animal, prese|nted to Gardens.	(en- nager)
(228) misquo is £18	Ap. 8. *Cheetham & Sharp,* you|te enclosed letter: limit named|o.	222 237
(229) case de Port — quet —	Ap. 9. *Director, Zoo. Gardens.* livered to us contained 1 doz. consumed at Directors' Ban-many thanks.	227 230
225 ⊙	(230) do. T *Jones, Mrs.* why|call a doz. of Port a 'White Elephant?	
(231) joke'.	do. T *Jones, Mrs.* 'It was a| joke'.	⊙

29233	/90.	
	(233) Ap. 10. (Th) *Page and Co.*	orderg
	Macaulay's Essays and "Jane	Eyre"
242	(cheap edtn).	
(234)	do. *Aunt Jemima* — invitg for	
2 or 3	days after the 15th. [	236
(235)	do. *Lon. and West. Bk.* have	
recevd	£250, pd to yr Acct fm Parkins	
& Co.	Calcutta. [en	
234.	(236) do. *Aunt Jemima* — can	not
	possibly come this month: will	write
239	when able. [	
228	(237) Ap. 11. *Cheetham and*	Co. re-
240	turn letter enclosed to you.	[×
	(238) do. *Morton, Philip.* co	uld you
	lend me Browning's 'Dramati	s Per-
245	sonæ' for a day or 2?	
(239)	Ap. 14. *Aunt Jemima,* leav-	236
ing ho	use at end of month: address	
'136,	Royal Avenue, Bath.' [	
(240)	Ap. 15. *Cheetham and Co.,*	237
returng	letter as reqd, bill 6/6/8. [	244

29242	/90.	
(242)	Ap. 15. (Tu) *Page and Co.* bill for boo|ks, as ordered, 15/6 [	}233
(243)	do. ¶ *do.* books.	}247
240 248	(244) do. *Cheetham and Co.* c|an un-derstand the 6/8 — what is £6 |for?	
(245) matis	Ap. 17. ¶ *Morton. P.* 'Dra-Personæ', as asked for. [retd	238 249
221 250	(246) do. *Wilkins and Co.* wi|th bill, 175/10/6, and ch. for do. |[en	
243	(247) do. *Page and Co.* bill, postal ⅟E 107258 for 15/. and	15/6, 6 stps.
(248) was a	Ap. 18. *Cheetham and Co.* it|244 'clerical error' (!)	
245	(249) Ap. 19. *Morton, P.* retu|rning Browning with many thanks.	
(250) bill.	do. *Wilkins and Co.* receptd	246

I begin each page by putting, at the top left-hand corner, the next entry-number I am going to use, *in full* (the last 3 digits of each entry-number are enough afterwards); and I put the date of the year, at the top, in the centre.

I begin each entry with the last 3 digits of the entry-number, enclosed in an oval (this is difficult to reproduce in print, so I have put round-parentheses here). Then, for the *first* entry in each page, I put the day of the month and the day of the week: afterwards, "do." is enough for the month-day, till it changes: I do not repeat the week-day.

Next, if the entry is *not* a letter, I put a symbol for "parcel" (see Nos. 243, 245) or "telegram" (see Nos. 230, 231) as the case may be.

Next, the name of the person, underlined (indicated here by italics).

If an entry needs special further attention, I put [at the end: and, when it has been attended to, I fill in the appropriate symbol, e.g. in No. 218, it showed that the bill had to be *paid*; in No. 222, that an answer was really *needed* (the "×" means "attended to"); in No. 234, that I owed the old lady a visit; in No. 235, that the item had to be entered in my account book; in No. 236, that I must not forget to write; in No. 239, that the address had to be entered in my address-book; in No. 245, that the book had to be returned.

I give each entry the space of 2 lines, whether it fills them or not, in order to have room, in the margin, for a head-reference and a foot-reference. And, at the foot of each page I leave 2 or 3 lines *blank* (for entering omitted Letters) and I miss one or 2 numbers before I begin the next page.

At any odd moments of leisure, I "make up" the entry-book, in various ways, as follows:

(1) I draw a *second* line, at the right-hand end of the "received" entries, and at the left-hand end of the "sent" entries. This I usually do pretty well "up to date." In my Register the first line is *red*, the second *blue*: here I distinguish them by making the first thin, and the second *thick*.

(2) Beginning with the last entry, and going backwards, I read over the names till I recognise one as having occurred already: I then link the two entries together, by giving the one, that comes first in chronological order, a 'foot-reference', and the other a 'head-reference'. When the two entries belong to the same *thousand*, I use only the last 3 digits of their reference-numbers (see Nos. 221, 246): otherwise, I write the number in full (see head-reference of No. 217). I do not keep this "up to date," but leave it till there are 4 or 5 pages to be done. I work back till I come among entries that are all supplied with "foot-references," when I once more glance through the last few pages, to see if there are any entries not yet supplied with head-

references: *their* predecessors may need a special search. If an entry is connected, in subject, with another under a different name, I link them by cross-references, distinguished from the head- and foot-references by being written *further from the marginal line* (see No. 229). When 2 consecutive entries have the same name, and are both of the same kind (i.e. both "received" or both "sent") I bracket them (see Nos. 242, 243); if of different kinds, I link them with the symbol used for Nos. 219, 220.

(3) Beginning at the earliest entry not yet done with, and going forwards, I cross out every entry that has got a head- and foot-reference, and is done with, by continuing the extra line *through* it (see Nos. 221, 223, 225). I also cross out every entry that is done with, even if it have no head-reference, provided it is the *first of its kind*, so that no head-reference is possible: also every entry that is done with, even if it have no foot-reference, provided it is likely to be the *last of its kind*: but in this case it is convenient, in order to find it again if the correspondence should ever re-commence, to enter it in an alphabetical index of "Closed Correspondences." The result of this system of crossing-out is that, wherever a *break* occurs in this extra line, it shows there is some matter still needing attention. I do not keep this anything like "up to date," but leave it till there are 30 or 40 pages to look through at a time. When the first page in the volume is thus completely crossed out, I put a mark at the foot of the page to indicate this; and so with pages 2, 3, &c. Hence, whenever I do this part of the "making-up," I need not begin at the beginning of the volume, but only at the *earliest page that has not got this mark*.

All this looks very complicated, when stated at full length: but you will find it perfectly simple, when you have had a little practice, and will come to regard the "making-up" as a pleasant occupation for a rainy day, or at any time that you feel disinclined for more severe mental work. In the Game of Whist, Hoyle gives us one golden Rule, "when in doubt, win the trick." I find that Rule admirable for real life: when in doubt what to do, I "make up" my Letter-Register!

Index of Recipients

About the Editor

Born in Alberta, Canada, Morton N. Cohen is Professor Emeritus of English at the City University of New York. He has spent twenty years researching the letters of Lewis Carroll and was the editor of a two-volume edition of the letters published by Oxford University Press in 1979. He is also the author of *Rider Haggard: His Life and Works* and *Rudyard Kipling to Rider Haggard: The Record of a Friendship*.

Morton Cohen is at work on a biography of C. L. Dodgson.